Donald T. McGuire

Acts of Silence

Altertumswissenschaftliche Texte und Studien

Band 33

Donald T. McGuire

Acts of Silence

1997
Olms - Weidmann
Hildesheim · Zürich · New York

Donald T. McGuire

Acts of Silence

Civil War, Tyranny, and Suicide in the Flavian Epics

1997
Olms - Weidmann
Hildesheim · Zürich · New York

This work and all articles and pictures involved are
protected by copyright. Application outside the strict limits
of copyright law without consent having been obtained from
the publishing firm is inadmissible and punishable.
These regulations are meant especially for copies,
translations and micropublishings as well as for storing and
editing in electronic systems.

Das Werk ist urheberrechtlich geschützt.
Jede Verwertung außerhalb der engen Grenzen des
Urheberrechtsgesetzes ist ohne Zustimmung des Verlages
unzulässig und strafbar. Das gilt insbesondere für
Vervielfältigungen, Übersetzungen, Mikroverfilmungen
und die Einspeicherung und Verarbeitung
in elektronischen Systemen.

Die Deutsche Bibliothek - CIP-Einheitsaufnahme

MacGuire, Donald T.:
Acts of silence : civil war, tyranny, and suicide in the Flavian
epics / Donald T. McGuire. - Hildesheim ; Zürich ; New York :
Olms- Weidmann, 1997
   (Altertumswissenschaftliche Texte und Studien ; Bd. 33)
   ISBN 3-487-10334-6
NE: GT

© Georg Olms Verlag, Hildesheim 1997
Alle Rechte vorbehalten
Printed in Germany
Gedruckt auf säurefreiem und alterungsbeständigem Papier
Umschlagentwurf: Prof. Paul König, Hildesheim
Herstellung:
ISSN 0175-8411
ISBN 3-487-10334-6

FOR
FEE
FRANCES
&
ANDREW

AND FOR
MY PARENTS
(PARENTIBUS OPTIMIS!)

TABLE OF CONTENTS

Foreword... IX

Chapter 1: A Flavian Overview........................1

Chapter 2: Reading the Epics...........................40

Chapter 3: Flavian Epic and Civil War.......................88

Chapter 4: Facing the Tyrant..............................147

Chapter 5: Suicide--The Opposition Self-destructs........185

Chapter 6: Epic Silence..230

Selected Bibliography...249

ACKNOWLEDGMENTS

Several people deserve thanks for their support and their input into this book. I would like to thank the following friends in particular: Fred Ahl, Tony Boyle, Caroline Dewald, Judy Ginsburg, Jeff Henderson, Ralph Johnson, Carole Newlands, Michael Putnam, and Amy Richlin. Thanks on a different scale altogether go to Martha Malamud.

FOREWORD

In the years following his triumph over Antony and Cleopatra in 31 BC, Octavian set a new governmental system in place at Rome, one that retained most of the components of the Republican oligarchy (which Octavian claimed to have restored) but that in fact was subject to the control of a single ruler, Octavian himself. Octavian even shaped his own image in accordance with his new position of magisterial pre-eminence, adopting the title Augustus (at the Senate's behest, he claims), and leaving behind his own name, Octavianus, redolent as it was with suggestions of the strife, proscriptions, and land seizures that followed Julius Caesar's assassination.

The writers of the Augustan era--Vergil, Horace, Propertius, Livy, and Ovid, among others--testify to the concerns harbored by the educated and privileged classes at Rome regarding both the nature of the Augustan principate and the manipulation of images and facades which helped Augustus maintain his popular support. The literary work of this era constantly grapples with questions of self-representation and of the telling gaps that often separate image and reality, and it also explores the nature of personal and political power from several different perspectives. The writers and their *princeps* slowly define the limits of free expression and criticism as well: Suetonius credits Augustus with considerable tolerance for criticisms from the literary world, and yet late in his reign

Augustus banishes Ovid from Rome, in part because of his poetry.

One hundred years later, during the Flavian principate, the system that Augustus gradually put in place during his reign is still in operation; indeed, it has gained far greater operational stability, gradually bringing more and more of the state's functions under direct Imperial control. But several of the problems that the Imperial system entails are still in evidence during the Flavian era: the civil wars that bring Vespasian to power in AD 69 make clear the potentially divisive and intrusive role of the military in the Roman power structure; Domitian's reinstitution of the *maiestas* laws, after their suspension by Vespasian and Titus, reflects the emperor's instinct to seek out and suppress opposition; and as Domitian's reign continues, the fact that he has lined up no obvious successor, natural or adopted, underscores the problem of succession, for which the Julio-Claudians had established no systematic solution.

This book offers a literary analysis of the three epic poems of the Flavian era (the *Thebaid* of P. Papinius Statius, the *Argonautica* of G. Valerius Flaccus, and the *Punica* of Silius Italicus) in light of their contemporary political world; in doing so it aims to fill a sizable gap in our scholarly appreciation of Latin literature, for at present there are still no full-length, comparative studies of these three epics, even though they were all produced in a short span of time during the reign of Domitian. The basic purpose of the book, then, is to introduce students of Imperial Roman literature and history to a significant body of material common to all three of the Flavian epics.

The book focuses in particular on the ways in which the authors shape their poems in terms of various modes of political behavior: it argues that all three poets concern themselves with specific types of political behavior closely linked to contemporary events. In each of the epics images of civil war, tyranny, and suicide are represented with surprising frequency; the images are used to examine not only the workings of monarchical power itself, but also the type of conflict that in the Flavian era produced such power, and produced as well the most extreme type of personal response to authoritarian oppression.

The fact that all three of these poets share such a strong preoccupation with these issues and images is important and ironic in its own right, for in doing so they narrate events that regularly earn the epithet *nefanda*--things that should remain *un*spoken. Civil war itself is regularly termed a *nefas* in Roman poetry in general, and the Flavian era in particular. We find tyrants in these epics not only committing various unspeakable acts but also using their own calculated silences as a form of manipulation and demanding silent obedience from their subjects. Finally, in turning repeatedly to the image of suicide, the poets dwell on an action which, however eloquent a protest in itself, also (in their representations of it) permanently silences the protester.

In fact, in speaking about the unspeakable the Flavian epicists stretch the irony even further, for they also draw emphatic links between their own poetic voices and these modes of political behavior, identifying their own poetic voice and power with acts and individuals that either generate or entail silence. The consistency of this perspective is what particularly distinguishes these poems from earlier generations of Roman epic, and it raises several questions about the place of epic poetry in the Flavian era.

There is, first of all, the question of the relationship among the three poets in the Flavian era. The fact that they offer such strong parallels in terms of subject matter and treatment suggests that they were aware of, and responding to, each other's work. While a detailed analysis of common poetic diction is beyond the scope of the present study, I hope at least to encourage further work in this area by pointing out the more general areas of common concern.

Second, in their continued emphasis on Pharsalian visions of civil war and on stereotypical portraits of tyranny the Flavian poets raise several questions regarding epic's evolution and its relationship to the Principate at the end of the first century AD. Though these poets all write in the period after Vespasian had supposedly restored much stability to the Principate, they return again and again to visions of civil strife and the devolution of political order. This emphasis might reflect not only a strong awareness of Rome's own past experiences with civil war, but also the argument that a monarchic system such as the Principate necessarily entails the potential for further strife. The characterization of tyranny itself encourages a systematic reading of the political world contained in these epics. The tyrant, so familiar in rhetorical and mythic models of earlier generations, remains the only sort of political being to amass power with any regularity, and the characterization of tyranny becomes frozen and unchanging. There is a significant degree of anti-Imperial commentary, however basic, in such a consistent portrait of rulership--that is to say, in an era when the Principate itself continues to develop its own monolithic facade and self-image, the poets offer their own monolithic vision of monarchy. But there is a further point regarding tyrants and the opposition (whether literary or more practical) that they generate, for the Flavian writers suggest in their representations of authority, that tyranny (and, perhaps, the Principate itself) manages to co-opt and foil many constructive avenues of opposition.

Finally, there is the emphasis on suicide in these epics (itself the most striking sort of political opposition) and a tendency in all three poems to link suicidal moments to the poet's own voice--that is to say, the poets use suicide scenes as their chief occasion for explicit meditations on the commemorative power of poetry.

This link between the ferocious suicides of Flavian epic and references to poetic power reflects an increasing sense of self-conscious despair burdening the poets of this era: in adopting the most full-throated of Roman poetic genres they identify their own powers with figures who have been silenced--who in fact have silenced themselves. Such a pessimistic stance regarding their own material and their own creative efforts certainly differentiates these poets from their epic predecessors and might stand as indirect evidence of their awareness of epic's increasing marginalization. And, as we shall see, Statius and Valerius both include more explicit references to this same sensibility.

Other literary evidence also points to the possibility that these poets might have been prescient in suspecting the genre's increasing marginalization, for as best we can tell, they represent the last significant period of Imperial Latin epic composition: whereas we know of over 20 epics that were being composed in the Augustan era alone, under the Flavians we know of only four other poets who take on the genre (one of whom is the *princeps* himself, Domitian). More surprising, in the 94 year span between Trajan's accession and Commodus' assassination, we know of a grand total of 2 epic poets, though other genres of Latin literature continue to thrive.[1]

The Flavian epicists, then, stand at a significant juncture, for they look back at the tremendous body of material passed on to them by earlier generations of Greek and Latin epic, and yet their genre of poetic endeavor is poised (as best we can tell) on the brink of silent disappearance, not to

---

[1] See Bardon (1956), v.2, 229-231 and Fantham (1996), 215-216.

reemerge until a very different literary landscape evolves in the fourth century.

These epics also offer valuable literary testimony regarding the broader issue of artistic expression in a politically repressive society. The imagery and themes that they foreground find intriguing counterparts in more contemporary cultures of repression--in the literatures of Stalinist Russia and contemporary Latin America, to name but two, where visions of tyranny and images of suicide and silence are particularly prominent. Unlike their twentieth-century literary kin, however, the literary works of Flavian era have few supplementary sources to help us appreciate their coded world, and so the parallels that modern literatures might offer must, for the moment, remain more evocative than definitive, more suggestive than quantitative.

CHAPTER 1: A FLAVIAN OVERVIEW

...I'd rather compose romances for you--
more profit in it and more charm.
But I subdued myself, setting my heel
on the throat of my own song.
Listen, comrades of posterity,
to the agitator, the rabble-rouser.
Stifling the torrents of poetry,
I'll skip the volumes of lyrics;
as one alive, I'll address the living.
I'll join you in the far communist future,
I, who am no Esenin super-hero.
My verse will reach you across the peaks of ages,
over the heads of governments and poets...

My verse by labor will break the mountain chain
      of years,
and will present itself ponderous, crude,
      tangible,
as an aqueduct, by slaves of Rome
constructed, enters into our days...

Let fame trudge after genius
like an inconsolable widow to a funeral march--
die then, my verse, die like a common soldier,
like our men who nameless died attacking!
I don't care a spit for tons of bronze;
I don't care a spit for slimy marble...
My verse has brought me no rubles to spare:
no craftsmen have made mahogany chairs for my
      house.
In all conscience, I need nothing
except a freshly laundered shirt...
      V. Mayakovsky, "At the Top of My Voice"[1]

---

[1] Mayakovsky (1975), 223-233.

In the 1930's and in subsequent decades Soviet writers responded in different ways to the draconian controls imposed on them by Stalin and his successors.[2] Some committed suicide; many were denied the luxury of such a decision and were executed by the government because of their literary work; many simply accepted, to different degrees, the tenets of Socialist Realism, working within the confines of the doctrine, whether they supported or opposed the doctrine itself.[3] One writer, Isaac Babel, tried yet another response; he announced at the 1934 Congress of Writers that he was working in a new genre which he entitled "the genre of silence," and he published little work after this date. Silence afforded Babel no protection, however, as he was arrested in 1939 and died in a labor camp two years later.[4]

Vladimir Mayakovsky was one of the poets who committed suicide; in April, 1930 he shot himself, in the midst of work on a new poem, "At the Top of My Voice." What survives of the poem is apparently the first of two parts; in it the narrator, defiantly alive, and speaking in a civic or declamatory voice, describes to his Soviet comrades his commitment to living and his concomitant rejection of lyric poetry; he exhorts

---

[2] For a survey of Soviet literature in the Stalinist and post-Stalinist eras, see Brown (1982). An excellent essay on the Stalinist era in particular is Roman Jakobson's "On a Generation that Squandered its Poets" in Brown (1973), 7-32. See also selected articles in Conquest (1989).

[3] Milosz (1981) provides a series of examples of different ways that writers worked within the confines of this doctrine, articulating the difficulties these writers faced in transcending its constraints.

[4] See Brown (1982), 94.

these comrades to face the future with the help of his verses. Yet notes that Mayakovsky left behind show that the second half was to have been written in a lyrical, intimate voice-- precisely the sort that the narrator strangles in the opening section.[5] Clearly, the poem would have generated a series of strong internal tensions-- between the initial suppression of a lyrical sensibility and its later reassertion; between the narrator's (or anyone's) power to stifle his lyric voice in the first half and the power that lyric itself assumes in the second; between the human life of a poet and the independent life of a poem. Scholars of Soviet literature differ in their explanations of the young poet's suicide (he was 36 years old),[6] but part of its explanation certainly lies in the difficulty Mayakovsky had in accepting both the growing governmental control of literature and the emerging principles of Socialist Realism that characterized the 1930's in Stalinist Russia. Like Mayakovsky's suicide itself, "At the Top of My Voice" offers ample testimony of this fact in its references to the impossibility, indeed the unacceptability, of writing lyric under Stalin, in an age when the historically real and ideologically correct novel became the approved form of literary expression. Even within the first section of the poem Mayakovsky simultaneously endorses this control ("But I subdued myself,

---

[5] Brown (1982), 42-44.
[6] Brown (1982), 19-49, balances the political and personal factors; Mandelstam (1970), 27 and 158, describes how his fellow writers primarily acknowledged the political aspects of his death.

setting my heel / on the throat of my own song") and rejects it ("My verse will reach you across the peaks of ages, over the heads of governments and poets..."). He silences one type of verse at the same that he shouts (at the top of his voice) in another, weaving images of silence, death, and suicide together with visions of poetry's power and voice, and its promise of eternal fame.

Roman images abound in the poem as Mayakovsky reappropriates both literary and physical remains from the Imperial era. His verses reject Horace's model of material permanence[7]--marble and bronze are to be spat upon; Roman aqueducts only testify to Rome's imperialist oppression of slaves. And yet, those Roman aqueducts have endured for centuries, and Mayakovsky's poem lays claim itself to the same durability as Horace's poem did, no matter what the consequences. Fame, after all, follows poetic genius "like an inconsolable widow" in a funeral march, and so the act of writing itself, with fame as its final product, becomes an act of prolonged self-destruction.

The voice and genres adopted by Mayakovsky here are both distinctly Horatian; but the poem's images of silence and suicide, and its self-consciousness regarding its place in both local and global literary traditions (the references to Esenin, another Soviet poet and suicide, on the one hand, and to Horace on the other) are more in line with a subsequent period and

---

[7] Horace, *Carm.* 3.30.1.

different genre of Roman literature--the epics of Flavian Rome. It is in the Flavian era, and in the epic genre in particular, that we find a steady preoccupation with visions of tyranny, silence, suicide, and civil war, and it is the Flavian epics that present these visions in contexts very conscious of their epic predecessors.

Flavian Rome

Valerius Flaccus, Statius, and Silius Italicus all produced their epics--the *Argonautica*, the *Thebaid*, and the *Punica*, respectively--within a twenty year span (perhaps, even, only a 10-15 year span), between AD 80 and 100. These poems occupy a singular position in the field of Roman literature, as they provide us with three finished epics (or nearly finished, in the case of the *Argonautica*) all composed during one brief span of time. They thus offer their readers a unique perspective on the Latin epic tradition, on the literary world of Domitian's day, and on the Roman world in which they were written.

The era in which these writers worked is often looked on as a transitional stage of Roman history bracketed by Neronian flash and turbulence at one end and Trajanic enlightenment and control at the other. Perhaps Gibbon is to be blamed, or credited, for this perception, as, at the very outset of his *The History of the Decline and Fall of the Roman Empire*, he identifies the second century AD. as the acme of Roman

Imperial existence. As a result, Trajan and his Antonine successors get all the credit, and more people probably remember the Flavian era for the ludicrous hairstyles sported by its portrait busts than for any of its impact on politics and literature.[8] In fact, Trajan might reap the profits from what the Flavians sowed and harvested. Among other things, the Flavian era can boast that it was the last great period of Latin poetry before the relative poetic silence of the second and third centuries;[9] it was a period of dramatic urban renovation and social transformation; it was, finally, a period in which the principate reestablished itself after the instability of AD 69, no doubt taking on much of the shape that we see in Trajan's own regime.

But the Flavian principate also exhibits several problematic and conflicting facets, and perhaps it is on their account that posterity is inclined to glide over the Flavians and fix on the apparent security offered by Trajan and his successors. The stability that Vespasian seemed to restore to the principate is shattered first by the sudden and early death of Titus and then by the latter years of Domitian's reign, when there is neither a son nor successor in sight, and both palace intrigue and provincial revolt threaten to return Rome to the chaos of AD 69. The credit that Domitian might take for fostering literary arts diminishes when we contemplate both the

---

[8] See, for example, the portrait of a "Flavian Beauty" in Hanfmann (1975), page 95 and Plate 78.

[9] See the excellent surveys of d'Esperey (1986) and Coleman (1986).

comments of later writers on literary censorship in Domitian's day and the writers and thinkers who were executed under Domitian on charges of *maiestas*. Finally, the new stability of the principate rests, ultimately, on its increasing monopolization of power: there may debate about whether Domitian actually called himself *dominus et deus*;[10] but all agree that the term *dominus* is, at least by Trajan's reign and quite plausibly in Domitian's own day, a standard form of Imperial address.[11]

There are obvious dangers and problems in drawing too precise an analogy between Stalinist Russia and Imperial Rome. But scholars of Roman history and literature are generally more inclined to downplay the importance of authoritarianism and censorship in Rome; and so, before we turn to the Flavian poems themselves we might consider some basic facts regarding the principate, censorship, and the lives of these poets themselves.

While Vespasian may have steadied the principate, its nature also underwent some gradual and significant transformations during the second half of the first century AD, in relation to both individual citizens and governing bodies (i.e. the magistrates and the Senate). The century that began with the image of a restored Republic ends with the accession of Trajan, the *optimus princeps*, who presents no illusions about

---

[10] See Jones (1992), 107-109, for the most recent discussion; Jones argues as effectively as possible against trusting Suetonius's claim (*Dom*.13.2); I find the cumulative weight of the ancient comments and references too significant to explain away.
[11] Sherwin-White (1985), 557-558.

sharing power with others.

On the individual or private level, we find the *princeps* gradually assuming broad juridical powers at Rome; he becomes, in essence, the sole dispenser of both private *beneficia* and wise justice.[12] This is a key change in the Roman legal system, for one man, the *princeps*, now monopolizes the same judicial powers that several magistrates and judicial boards had shared in the Republic. As Millar notes,[13] such a system requires, but might not always receive, a constant and skillful balance of interests and powers, for as much as it is in the interests of the *princeps* to dispense justice and law, he also has the power to override the law simply by invoking the principle of *clementia*.

The emperor's relationship to the institutional components of the Roman state, especially the annual magistracies and the Senate, reflects a similar trend toward imperial monopolization of power.[14] By Domitian's day the *princeps* has taken on several tasks formerly performed by the Senate--establishing laws by edict or mandate, appointing candidates for magistracies, and appointing officers within the Senate itself, to name just a few. He also eliminates many of the various assemblies' functions, as his appointment of all consuls attests--indeed the very existence of both ordinary and

---

[12] Millar (1977), 465-551.

[13] Millar (1977), 516-517.

[14] Millar (1977), 275-363; Talbert (1984) also recognizes this general trend, though his study of the Imperial Senate aims to identify those areas in which the Senate retained some influence.

suffect consuls points to the devalued status of the curule magistracies under the Principate.[15]

By Domitian's time, the *princeps* has also readapted a further set of laws to be used at his discretion, the laws involving *maiestas*, and the writers of Domitian's day must have been especially sensitive to his extended powers in this area.[16] It is important to note the frequency with which published literary works provided key evidence in the treason trials of Domitian's day--the chief cases are those of Herennius Senecio, Arulenus Rusticus, the younger Helvidius Priscus, and Hermogenes of Tarsus, each of whom was then executed (no *clementia* here!) after conviction.[17] Domitian's actions in this area become more striking when we compare him to his father and brother, both of whom abolished prosecutions for *maiestas*.

These cases also demonstrate how different types of writing could be construed as treasonous. Arulenus Rusticus and Herennius Senecio were both sentenced to die for their published *laudes* of Thrasea Paetus and Helvidius Priscus.[18] The younger Helvidius Priscus was executed for dramatizing mythic material to which Domitian took offense.[19]

---

[15] Millar (1977), 308-309.

[16] The chief studies of this issue are Rogers (1960) and Baumann (1974).

[17] Rogers attempts to downplay the importance of written material in these cases, but is corrected on this point by Baumann; see Baumann (1974),159-160, and note 165 in particular.

[18] Tacitus, *Ag*. 2.1.

[19] Suetonius, *Dom*. 10.3.

Hermogenes of Tarsus was put to death because of his historical writings--according to Suetonius, his histories contained some unfortunate allusions to Domitian.[20] We might note as well the execution of Aelius Lamia, who was not punished for his writings, but for spoken witticisms critical of the *princeps*.[21]

These cases occur both early and late in Domitian's reign and argue against Suetonius' schematic identification of 2 distinct periods in Domitian's principate, the first mild and the second cruel.[22] While one might summon several arguments to downplay the significance of these cases--they are often grouped together, for example, as representative works of some philosophical or Stoic opposition[23] their importance for fellow writers under Domitian should not be underestimated. One prosecution alone (not necessarily a conviction even) would serve to warn writers that their material was being monitored and that current Imperial favor might always turn to disfavor.

To appreciate how this fact might influence writers of the time, we can look to Tacitus' *Dialogus de Oratoribus*, whose dramatic date is ca. AD 75.[24] At the very opening of the work Maternus' visitors (Marcus Aper, Julius Secundus, and

---

[20] Suetonius, *Dom.* 10.1.
[21] Suetonius, *Dom.* 10.2.
[22] Suetonius, *Dom.* 9-10.
[23] Jones (1992) 119-124; Coleman (1986) 3111-3115.
[24] Bartsch (1994), 98-147, offers a detailed and wonderfully persuasive reading of the *Dialogus* and its articulations of how *princeps* and poet both avail themselves of the rhetorical strategies that Bartsch terms "doublespeak."

the young Tacitus) express surprise that he is not frightened at the offense to the court that his *Cato* gave on the previous day. Far from being frightened, Maternus assures them, he not only will refuse to edit his *Cato* in order to make it safer (*securiorem*), but he will also put anything that he left unsaid into his next play, the *Thyestes* (*Dial.* 3.1-3).

Maternus and his friends speak matter-of-factly about the dangers inherent in literary and dramatic presentation, and their comments suggest that this danger existed even in Vespasian's day, though the *maiestas* laws were at that time in abeyance. A poet could choose to edit his material in order not to give offense, and a poet had to weigh his options carefully, whether he was writing about historical figures (as in the *Cato*) or mythic ones (*Thyestes*). The remarks of Maternus and his visitors take on added irony and force if, as Williams has argued, Maternus was executed in the years between the setting of the dialogue and Tacitus' publication of his work.[25]

The Poets Themselves

By Domitian's time, with his resumption of *maiestas* laws, and with his prosecution of writers, these dangers would have been even more obvious, and Pliny and Tacitus both claim to feel relief at their ability to express themselves in the freedom of the Trajanic period.[26] And yet, Silius, Statius, and Valerius

---

[25] See G. Williams (1978), 34.
[26] e.g. Pliny, *Pan.* 47.1-3; Tacitus, *Hist.* 1.1. Jones (1992), 124, is right to

all are taking part in an extremely active literary scene under Domitian, and the scene reaches into Imperial circles, where Statius stood in good favor.[27]

When we turn to these writers themselves in order to locate them in their Flavian world, we find that, despite the wealth of historical and literary material surviving from this era, our knowledge about the poets and the circles in which they moved remains disappointingly imprecise. For, though we know the general outline of literary history from the death of Nero to the accession of Trajan, precise biographical facts about Valerius Flaccus, Statius, and Silius Italicus elude us.

All that we know about Valerius Flaccus is based on a couple of slim pieces of internal evidence in his poem and a passing remark about his recent death made by Quintilian, who says, tersely, *multum in Valerio Flacco nuper amisimus* (*Inst. Or.* 10.1.90). Regarding his own life, the evidence is scanty, at best, and hypotheses about his career are built on shaky ground. Arguments regarding the date of his epic's composition span two decades, between AD 70 and 92, but few now maintain that it took any significant shape before AD 80. While his literary career might reach well back into the reign of Vespasian, it most likely extends well into the Domitianic era as

---

observe that such comments say nothing about the contemporary dynasty's (in)tolerance of opposition.

[27] See the comment of Coleman (1986), 3115: "The literature of Domitian's period was determined by two opposing attitudes on the part of the emperor: a concern for literature and a tendency to smother it."

well.[28]

What little we know about Valerius still does suffice to link his work chronologically with that of Statius and Silius. We know more about Statius and about the chronology of his literary activity, thanks primarily to his own statements about his life in his *Silvae*.[29] He came from a prosperous and learned family that had once enjoyed, but then lost, equestrian status; he was active in the literary circles of Rome and Naples; he received some favors from Domitian, and wrote many of his shorter poems, the *Silvae* to Domitian and his colleagues. In particular, we know that the *Thebaid* was published in the early 90's AD, before Statius moved on to publication of his *Silvae* and to his unfinished *Achilleid*; thus, it was being composed at roughly the same time as the *Argonautica*, probably a few years later.[30]

Silius' poetic activity, too, can be assigned to the period of Domitian's rule. The chief piece of evidence is a letter (*Epist.* 3.7) written by the younger Pliny to Caninius Rufus reflecting on Silius' recent death and on his career--both political and literary. We learn from it that Silius was a member of the Senate, an accuser, and a suffect consul under Nero; after serving as governor of Asia in the late 70's he retired to the Naples area and involved himself in the literary scene there; in

---

[28] For the most recent summary and analysis of this issue see Lefevre (1971).
[29] Detailed summaries of these statements can be found in Vessey (1973), 15-54, and A. Hardie (1983), 58-72.
[30] Vessey (1973), 55.

AD 101 he starved himself to death in order to escape a long illness. In addition to Pliny's letter we have several references in Martial to Silius,[31] and while these external pieces of evidence do not allow us to reconstruct the exact chronology of the *Punica*'s publication, they do suggest that Silius was at least reading from his work in the early 90's AD, and that a publication date from the mid-90's to around 100 is probable.[32]

The evidence about these authors provided by other Roman writers also indicates the general reception of these poems by their contemporaries. Quintilian's comment about Valerius, however brief, confirms that he held Valerius' poetry in high regard, as it is made in a purely literary context. For the reception of Statius' epic poetry, we can look to Juvenal's comment at *Sat.* 7.82-86, describing the crowds that turn out when Statius reads from his Theban epic. Silius too was well enough received by his contemporaries. True, Pliny writes that he wrote with more industry than innate talent (*Epist.*3.7, *scribebat maiore cum cura quam ingenio*), but this statement, taken by scholars as a remark critical of Silius, need not be entirely negative--though excessive *cura* could be construed as a fault in rhetorical circles,[33] it was also a quality that many

---

[31] Martial 7.63, 8.66, 9.86, 11.48, and 11.49.

[32] On the basis of other scholar's analyses, and based on material we will subsequently encounter in this study, I take it as a working premise that Valerius Flaccus was the earliest of the three poets to circulate his material, and that Silius published his *Punica* after Statius published the *Thebaid*.

[33] See, e.g. Quintilian's description of Julius Africanus at *Inst.* 10.1.118, *hic concitatior, sed in cura verborum nimius et compositione nonnunquam longior et translationibus parum modicus.*

poets, Horace for one, esteemed.[34] In addition to Pliny, moreover, we should keep in mind Martial's several positive comments about Silius--in 7.63 he describes Silius' poetry as *perpetui numquam moritura volumina Sili* and *Latia carmina digna toga*. Such praise is especially significant, as it comes from a poet not inclined to bestow literary praise with any frequency.[35]

The available testimony, then, suggests that all three of these writers enjoyed respect, and even popularity, for their literary efforts; it further suggests that they should be read together, for the *Thebaid* and the *Punica* especially display a great awareness of the other epics being composed contemporaneously. Statius and Valerius both include in their poems lengthy treatments of the Lemnian massacre, and Statius might well be revising and commenting on what he knew of the Valerian version;[36] the several references to the Argo and to the *Argonautica* that we find in the *Thebaid* also testify to Valerius' influence on Statius.[37] Silius, too, was arguably influenced by Valerius' Lemnian episode, shaping his final scenes at

---

[34] See, e.g. Horace, *Ars* 291-298.

[35] Sullivan (1991), 74 n34, suggests that Martial held back on any criticisms of the *Punica*--and certainly the *Punica* did not conform to any of Martial's neo-Callimachean instincts--out of friendship. I see no reason not to presume that Martial also saw a fair amount of literary merit in the work. Perhaps Wilson (1993), 235, best frames the issue of contemporary attitudes to Silius: "Pliny's reaction shows what scholars have subsequently demonstrated over and over again, that the *Punica* is liable to discompose the prosaic mind."

[36] Vessey (1970) and (1985) provides some analysis of the interrelationship between the two accounts.

[37] e.g. *Theb.* 2.281; 3.351-3; 3.517-521; 8.212-214.

Saguntum in *Punica* 2 partly along Valerian lines; and there is no doubt that he frequently uses the *Thebaid* as a model for his narrative--the best example being the games that Scipio puts on in Spain in *Punica* 16, in which Silius includes a miniaturized vision of the end of the *Thebaid*.[38]

To sum up, we have some information on which to build a basic picture of the these poets' careers; the details are few, however, and the biographical outline is skeletal at best. No dramatic suicides in the face of Imperial prosecution, only a suicide to end a long and tired life; no tales of literary rivalries, only hints of each poet's appreciative awareness of his peers' efforts; no myths of last wishes for work to be burned (cynics might say that this is the one Vergilian path not followed); only two clearly finished products and one *opus interruptum.*

In fact, our epic poets, in one further respect, give us an opportunity rarely found in Latin literature: a chance for the poetry to speak for itself, and it is the poetic material they give us that takes us into the realms of Mayakovsky and Stalin, for the material that fills these poems speaks as powerfully to the conditions of their era as Mayakovsky's poem does to Stalinist Russia. As we noted earlier, they dwell repeatedly on images of tyranny, suicide, silence, and civil war, and they speak in sadly ironic terms about the powers and limitations of the poet's own voice in chronicling such matters.

---

[38] See Ahl (1986b), 2814-2815 and his bibliographical note.

Dymas at Thebes

For a case in point we might look at the Dymas episode in *Thebaid* 10.[39] In the first half of this book, during the night before the final battle between Eteocles and Polynices, Statius traces the movements of two raiding parties, one Theban and one Argive, sent out on night missions (*Theb*.10.1-448). His account closes with the story of two young Argives, Hopleus and Dymas, who die while trying to recover the corpses of Parthenopaeus and Tydeus, both killed in the previous day's fighting. Statius' narrative draws on two familiar models, moving back and forth between allusions to Dolon's encounter with Odysseus and Diomedes in *Iliad* 10, and to the ill-fated mission of Nisus and Euryalus in *Aeneid* 9.[40]

Like Nisus, Dymas sees his companion killed and steels himself to take on all the Thebans who surround him (10.409-422); later, like Dolon, he is presented by his captors with an opportunity to save himself in exchange for information (10.431-434). And yet, at the last moment, Statius dramatically veers away from the expectations that each of these epic models generates; Dymas finds death not in the middle of a battle (like Nisus), and not (like Dolon) at the hands of a cunning captor. On being offered his life by Amphion, he abruptly stabs

---

[39] For discussions of this passage, see Vessey (1973), 116-131, and R.D. Williams (1972), 76-86.

[40] Juhnke (1972), 144-147, provides a brief exposition of the connections between the Statian and Homeric episodes.

himself:

> "immo" ait Amphion, "regem si tanta cupido
> condere, quae timidis belli mens, ede, Pelasgis,
> quid fracti exanguesque parent; cuncta, ocius effer,
> et vita tumuloque ducis donatus abito."
> horruit et toto praecordia protinus Arcas
> implevit capulo. "summumne hoc cladibus" inquit
> "derat, ut adflictos turparem ego proditor Argos?
> nil emimus tanti, nec sic velit ipse cremari."
> (*Theb.*10.431-438)

> Amphion speaks. "hmmm...If you have so strong a desire to bury your king, tell me what intention your terrified Pelasgians have for battle--what are they devising in their broken and weakened state? Tell us all, and quickly, and you can get away, granted both your life and a tomb for your leader." The Arcadian shuddered and immediately filled his breast with his sword--hilt and all. He asks, "Were we missing this last thing to cap off our suffering, that I should foully betray the Argives when they are already so troubled? That is too high a price for me; nor would he himself want a pyre so."[41]

The suicide takes but a moment (we proceed from Amphion's guileful words directly to a description of Dymas plunging home his sword); yet Statius still manages to give the act some significant coloring. Dymas' suicide is a ferocious one, for Statius tells us that the sword enters Dymas' breast hilt and all (*toto praecordia ...implevit capulo*).[42] His suicide,

---

[41] All translations are, I should note, my own.
[42] See R.D. Williams (1972), 84-85, for the inescapability of this interpretation.

moreover, comes in response to a verbal offer from his captor; but Dymas only responds verbally to the offer after he has already driven his sword home--the act of suicide thus becomes the primary means of expression here, and speech itself becomes secondary.

As we have already noted, there is a significant amount of Homeric and Vergilian shading in this passage--especially Vergilian, for not only do Nisus and Euryalus clearly stand as literary models for Hopleus and Dymas, but Statius also specifically invokes the Vergilian pair in his salute of the Argives:

> tales optatis regum in amplexibus ambo,
> par insigne animis, Aetolus et inclytus Arcas,
> egregias efflant animas letoque fruuntur.
> vos quoque sacrati, quamvis mea carmina surgant
> inferiore lyra, memores superabitis annos.
> forsitan et comites non aspernabitur umbras
> Euryalus Phrygiique admittet gloria Nisi.
> (*Theb.*10.442-448)

> Such was the pair, in the longed for embrace of their kings, equally distinguished for their courage, the Aetolian and the celebrated Argive; they breathe forth their remarkable spirits and enjoy their death. You too have been anointed, though my song rises from an inferior lyre, and you will overcome the unforgetting years. Perhaps, too, Euryalus won't spurn your shades' companionship, and the glory of Phrygian Nisus will welcome you.

There are, however, significant shifts in Statius'

representation of the scene, for while Nisus' death in *Aeneid* 9 has obvious self-destructive aspects to it, Dymas simply kills himself, confounding any expectations of further complication or delay that the Homeric and Vergilian scenes raise in the *Thebaid*'s readers. Statius' subsequent linkage of his own poetic powers to Dymas' fate recalls Vergil's meditation on his song's commemorative power after the deaths of Nisus and Euryalus (*Aen*.9.446-449). But it shifts the focus of its Vergilian model in one key respect, for as we will see in our extended discussion of suicide, the Flavian poets (unlike their epic predecessors) repeatedly append their expressed hopes for the commemorative power of their songs to acts of suicide, ironically linking claims of poetry's permanence to visions of self-destruction.

Dymas' suicide takes place in the midst of a civil, indeed fraternal, war; it is a profoundly paradoxical action of defiance and self-destruction, committed in order to deny control to another; an act that silences its doer, it occasions the poet's contemplation of his own words' durability. We can, then, see in this suicide a network of images and themes that in fact runs through all three of the Flavian epics, and we might turn now to explore the parameters of these themes in all three epics. Our discussion, like the chapters that follow, will focus on suicide, tyranny, and civil war; the issues of silence and poetic power will surface within these different frameworks.

Suicide

Dymas' actions in *Thebaid* 10 raise several large questions about the poetic material on which these writers draw, chief among which is the question of how we account for the sheer number of suicides we find in these poems:

Dymas pursues the same course of action as Maeon in *Thebaid* 3,[43] and as Menoeceus later in *Thebaid* 10.[44] In the *Punica*, in addition to several kamikaze forays on the battlefield, the entire population of Saguntum commits mass suicide in *Punica* 2;[45] the younger Scipio tries twice to kill himself in *Punica* 4;[46] a young Roman kills himself (after mistakenly killing his father) on the morning of the Cannae disaster;[47] and a series of Capuans named Decius, Virrius, and Taurea, promote and commit suicide at different points in *Punica* 11-13.[48] Finally, we find Valerius Flaccus similarly engaged with the issue in what he finished of the *Argonautica*; in the opening book he narrates in great detail the suicide of Jason's parents;[49] and in *Argonautica* 7, Medea contemplates suicide as a solution

---

[43] *Theb.* 3.87-91.
[44] *Theb.* 10.774-782.
[45] *Pun.* 2.612-695.
[46] *Pun.* 4.457-459.
[47] *Pun.* 9.173-177.
[48] Decius: *Pun.* 11.186-188; Virrius and his followers: *Pun.* 13.261-298; Taurea: *Pun.* 13.374-380.
[49] *Arg.* 1.767-851.

to her troubles.[50] This is a *lot* of suicide.

Part of the reason for its prominence revolves around the peculiar aura taken on by suicide in the first century AD--in fact from the time of Cato Uticensis on.[51] In addition to its fashionable status as an action, it has become an occasional topic in rhetorical exercises, in epic, in tragedy, and in parody.[52] All of these traditions come to bear on the Flavian epics, but they do not explain the frequency with which these poets present the act. Moreover, as we remarked above, all three poems draw a strong link between their several suicides and epic *fama*, as the suicides provide the most common occasion for comments by the poet about the commemorative power of his poetry. This makes for a very different epic world from that in which Homer or Vergil operated: The *Iliad* and *Odyssey* celebrated the *kleos andron* primarily as epitomized by those feats (of strength, of cunning, and of wisdom) by which the many heroes helped themselves, their comrades, and their leaders; the *Aeneid*, written in the post-Catonian world, makes room for devotional deaths on the battlefield and for more contemplative suicide in the case of Dido--but no reference is

---

[50] *Arg.* 7.331-337.

[51] The best recent discussions of suicide in Imperial Rome are those of Grise (1982) and Griffin (1986); for explorations of specific aspects of suicide, see Bayet (1951), Rutz (1960), and Dutoit (1936).

[52] For its presence in rhetorical exercises, see the elder Seneca's *Suasoriae* and *Controversiae, passim*; in epic, Dido's suicide in *Aeneid* 4 and the suicide of Vulteius and his comrades in *Pharsalia* 4. Suicide is frequently considered in Seneca's tragedies; and we find it parodied at several points of Petronius' *Satyricon*, in sectioons 94 and 108 for example.

made to suicide when Cato appears on Aeneas' shield, and Vergil generally reserves his comments about his poem's commemorative power for noble deaths at the hands of one's enemies.

It is the Flavian epics that first draw a consistent connection between writing / commemoration and suicide, and this equation creates some significant oppositions, for now the *fama* that Cato and his imitators earn by their actions is pitted against the *fama* imparted by poetry; an act of total self-destruction becomes the measure of a person's lifelong achievements; and the same act of self-obliteration becomes the focus of the poet's powers of creation.

Their frequency is not the only characteristic to mark these suicides, for the poets make it clear that the stress they put on suicide is deliberate: all three of them alter their mythic and historical traditions in order to bring suicide into their poems. Valerius alters the mythic tradition of the Argo voyage to unite Jason's parents in suicide immediately after Jason's departure. Statius invents suicide scenes for Maeon (*Thebaid* 3) and Dymas (*Thebaid* 10), and includes a lengthy description of Menoeceus' suicide (also *Thebaid* 10). Silius spends the first two books of his poem, nearly one eighth of his entire epic, on the fall of Saguntum, altering the historical tradition of Saguntum's end to give suicide greater prominence; and he later creates suicide scenes at Cannae and Capua.

The suicides at Capua, furthermore, have a momentum common to much of the *Punica*'s action--in the first scene, suicide is urged in the face of Hannibal's occupation of the city; later two other Capuans named Virrius and Taurea commit suicide in the face of the subsequent *Roman* occupation. Silius singles out the last of these suicides, Taurea's, for particular praise, saying he couldn't possibly approve the suppression of such a noble deed (*decus*), even if it was done by an enemy of Rome (*Pun*.13.369-370). Silius frequently sets the Carthaginians up as monstrous and cruel oppressors, and later, as Rome gains the upper hand, attributes the same actions to the Romans.

All three of these poets take particular advantage of the rhetorical tradition surrounding suicide in that they are clearly engaging in a debate about suicide's justifiability as a *political* act. Suicide is not presented as a means of escaping sickness or old age in these poems--not even in the *Punica*--nor is it seen primarily as an altruistic act of self-sacrifice done to save others (though altruism is a factor in the suicides of Dymas and Menoeceus in *Thebaid* 10). Almost all of the suicides in these poems are committed in the face of tyranny, as acts of defiance meant to deny a tyrant control of the individual's fate.

So far we have the following facts about suicide in these poems: it is a remarkably frequent occurrence; its presence often involves dramatic changes in literary and mythic traditions; it is the prime locus for the poets' comments about their own powers; and it is presented as a political act. There is one final and important point: all three poems suggest, in varying degrees, their own skepticism about the ultimate value of suicide, especially as a defiant response to tyranny. In so doing, the poets can be seen to add their voices to the debate about suicide that took place primarily in philosophical circles. Most surprisingly, at the moment of suicide, they repeatedly describe the individual about to commit suicide in terms that they otherwise reserve solely for tyrants. The suicidal characters possess as fanatical a zeal for self control as the tyrants possess for political control, and their assertions of this control come in actions as destructive and deadly as any tyrannical acts. There is a black and sterile shading to the suicide scenes that has yet to be recognized.

The suicide scenes of these poems, then, create a rich poetic matrix in which the issues of writing, self-determination, and self-destruction, all intersect. They also come to bear on the other two major concerns of this book, the portrayal of rulers and the presence of civil war.

Tyrants and subjects

> et ideo ego adulescentulos existimo in scholis stultissimos fieri, quia nihil ex his, quae in usu habemus, aut audiunt aut vident, sed piratas cum catenis in litore stantes, sed tyrannos edicta scribentes, quibus imperent filiis ut patrum suorum capita praecidant...
> (*Satyricon* 1.3)
>
> Furthermore, I am of the opinion that young men are becoming exceedingly dim-witted in the schools, since they neither hear nor see anything of real

practicality in these places, but only hear of pirates standing on the beach carrying chains, and tyrants scribbling orders in which they command sons to chop off their own parents' heads...

> ibi durum Eteoclea cernit
> sublimem solio saeptumque horrentibus armis.
> iura ferus populo trans legem ac tempora regni
> iam fratris de parte dabat; sedet omne paratus
> in facinus queriturque fidem tam sero reposci.
> (*Theb*.2.384-388)

There he finds stern Eteocles high up on his throne and fenced in with bristling weapons. Eteocles is wildly imposing laws on his people, in spite of the law and terms of his rule, in his brother's place; he stays seated, primed for any crime and he complains that the agreement is being invoked too late.

As the passage from *Thebaid* 2 should indicate, by the time of the Dymas episode Eteocles has long since been established as an archetypal tyrant, familiar from both rhetorical and poetic models. His presence in the Dymas scene is indirect, but important, for Dymas' captor, Amphion, is on a scouting mission for Eteocles, and both before and after Dymas' suicide Statius emphasizes Eteocles' connections to the scene (*Theb*.10.387-89,449-52).

Tyrants figure in most of the suicides we find; in fact they loom large everywhere in these poems, and this pervasiveness of tyranny is significant in itself. It is stranger to note how, when tyrants appear, our poets pause again and again to catalogue the same tyrannical attributes: purple rage, paranoia, cruelty, and lust for power--we see these details over and over in each epic, even in the *Punica* where Silius sometimes has to work overtime to squeeze tyrants into the Hannibalic war.[53]

Although tyrants populate most Greek and Roman epics, the poets of previous eras never dwell so consistently on their various characteristics. Why bother? As the opening of the *Satyricon* would suggest, one need only mention a name such as Pelias in Rome and everyone can imagine his various characteristics and habits. Ovid's *Metamorphoses* offers some proof of this point; it is a poem absolutely crammed with tyrannical types, but once Ovid sketches out the type with a couple of figures, Lycaon and Tereus most notably, he never bothers to rehearse all of the formulaic details. Rather than assuming that the Flavian poets repeated a typology because of their rhetorical training or simply for the sake of repetition, then, let us assume that such repetition carries some significance.

We first need to acknowledge the anti-Imperial force that these literary types can bear. Maternus' writings and remarks in Tacitus' *Dialogus* once again serve to remind us that this level of signification is one which the Romans recognized. Indeed, one of the characteristics common to most of the Flavian epic tyrants is the control or manipulation of silence--a

---

[53] Compare, for example, his transformation of Hasdrubal into a completely tyrannical figure (*Pun*. 1.144-164) to Livy's description of a more benign Hasdrubal (21.2.3-5).

tool mastered by Tiberius and Domitian both. Here our Flavian poets might well be constructing their model with specific *principes* in mind.

But there is more to the tyrants than this. If we read these epics as models of different types of political and social behavior, we find these tyrants, impressively uniform in character and action, triggering extremely different reactions in their different contexts--much as in the elder Seneca's *Controversiae* and *Suasoriae*, where the alteration of one detail in a proposition changes the entire nature of the arguments. In the Flavian epics the tyrants stand as a major constant in the models created by each poet; their presence keeps the models focused on authoritarian rule, but the reactions of others are as important as the tyrannical essence itself.

The Flavians reshape the tyrannical model they receive from earlier literature: they distill it somewhat, strip it down (by eliminating lust and sexual crimes from the list of attributes). They give their tyrants new weapons--silence and the ability to conceal emotions and intentions. And, perhaps in response to the younger Seneca's various discussions of tyranny, they devote a great deal of poetic energy to the balance, the give and take, that exists between ruler and subject. Silence in a tyrant generates silence--or anonymous complaint--in his people. Fear and hatred are set in the same equilibrium. A tyrant's moments of instability produce instability and fickleness in the *populus*. These balances, though, stand in contrast to all the ways in which the poets show tyranny and authority transgressing normal personal, societal, and even literary bounds; these transgressions keep the relationship between tyrant and subject in permanent imbalance.

Such representations of rulership make sense in Flavian Rome. As we have already discussed, this is a period of growing authoritarianism in the Principate, and the expansion of Imperial power no doubt intruded on all classes in Rome. In fact, the classes to which these writers belonged were losing the most in terms of political power and *auctoritas*; and the population at large was confronting consequences, both global and trivial, of an expansionist administration--the same Imperial family that introduced a tax on public latrines, for example, also exercises an increasingly tight control on the most prominent of the surviving magistracies--Domitian held the consulship ten times during his own Principate. The tyrants, models of absolute monopolization of power, offer the poets a steady opportunity to explore, each in his own way, the dynamics between ruler and subject, the mechanics at play in a monarchic state.

Civil war

Dymas' suicide takes place in the midst of a civil war, and is itself emblematic of that war. Lucan had, after all, opened his epic about the civil wars of the first century BC with an image of Rome turning its sword on itself as a metaphor for these wars,[54] and so the equation had been drawn between suicide and civil war by the time the Flavian epics were written.

This book will also examine the several means used by each poet to introduce the issue of civil war into his text. Granted, in the *Thebaid* the theme of civil war is an inescapable fact;[55] but even Statius raises the issue more frequently than a reader might expect. Valerius and Silius, on the other hand, drawing on mythic and historical traditions less evocative of civil war, bring the issue before the reader's eyes with surprising frequency.

In making civil war such a focal point in their works, all three poets are certainly responding to conditions that they experienced in their own lifetimes. For shortly after Lucan's *Pharsalia* was published, civil war reared its head again at Rome in the wars of AD 68-69, at a time when all three of the Flavian epic poets were developing their poetic perspectives.[56] So too, they were without a doubt well into their work when Domitian, with no male heir or successor-designate, quelled the revolt of Saturninus in AD 89 in the same general area (Upper Germany as opposed to Lower) that had witnessed Vitellius' entry into the strife of AD 69. Even aside from the rumors about the animosity between Vespasian's two sons and about Domitian's possible hand in Titus' death, several historical

---

[54] *Phar.* 1.2-3, *canimus populumque potentem / in sua victrici conversum viscera dextra.*
[55] Henderson (1993), 162-167 offers a vivid articulation of this point.
[56] Henderson (1993), 166.

events took place in the post-Neronian world to keep the issue of civil war alive at Rome.

Of the three epics, the *Argonautica* and the *Thebaid* maintain the most consistent emphasis on the theme of civil war, though they approach the issue from different angles. During the Argo's voyage, the crew encounters a variety of societies and peoples, yet civil war seems to be a common denominator at every step of the voyage: the potential for it exists at Iolcus in *Argonautica* 1 and it breaks out on Lemnos in the second book; a war that is all but civil is fought in the Cyzicus episode of *Argonautica* 3; and Valerius devotes an entire book to his unprecedented account of civil war at Colchis (*Argonautica* 6).[57] Valerius' repeated turns to incidents of civil war seem to suggest that there is an inevitable tendency toward strife in all societies, an understandable enough suggestion given Rome's own experiences between 100 BC and AD 100.

Statius, on the other hand, focuses on civil war at Thebes alone, expressing bewilderment at the outset as to how to limit his discussion, given the long tradition of strife in that city. Fraternal warfare can be traced back right to Thebes' origins (the same is true of Rome), and Statius' poem focuses on one stage in the unending cycle of Theban civil war. Yet even in the *Thebaid* civil strife can break out at surprising moments--most notably at Nemea at the close of *Thebaid* 5--and in *Thebaid* 12, after the war between Polynices and Eteocles

---

[57] We will discuss these episodes in more detail in subsequent chapters.

has run its course Thebes is immediately plunged back into war against Theseus. Statius' cyclic conception of strife at Thebes is no less appropriate than Valerius' to 1st century Rome, for as we have pointed out, though the Julio-Claudian and Flavian houses had each brought decades of respite and political stability to Rome, the specter of civil war and governmental collapse still reared its head repeatedly.

When we turn to the *Punica*, we have to take into account the unique problems posed by Silius' historical material; yet Silius too is able to bring the theme of civil war before his reader's eyes in several ways. He uses three chief vehicles to accomplish this:

1. the Saguntum episode of *Punica* 1-2 which sets the stage for many of the thematic programs of the epic.

2. his poem's repeated allusions to scenes of civil strife in Statius' *Thebaid*.

3. his remarkable and anachronistic use of Roman names throughout the epic (he fills his Roman legions with soldiers bearing such names as Marius, Sulla, Milo, Brutus, Catilina, and Casca).

Our analysis of these three points should clarify one of my chief arguments regarding the *Punica*: it uses the *Aeneid* and the *Pharsalia* as epic termini, or "bookends"--where the *Aeneid* traced Rome's epic, historic, and political origins, and the *Pharsalia* charted Rome's political demise, the *Punica* slips inside these boundaries to define the key moment at which Rome's energy finally and irreversibly shifted from positive evolution to strife-torn devolution.

Towards a new perspective on Flavian epic

If we return for a moment to the passage from Mayakovsky's final poem cited at the outset of this chapter, we might now better appreciate how it sets into relief many of the issues involved in a reading of Flavian epic. As I have already noted, the material of Mayakovsky's final poem offers an immediate parallel to some of the material of Flavian epic in the links that it draws between acceptable and unacceptable poetic voices, between overt and coded appropriations of literary independence, and between suicide and literary creation.

The first of these points, the contrast between acceptable and unacceptable poetic voices in Mayakovsky's poem, finds some correspondence with Flavian epic in the proems of both the *Argonautica* and the *Thebaid*, for Valerius and Statius both begin their mythic works by contrasting their choice of material to works more directly concerned with the Flavian regime itself. Valerius does not press this point too far, only noting that he will sing of the great deeds of men of old (*Arg*.1.11-12, *veterumque... veneranda canenti / facta virum*) while Domitian himself will sing of Titus' and Vespasian's Judaean victories (*Arg*.1.12-14, *versam proles tua pandet Idumen / (namque potest), Solymo ac nigrantem pulvere fratrem / spargentemque faces et in omni turre furentem*). While the contrast here seems simply that between the mythic past and current events, with neither topic seeming more appropriate than the other, Valerius' words nevertheless imply a refusal to sing of Flavian achievements himself.

Statius, on the other hand, openly contrasts his topic of the Theban wars and the house of Oedipus to a poem about Domitian's German campaigns in a way that emphasizes the potential inappropriateness of his epic's theme: he says "let the mixed-up house of Oedipus provide the limit for my song, *since* I would not yet dare to sing of Domitian's northern triumphs (*Theb.*1.16-18, *limes mihi carminis esto / Oedipodae confusa domus, quando Itala nondum / signa nec Arctoos ausim spirare triumphos*). Shortly after this statement he claims that he will only sing of Domitian's deeds when he has been incited to boldness by a Pierian gadfly (*Theb.*1.32-33, *tempus erit, cum Pierio tua fortior oestro / facta canam*). Statius' Theban topic, unnatural and horrific, is thus cast as the alternative choice to an epic about Domitian's own campaigns.

Mayakovsky's poem also provides a model of some means afforded the individual poet to bypass governmental control, for in his poem's two separate sections he is still able to juxtapose his public and civic poetic voice with a freer and more romantic private voice, leaving it to surviving readers to appreciate the tension and irony created by the two conflicting voices. Mayakovsky's contemporaries and successors used other literary devices to evade and defy Soviet censorship as well--for example, during the Stalinist period and in subsequent eras, Soviet writers developed a type of ambiguous and coded language known as "Aesopian," which was designed to maintain literary independence and provide a language of opposition.[58]

Similar rhetorical and literary devices were available to the poets of the Roman world, especially the rhetorical uses of *emphasis* and *schema*, as defined by Quintilian and other rhetoricians.[59] Quintilian and his fellow rhetoricians describe how these rhetorical techniques (*emphasis* = to conceal additional meanings inside a statement; *schema* = to arrange one's statements in such a way as to protect one's self[60]) come into play when open speech and criticism are unsafe, and Quintilian notes their pervasiveness in his own day.[61] By using these techniques, a writer or speaker could avoid punishment; indeed, even if a ruler recognized the criticism, the critic could remain safe, so long as his words offered some alternative interpretation.

As we have already argued, censorship and prosecution of writers existed in Flavian Rome, but these rhetorical devices offer a writer room for literary and rhetorical attack upon the *princeps*, so long as it took other forms--even the form of flattery, for, as all rhetoricians suggest, and as the emperor Tiberius himself appreciated, flattery is a highly suspect form of

---

[58] See, especially, the discussion of "Aesopian" language in Russian literature of the twentieth century in Loseff (1984).

[59] These rhetorical techniques and their use by Greek and Roman orators and poets are discussed by Ahl (1984).

[60] Ahl (1984), 176-179. Among the relevant passages cited by Ahl are Demetrius, *Eloc.* 287, and Quintilian, *Inst.* 9.2.64ff.

[61] *Inst.* 9.2.65; he is speaking primarily of *schema.*

communication.[62] We need, then, to appreciate more fully the ways in which the Flavian poets encoded their criticisms and built them into their poetic works.

By the same token, my chief objective is not simply to determine whether or not these epics were pro-or anti-Domitian.[63] Reading these epics solely as anti-imperial statements flattens out their contours as irreparably as any other single-minded approach. My initial point is that these poets work with literary forms recognized by both the public and the *princeps* as an appropriate medium for political commentary and critique. We then need to move on to see how the poets use these forms to create different models of political behavior--they explore such issues as personal freedom, tyranny, and civil war from different vantage points, examining the effects of different political activities on both the individual and society as a whole.

The third point of correspondence between Mayakovsky's poem and the Flavian epics lies in the despairing links they draw between suicide and poetic expression. Mayakovsky extended this poetic conceit to its ultimate extent, using "At the Top of My Voice" as his own suicide note; none of the Flavian writers were as extreme in their approach to this issue, limiting their exploration of suicide and poetic voice to more literary levels (Silius Italicus' suicide does not seem to

---

[62] See Tacitus, *Ann.* 1.52.2, where Tiberius' excessive praise of Germanicus marks the emperor's displeasure at Germanicus' achievements.

[63] The recent volume on poetry and propaganda in the Augustan era, Powell (1992), reflects, in most of its essays, a similar disinterest in defining the politics of poetry in such absolute and polarized terms.

have been connected in any way with literary production or censorship).

Valerius Flaccus draws an intriguing link between poetry and suicide in his poem's opening lines, when he asks his emperor's favor in undertaking his literary task:

> eripe me populis et habenti nubila terrae,
> sancte pater, veterumque fave veneranda canenti
> facta virum.
> *(Arg.*1.9-11)

> Take me away from people and the earth with its clouds, blessed father, a grant me favor as I sing of the glorious deeds of men of old.

His words here, *eripe me populis et habenti nubila terrae*, are cast in Horatian tones, drawing on the language of poetic apotheosis and recalling Horace's claim at the close of his first ode, *me gelidum nemus / nympharumque leves cum Satyris chori / secernunt populo (Carm.*1.1.30-32). But, whereas Horace's entire first ode explores different ways of life and describes the aspects of his own calling that distinguish it from other livelihoods, Valerius simply wishes for separation from other people and from his earthly existence. Moreover, before *Argonautica* 1 draws to a close, Valerius uses similar language specifically in connection with suicide, as the ghost of Cretheus, in trying to persuade his son Aeson to commit suicide, says at *Argonautica* 1.749, *quin rapis hanc animam et famulos citus effugis artus*?

The Flavian epicists seem far more preoccupied with the

prospect of literary death and silence than earlier generations of Roman poets. Statius and Valerius question the durability and popularity of epic at several points in their poems; Silius saves his meditations on epic for *Punica* 13, where Scipio's journey to the Hades includes an encounter with the ghost of Homer and a suggestion that epic now belongs more to the Underworld than to the human world.

There is in the Flavian epics, then, an ambivalent and conflicting set of tendencies that distinguishes them from their predecessors. On the one hand they are heirs to the most public of Roman poetic genres--a genre which, as lyric *recusationes* suggest, was expected to engage itself in open dialogue with the Principate regarding Imperial policy and achievements, and which could couch its more critical commentary in the literary and rhetorical figures familiar to its Roman audience. At the same time, as we will see more clearly in later chapters, these poems mark the possible futility of such a stance in their preoccupation with suicidal heroes and in their comments on poetry itself.

This book will explore these issues and the thematic material common to all three epics primarily from a broad, content-oriented perspective, focusing more on the types of scenes, characters, and events, that the poets choose to include, than on narrower questions of comparative philology. While my critical sensibilities lie generally with the work of Ahl, Henderson, Masters, and Dominik, I am also firmly of the opinion that there is still a great deal of initial discussion that needs to be covered with each of these epics--especially with the *Argonautica* and *Punica*. Where Augustan poetry has benefitted from generations of literary discussion, Flavian epic still begs some very basic sorts of literary and thematic analysis that can make the poems more accessible to different levels of readers. The generally positive reception these poems found in their own day testifies to the pertinence Romans saw in them. The fact that these poets focus so consistently on tyrants, civil war, suicide, and silence and that they shape this material in relation to their epic predecessors, suggests that we might find in them important commentary on the Flavian world and on the poet's place in it.

CHAPTER 2: READING THE EPICS

References to Valerius, Statius, and Silius in other contemporary sources, rhetorical theory, and historical data all provide some context for these epics. From these sources we can construe an active literary scene in Flavian Rome (active especially in terms of epic poetry) taking place within a restrictive environment created by the principate's expanding powers and its control of literary activity. Rhetoric clearly influenced the shaping of these poems in several ways (again, one thinks of the ways in which their subject matter parallels the material of the elder Seneca's *Suasoriae* and *Controversiae*) among which we must include the techniques of *emphasis* and *schema*.

But these poems also provide their own clues about their various connections to Flavian Rome. In each one the mythic or historical field of the narrative is mapped onto a particularly Flavian grid, and the points at which the Flavian grids surface occur at significant moments in each text. Before we move on to a more detailed exploration of specific themes within the poems, then, we need to define some of the techniques that each of these poets uses in constructing such a contemporary grid, for these contemporary references allow each poet to create a dual perspective for his poem--a perspective from which the reader can view both the action within the narrative and the figured ways in which this action comments on the poet's own world.

Even such elemental issues as choice of subject matter are involved here: we might recall Maternus' words to his visitors in Tacitus' *Dialogus*, (*Dial.* 3.2, *Quod si qua omisit Cato, sequenti recitatione Thyestes dicet*), as they underscore the power Romans saw in mythic and historical topics alike to speak to contemporary political and social issues. In light of Maternus' statement we can see that each of our poets has chosen a narrative tradition with clear allusive potential.

Valerius, for example, in turning to the voyage of the Argo, has fixed on a mythic tradition ideally suited to a Roman treatment in that it can take great advantage of two systems of imagery well established in all Latin poetry: the ship as a ship of poetry, and the ship as a ship of state.[1] The Argo, as it travels toward Colchis, becomes the vehicle for Valerius' poem as well as for the Argonauts (or perhaps we should say that Valerius' poem is as efficient a vehicle for the Argonauts and their achievements as the Argo); and Valerius' own vatic powers match the oracular capacity of the Argo, which is built with wood from Jupiter's grove at Dodona. So too, the Argo's capacity to stand as a ship of state should be clear: the *topos* is as well established in the Roman poetic tradition as that of the poetic ship; and the Argonauts led by Jason constitute their own

---

[1] For this point see Davis (1990), *passim*. Of the Flavian writers, Valerius has received the least analysis in recent years. The most extensive general discussion of his poem can be found in Burck (1979), 208-253.

political body on board their ship, debating and interacting among themselves and among the peoples that they encounter.

Valerius, like Catullus, treats the Argo voyage in paradoxical terms as both the consummate achievement of a more heroic and golden era and the first cause of later commercial and material corruption.[2] The voyage represents the greatest cooperative effort of a multitude of mythic heroes who embark on the first nautical voyage by man; yet their successful completion of their mission, the capture and transport of the Golden Fleece, will bring man into an age in which gold and travel both will corrupt society irreparably.

Statius' poem finds fewer precedents in the Roman literary tradition than does Valerius', and of the three Flavian epicists he seems the most at risk in his choice of topic--the *confusa domus* of Oedipus and the *nuda potestas* that corrupted his sons and Creon.[3] Nevertheless, despite the unpleasant implications the Theban tale bears for the Flavian principate, Statius is able to distance his poem sufficiently from direct association with the Imperial house. He states simply at his poems outset that he is not yet ready to write of Domitian

---

[2] For the connections between Valerius and Catullus, and for the relationship between the Argo voyage and subsequent corruption, see again Davis (1990), and also Boyle's introductory essay on Valerius Flaccus in Boyle and Sullivan (1991), 270-277. Feeney (1991), 330-335, rightly emphasizes the links between Valerius' poem and Seneca's *Medea* in their similar visions of the connection between the Argo voyage and the end of the Golden Age.

[3] The most recent, detailed studies of the *Thebaid* can be found in Ahl (1986b), Burck (1979), 300-351, Dominik (1994a) and (1994b), Henderson (1993), and Vessey (1973) and (1986). For the linkage between the house of Oedipus and Roman Imperial families, see Henderson (1993), 166.

himself, and has chosen the Theban myth as an interim topic. Such a statement is loaded with its own connotations, for it implies--but does not openly state--that the Theban myth provides a logical step on the way to writing about Domitian; but Statius leaves it to the reader to make this deduction, effectively shielding himself in the process.[4]

In its topic, the Second Punic War, Silius' poem is certainly the most Roman of the three,[5] and it does not involve material so obviously dangerous as the *Thebaid*.[6] It does, however, afford Silius two general areas within which to explore the links between his own Rome and its past. First, the poem treats a period of Roman history to which Romans regularly turned for models of individual and collective behavior, both positive and negative--Hannibal, the various Scipios, Fabius, Varro, Marcellus, and Claudius Nero, all can be found in Imperial literature as exemplars of different human (and Republican) traits and actions. One might well look at the *Punica* as a work that re animates all of these figures in a non-historical, non-biographical setting. Second, the chronological progress of the war from Punic to Roman triumph provides Silius with an opportunity both to examine Rome's victory in light of earlier Carthaginian successes and implicitly to compare

---

[4] Ahl (1986b), 2817-2819.

[5] For general studies of the *Punica* see Ahl (1986a), Burck (1979), 254-299, and (1984), Kissell (1979), Küppers (1986), Reitz (1982), and von Albrecht (1964).

[6] It is, nevertheless, worth recalling the fact that Domitian executed Mettius Pompusianus, in part because he named two of his slaves Mago and Hannibal. See Suetonius, *Dom*.10.3.

Rome's Flavian status as a supremely victorious state to its status within the narrative as an emerging power.

The topics of these epics themselves, then, suggest some very basic ways in which these writers can configure their work to meet contemporary issues and interests. The shape that they give these topics also has some bearing on how we see these poems relating to their era; these points might best be articulated by presenting a brief summary of each epic and its scope.

Outline #1: The Argonautica

Incomplete as it might be, Valerius' *Argonautica* covers a vast amount of mythic terrain. The Argo voyage always stood as one of the seminal events in the Greco-Roman mythic tradition an event which, like the Calydonian boar-hunt or the Trojan War, gathered together dozens of mythic heroes and allowed them to visit many different parts of the Mediterranean world. Valerius is ready at every turn to take his own advantage of the Argo tradition's originative capacity: he fits Troy and the origins of the Trojan War into his scheme of things; he gives far greater place than did Apollonius Rhodius to such mythic events as Hercules' freeing of Prometheus; mythic innovation is, in short, as important a keynote in his poem as mythic tradition.[7]

---

[7] For a more focussed study of how the *Argonautica* works on innovative levels within the mythic tradition, see Malamud and McGuire (1993).

Valerius certainly draws on Apollonius Rhodius' Hellenistic poem and on Catullus' briefer treatment of the myth in Poem 64. He most probably also avails himself of other epic and dramatic versions of the story that survived at least into his own day: Ovid's account of these myths in the *Metamorphoses* and his lost *Medea*; Seneca's *Medea*; and the *Argonautica* of Varro of Atax, from the first century BC.[8]

His *Argonautica* breaks off in the middle of Book 8, at the moment when Medea and Jason, in flight from Colchis, are about to kill Medea's brother and pursuer, Absyrtus. Debate carries on regarding the intended length of Valerius' epic; though some would argue that the poem would have ended with the eighth book, it needs pointing out that, if the poet were to maintain the same proportional relationship between his poem and Apollonius', we should expect that he had at least two books of material ahead of him.[9]

In *Argonautica* 1 Valerius makes clear his willingness to diverge from Apollonius' account. The entire first book focuses on the beginnings of the voyage, but while much of his treatment follows an Apollonian outline (Pelias' initial predicament and plan, and his catalogue of Argonauts), he abandons some of Apollonius' material (the debate over who should command the expedition; Orpheus' first song; the

---

[8] See Statius, *Silv.* 2.7.77, and Vessey (1982), 580.
[9] Schetter (1959) argues that in fact the poem was finished in eight books, and simply not preserved in its entirety; see also Davis (1990), 60, and Boyle (1991), 274.

argument between Idmon and Idas) and also creates several scenes of his own (the reaction of Mars and Sol to this expedition at *Arg*.1.498-560; and the final scene of his opening book--the suicide of Aeson and Alcimede which foils Pelias' plan to kill the couple, *Arg*.1.700-851). These additions to the mythic tradition are of special significance, and we will examine both episodes in later sections.

Valerius has a talent for both creating dramatic scenes and quickly moving from one to another. Once past the first book, his epic races from place to place, but on the way to Colchis the poem presents a series of powerful episodes. In *Argonautica* 2 the Argonauts stop for an extended stay at Lemnos, the recent victim of Venus' anger (2.82-428); they pause at Troy (2.450-578) in an episode not included by Apollonius--and their stop here is significant, for Laomedon seals Troy's doom by his mistreatment of Hercules;[10] they then move on, reaching the island of Cyzicus at the close of the book. *Argonautica* 3 narrates their ill-starred battle with the Doliones and the death of Cyzicus, who is punished by Cybele (3.1-459), and then describes the loss, at Juno's instigation, of Hercules and Hylas from the expedition (3.484-725). The Argonauts next encounter in the fourth book the boxer-king Amycus (4.99-343), and the Clashing Rocks (4.637-732), before landing among the Mariandyni, a people of the Black Sea ruled by Lycus.

---

[10] For which see Barnes (1981).

The Argonauts reach Colchis early in *Argonautica* 5, after losing two of their most valuable crew members, Idmon and Tiphys (5.1-62). They find there a situation somewhat different from that of Apollonius' account, for Aeetes is embroiled in a civil war against his brother (a war that Juno stirred up back in *Argonautica* 3 to distract Pallas). Valerius weaves details about this war and about Colchis together with a narrative of Medea's growing love for Jason in Book 5, and then after a full book devoted to an account of the civil war, he turns in *Argonautica* 7 to an account of Jason's and Medea's trials and triumphs. As in Apollonius' *Argonautica*, Medea here takes center stage. Even Jason's struggles against the fire-breathing bulls and the *terrigenae* take a back seat--indeed, Valerius devotes 114 verses to them, while Apollonius, the model of poetic economy, gave them 178.[11] Jason's feats end the book, and what we have of Book 8 details the departure of the Argonauts, with Medea's help, from Colchis.

Valerius' organization of his poem reflects the way in which his narratological concerns might have differed from those of Apollonius and others who worked within this mythic tradition. We see this especially in his additions to the Argo tradition, where he foregrounds such topics as civil war, tyranny, and suicide; but we also can find reflections of this fact in the different shape he gives to more traditional elements in the myth. For example, though he narrates several episodes

---

[11] Compare Valerius' account, *Arg.* 7.539-653, to Apollonius' *Arg.* 3.1225-1403.

found in Apollonius' poem, he changes the episodes' structures to include more frequent portrayals of divine machinations and retribution. Thus when the Argonauts inadvertently fight their allies, the Doliones, and kill the king, Cyzicus, Valerius alters Apollonius' account, explaining that Cyzicus had to die for offenses he gave to Cybele (3.20-31).[12] So too, when Juno and Venus scheme to remove Hercules from the expedition, they get Pallas out of the way by inciting the civil war at Colchis as a distraction for her (3.487-508).[13]

The different role Valerius gives to divinity takes us into a world that owes much to the *Aeneid* and the *Metamorphoses* in its depiction of the victimization of mortals by various divinities. Favoritism from one god often entails automatic hostility from another, and mortals can transgress divine interests unwittingly. But, while such sad realities might be the theme of literature in many previous periods, it means something different to represent divinity in this way in Valerius' day. For Valerius writes in a time when Romans are expected to acknowledge the divinity of the Roman emperor (though, as Vespasian's famous jest on his deathbed shows,[14] they did not necessarily have to believe in it); and Domitian, in particular, put great stock in his own divinity. Indeed, the fact that Juno

---

[12] In Apollonius' poem Cyzicus' death is simply attributed to fate (*Arg*. 1.1030-1035).

[13] Feeney (1991), 335-336, argues that any "hideous and frightening encounters between gods and humans" are balanced by scenes of positive interaction between these same two realms. I see no such equilibrium myself.

[14] Suetonius, *Ves*.23.4, *vae, inquit, puto deus fio*.

and Venus decide on civil war as the most appropriate distraction for Pallas bears directly on Domitian, for Minerva, the Romanized Pallas Athena, is a goddess whom Domitian especially favored.[15] Her role as protector of the Argo makes the *Argonautica* even more appropriate to Valerius' day; but in the course of the poem we find her linked on more than one occasion with such negative aspects of the poem as civil war.

Outline 2: The Thebaid

Where the *Argonautica* explores a series of cultures and events and encompasses a myriad of mythic traditions (in just the first half of the Argo's journey), the *Thebaid* focuses on one mythic tradition, and really on one moment in that tradition--the fight between the two sons of Oedipus, Eteocles and Polynices. Statius puts their fight, and the events leading up to it, under a high-powered microscope, but by the end of his epic, though he claims at times to be stripping the story down to its bare essentials (a fight between two brothers in which power pure and simple--*nuda potestas* Statius says--is at stake), he has demonstrated one mythic incident's capacity to involve countless other people and events in its momentum.

While it owes much to earlier dramatic treatments of the Theban legend, and draws on the Latin epic tradition in general,

---

[15] Suetonius, *Dom.*15.3, and Jones (1992), 100. Carradice (1983) provides an excellent summary of Domitian's coin types, and makes clear Minerva's frequent presence on Domitianic coins.

Statius' poem might, in organizational terms, rely a great deal on one of its few epic precedents, the fifth century BC *Thebais* of Antimachus of Claros. This long epic was familiar to Cicero,[16] and was notorious for its grand scope: by the 24th book of his poem Antimachus had yet to get the first Argive army to Thebes, even though the poem was to include the second expedition of the Epigonoi as well.[17]

In Statius' account, Polynices is already in exile and Jupiter has declared his intention of pitting the two brothers against each other on the battlefield by *Thebaid* 1.312; but Polynices will not return and the war will not get under way until *Thebaid* 7.452ff, when the Argive army, led by Polynices and Adrastus, arrives at Thebes.[18] In between these two points we read of the many events that transpire between the time of Polynices' exile and that of his return: his arrival at Argos and encounter with Tydeus (*Thebaid* 1); their weddings to the daughters of Adrastus, Tydeus' not very diplomatic mission to Eteocles at Thebes, and his single-handed destruction of forty-nine ambushers sent out by Eteocles (*Thebaid* 2); the report to Eteocles and suicide of Maeon, the sole survivor from the ambush, and the return of Tydeus to Argos, where he and his compatriots decide to wage war against Thebes and then take

---

[16] At *Brut.* 51 (191) he seems to refer to it as *magnum illud volumen*.

[17] More detailed comparisons of the two *Thebaids* are difficult to make with any certainty; see Vessey (1970).

[18] For a detailed discussion of the *Thebaid*'s organization, see Ahl (1986b), 2805-2822; see also Vessey (1973), 317-328 for a more schematic approach to the poem's architecture. Regarding the issue of narrative delay and the structure of the poem, see Feeney (1991), 338-340.

the auspices for such a war (*Thebaid* 3); the catalogue of troops at Argos and their subsequent arrival at Nemea, which bracket a description of the omens taken by Tiresias for Eteocles at Thebes (*Thebaid* 4); the story of Hypsipyle, both her troubles on Lemnos, and her subsequent difficulties at Nemea (*Thebaid* 5); the games held at Nemea by the Argives in honor of Opheltes, the son of Nemea's king Lycurgus, who was crushed by a snake while Hypsipyle, his nurse, told her story to the Argives (*Thebaid* 6).

Finally, at the start of *Thebaid* 7, we find Jupiter impatient at the slow progress of the war (so impatient that he threatens to institute eternal peace if Mars doesn't get on the ball), and the pace with which we move toward the brothers' final battle increases. Much still stands in the way of this duel, and between *Thebaid* 7.628 and *Thebaid* 10 Statius charts the violent elimination of nearly all of the Argive heroes (and several Thebans and many supporting troops as well) who came with Polynices. The poet does, however, satisfy the reader's expectations after such a build-up, devoting all of *Thebaid* 11 to the brothers' mutual slaughter and to the events immediately surrounding it. *Thebaid* 12 describes the aftermath of the fight: the cremation of the brothers, Theseus' intervention at Thebes on behalf of all the unburied Argives, and his defeat of Creon on the battlefield. Before the close of the poem there is a glimmer of hope when Statius describes in positive terms the altar of Clemency at which the Argive matrons petitioned

Theseus for help;[19] but when Theseus marches on Thebes we move right back to an ugly cycle of tyranny, warfare, and devastation surrounding the throne at Thebes, and the epic ends with visions of mourning and desolation, with Thebes' immediate future left uncertain.

Statius' story operates according to rules that modern physicists might reserve to define a black hole: It has a very precise point for its focus, and yet everything and everyone in Thebes' vicinity, indeed in much of Greece--Adrastus and the Argives, Theseus, and Hypsipyle--is sucked into the Theban turmoil. As the preceding outline suggests, I see a fair measure of black humor at work in the structure of this poem--in Jupiter's threat to Mars; in Opheltes' unhappy fate; and in the fact that it does take so long to get the war under way. The humor has a powerful effect on the poem as a whole, for it acts as a destabilizing force, keeping the reader, especially the modern reader, off balance. Ultimately, however, the relentlessness of his poem's momentum supersedes such elements as humor and exacts a heavy toll: the concluding books offer a sobering and ugly picture of power's corrosive force.[20]

Like Valerius, Statius gives his poem topical relevance to his day in his focus on fraternal strife, civil war, and power

---

[19] Vessey (1973), 307-316, offers a most optimistic reading of the *ara Clementiae*.

[20] Dominik (1994a) presents a detailed analysis of representations of power, both mortal and supernatural, in the *Thebaid*.

struggles; as in the *Argonautica*, too, Statius fits the divine machinery of his poem into a significant Roman framework. He is readier than Valerius to satirize openly the gods and their machinations, and he bases his first representation of them in *Thebaid* 1 on the council of the gods in *Metamorphoses* 1, thus taking advantage of the link that Ovid drew there between the Olympian seat of power and its mortal, Roman counterpart on the Palatine.[21] In the course of the poem, Olympus offers the reader a vision of bureaucratic tangles and conflicts of interests that is far more sardonic than what we saw on Ovid's Olympus and quite in keeping with Rome's own expanding Imperial machinery.

Outline 3: The Punica

With Silius, of course, we move from the world of myth to that of Roman history, but he is as adept as his peers at shaping and manipulating his material according to his own intents. He draws his material primarily--but not exclusively--from Livy's third decade,[22] and he shapes it in accordance with several epic models: the *Aeneid* especially, but also the

---

[21] Schubert (1984), 77-78, 99-103; Ahl (1986b), 2835-2841; Feeney (1991), 353-355.

[22] See Nicol (1936), whose entire study evaluates the amount of influence different factual sources had on Silius, and who concludes that Livy was by far Silius' prime source. The most recent consideration of the *Punica*'s relationship to its historical material can be found in Wilson (1993).

Metamorphoses, the *Pharsalia*, the *Argonautica*, and the *Thebaid*.

Unlike Statius and Valerius, Silius is bound by the confines of historical dates and facts--his epic *must* begin with the year 218 BC. and end in 201 BC.; the elder Scipios must die in Spain, as must Aemilius Paulus at Cannae, and Hasdrubal at the Metaurus; Rome must lose at Trebia, Trasimene, then Cannae, before it can win at the Metaurus and Zama. Still, within these unbreakable boundaries he gives rein to considerable powers of innovation, creating a narrative sequence that Livy would barely recognize: Saguntum (the first, minor skirmish in the war) occupies the first two books of Silius' poem; the first two years of a fifteen year war, including the great battles of Ticinus, Trasimene, and Cannae expand to occupy the next eight books of the 17 book epic, with Cannae as the poem's centerpiece (*Punica* 8-10); the last 13 years are compacted into the 7 post-Cannae books, along with some decidedly non-Livian incidents--Scipio Africanus' visit to the Underworld (*Punica* 13.381-895) and his judgment in the allegorical debate between *Virtus* and *Voluptas* (15.10-128), in which scene the two goddesses visit Scipio while he sits beneath a tree at his villa (he picks *Virtus*).

When reading the *Punica*, we need to take into account its unique and problematical relationship to epic and historical precedents: for Silius turns an analytical eye worthy of Livy or, in epic terms, worthy of Lucan to his historical period, but he also retains the entire mythic/Olympian framework of the

Aeneid. While such a construct might seem entirely appropriate in an epic about the mythic history of Rome's origins, the ancient or modern reader might be less inclined to accept it for a period of documented Roman history. Livy, after all wrote a Roman history of this era and never dared to describe any imaginary events on Olympus; instead, he confines the gods to their temples and oracles. This is not to say, however, that the presence of divine machinery in Roman historical epic is an automatically absurd proposition.[23] Rather, my point is that by introducing an Olympian administration to his poem, Silius is able to imbue the historical action of the *Punica* with an added level of unreality and artificiality, one that reinforces the readers awareness of the poem as a poetic construct. This sense of artificiality is further emphasized by the ways in which the poem reproportions and adjusts historical scale and scope, demanding that its readers reevaluate their historical perception of Rome's past; instead of defining the war in terms of its chronological progress, the reader must define it in terms of its broader effects on Rome's evolution. We need to ask, for example, why brief incidents in Livy's history have taken on a larger and different shape in the *Punica*, and what Silius has brought to his Cannae narrative in making it the war's pivotal event.

---

[23]Feeney (1991), 301-312, rightly avoids this argument in his analysis of the *Punica*.

Narrative Signs

Topic, structure, and general content thus tell us a fair amount about the operant strategies in these poems. All three of the Flavian epicists work with great creativity inside of well established traditions, and in their adaptations and reshaping of these traditions we can identify several ways in which they recommit their epic material to their contemporary audience.

But we can also identify several signs woven into the fabric of each poem that reinforce the connections the poems make to their own day. These signs range from the narrator's passing remarks about the state of his own world to narrative structures that involve Flavian Rome more directly in the poem's scheme of action. They frequently are set at pivotal moments in each narrative, and stand as markers of both the episode's immediate literary significance and its relevance to the Flavian world.

Some of these techniques are quite basic, but they still have a substantial effect on our reading of the poems. For example, both Valerius and Silius occasionally comment directly in their narrator's voice on the degree to which events and ideals within their poems differ from their own day. Thus Silius comments at the close of his Cannae narrative:

> Haec tum Roma fuit; post te cui vertere mores
> si stabat fatis, potius, Carthago, maneres.
> *(Pun.*10.657-658)

> This was the Rome of that era; and if it was fated
> that Rome's character would change after you were
> gone, Carthage, then it would have been better for you
> to survive.

This is an odd epilogue to what is certainly the most disastrous defeat that Carthage ever inflicted on Rome--Silius speaks directly to Carthage at the very moment of its bloodiest triumph over Rome, wishing that it still survived as Rome's opponent, and suggesting that Carthage played a significant part in the preservation of positive Roman *mores*.[24] As should become clear in the course of this book, this disconcerting apostrophe exemplifies the *Punica*'s preoccupation with the post-Hannibalic world, and its conviction that, after Hannibal, all that Rome could look forward to was a long, slow, downward spiral into moral decay and civil war. Silius' placement of this comment at the close of the Cannae narrative suggests that the seeds for Rome's decline were planted at Cannae or soon thereafter.

I have termed a second technique of linking epic material to contemporary reality "historical overlay." While it is difficult to define the full extent of this technique in the epics, its presence in all three poems also has some bearing on how we evaluate the relationship between these poems and their own day.

By "historical overlay" I mean to describe those episodes and events which are shaped in such a way as to

---

[24] Ahl (1986a), 2517-2518 and 2555-2558.

encapsulate contemporary events in their depictions of myth and earlier history. All three of our poets occasionally use this narrative strategy, at both the incidental and episodic level, and like many of their techniques, it too allows the author indirect access to representations of his own world.

Significantly, this strategy most often appears in the context of civil war, and each poet thus is able to frame occasional visions of the civil strife Rome experienced in AD 68-69 within the context of his epic. For example, as we have already noted, Valerius devotes all of *Argonautica* 6 to a description of civil war at Colchis. In creating his scenario, he is able to take advantage of two historical situations of his own time: the chaotic political situation at the eastern ends of the Empire in which Rome constantly intervened in the first century AD, and Rome's own return to civil strife in AD 68.

Valerius creates the link between his narrative in *Argonautica* 6 and the strife along Imperial Rome's eastern borders in the basic details of his war at Colchis: he locates his epic's civil war in the very territory that witnesses this turmoil in the first century AD, and, as Ronald Syme first pointed out, he includes in his cast of fighters peoples involved in the first century struggles, complete with their first-century weaponry.[25] Moreover, he specifically ties this war in with a vision of Roman civil strife in a simile that occurs in the course

---

[25] Syme (1929).

of his battle narrative;[26] in describing the destruction wrought by some out of control Scythian chariots on their own troops, Valerius equates the carnage to that produced in Roman civil war:

> Romanas veluti saevissima cum legiones
> Tisiphone regesque movet, quorum agmina pilis
> isdem aquilisque utrimque micant, eademque parentes
> rura colunt, idem lectos ex omnibus agris
> miserat infelix non haec ad proelia Thybris:
> (*Arg.*6.402-406)

> Just as when Tisiphone in her fiercest moments stirs up Roman legions and kings, whose ranks glitter on each side with matched pikes and eagles--the soldiers' parents till the same fields; the same unhappy Tiber had sent them forth picked from all the land for battles other than these.

The Scythian chariots actually compound the crime of civil war in this passage, as they are fighting in a fraternal war--Valerius refers to it as *impia proelia* at 5.221--and in the midst of this war they begin killing their own troops. More important for us here is the fact that, for Valerius, Roman civil war explicitly becomes the standard against which other strife can be measured. Indeed, Valerius' simile describes Roman legions and kings fighting in this civil war--a surprising conjunction in a world where the title *rex* was anathema. His simile calls a spade a spade, and it is especially appropriate to the civil wars of AD 68-69, when the victor was definitely going to become

---

[26] Preiswerk (1934) also notes this simile and its clear evocations of Valerius' contemporary world.

Rome's monarch and there was no chance of the Republic's return. In historical terms, then, the simile not only reflects the degree to which the post-Neronian wars confronted Roman citizens once again with the realities of civil war, but it also reflects Valerius' assessment of what type of power the *princeps* wields--regal power.

The simile is important on a literary level too, for it exemplifies the way in which the Flavian writers depend on both Vergil and Lucan as literary predecessors: Vergil first uses Roman strife as a measure for other events in *Aeneid* 1, where he compares Neptune's calming of the seas to the quieting effect a man of *pietas* and *merita* might have on a strife-torn *vulgus*.[27] Lucan subsequently creates a detailed poetic model of Roman fraternal strife in his *Pharsalia*. Valerius fuses these two models in his simile, measuring foreign deaths and self-destruction against Roman fraternal and legionary bloodshed on the battlefield.

We find similar linkages in the *Thebaid* between contemporary history and civil strife. For example, when civil war erupts at Nemea after Opheltes' death in *Thebaid* 5, Statius notes that the strife has reached such a pitch that a mob is ready to destroy the local temple of Jupiter[28]--clearly a worthy symbol of civil strife in the years after Rome's own temple to Jupiter Optimus et Maximus was destroyed in the fighting of AD 69. Indeed, Lycurgus himself urges the Argives to attack

---
[27] *Aen.* 1.148-153.
[28] *Theb.* 5.696-697.

his city and destroy the temple of Jupiter if they are so intent on civil war.[29]

On a larger scale, we find Statius drawing similar links between Roman wars against foreign foes and civil strife in his poem. Again, *Thebaid* 5 offers Statius the clearest opportunity for this: in her narrative of the Lemnian massacre, itself a model of domestic, familial bloodshed and strife, Hypsipyle specifically refers to the war waged by the Lemnian men in Thrace as a *Getic* war, and so the Flavian reader is encouraged to see in this war a vision of Domitian's own Getic campaigns in the 80's and 90's AD.[30]

Silius turns to this technique as frequently as his fellow epicists. The best example of this comes in *Punica* 10 in the final hours of the battle of Cannae, during which we witness a curious incident:

> Raptum Galbae procul (neque enim virtutis amorem
> adversa exemisse valent) ut vidit ab hoste
> auferri signum, conixus corpore toto
> victorem assequitur letalique occupat ictu.
> ac dum comprensam caeso de corpore praedam
> avellit tardeque manus moribunda remittit,
> transfixus gladio propere accurrentis Amorgi
> occidit, immoriens magnis non prosperus ausis.
> *(Pun.*10.194-201)

---

[29] *Theb.* 5.683-687. See also Dominik (1994a), 134, for additional examples of this technique.
[30] She describes Lemnos as an *insula...Getico nuper ditata triumpho* at 5.305-306.

> A standard was snatched some ways off from
> Galba, but even the present disaster could not
> extinguish his love of virtue. For when he saw it
> carried away by an enemy he strained with all his might
> to pursue the conqueror, and he laid him flat with a
> deadly blow. Even as Galba grabs the standard from
> the fallen enemy (whose dying hand yields it only with
> reluctance), another one, Amorgus, quickly intervenes,
> and Galba himself is stabbed, and he dies without any
> enjoyment of his great achievements.

Silius here invents a warrior named Galba who tries to save a legionary standard from Punic hands.[31] Yet Silius' description of this soldier might bring the emperor Galba all too quickly to mind--he spots a fallen standard (the consummate symbol of Roman military might), and races to seize it; but he then loses it almost immediately by his own death, *immoriens magnis non prosperus ausis*. We will return to this Galba in a later chapter, as he is not the only warrior in the *Punica* to bear such a suggestive name. For the moment, though, his presence can simply demonstrate the potential that the *Punica* has to mirror events from Silius' own day.

These glimpses of contemporary reality that each poet imposes on his narrative strongly influence one's reading of these poems, for they suggest that there is some connection, however distant, between these epic episodes and the historical emergence of the Flavian Principate from the strife of AD 68-69. Such a vastly overarching assertion of cause and effect

---

[31] The Galba described here is clearly not to be associated with either of the Galbas known to have fought in the Second Punic War. See McGuire (1995), 115-116.

strikes a twentieth century reader as improbable when distilled to its essence, and yet the same sort of implicit connection between mythic past and contemporary reality is regularly accepted as an important component of the *Aeneid*. In fact, this type of momentum running from distant past to present moment is a key element in all three of these poems, and it requires more detailed exploration.

From Mythic Past to Flavian Present

In drawing various broad connections between their epic material and their own world these poets are not necessarily claiming an actual and precise cause and effect relationship between mythic or earlier historical events and specific events in their own day. Rather, the epic topics provide a framework within which the poets can discuss different sets of political, societal, and individual problems; the links that the poets add between poem and contemporary reality allow them to involve their own world in the formal scope of their explorations and to create a sort of pseudo-origin for trends and situations that they see in their own world.

I say pseudo-origin because I see these poems as being written partly in response to the *Aeneid* and the way its topic fits into the Augustan world: Augustus and his adoptive father Julius Caesar had laid claim to their own descent from Venus and Aeneas as partial justification of their own right to rule; and Vergil, in the *Aeneid*, examines what this claim might actually mean, as he scrutinizes Rome's foundation legend and its connections to his own Augustan era. After Ovid has taken an opposite approach to the challenge of creating mythic models for his day, including virtually *every* myth in his progress toward the apotheosis of Caesar, the Flavian poets return to the perspective of the *Aeneid*, looking to a single myth or historical era, but seeking alternative myths and eras to those proposed in the *Aeneid*. They then impose on these alternative myths causal links that explicitly join the material of these epics and the Flavian world, forcing the reader to confront at every step the commentary which the epics' episodes might be making on Rome's own development.

Let us look briefly at each epic in turn to examine the details of these causal links more closely.

a. The *Argonautica*

In laying out the mythic groundwork of his poem, Valerius takes care to point out the ways in which it will accommodate Rome's own historical rise to power, including the rise of the Flavian Principate itself. He establishes this premise in the opening lines of the poem, in his salute to Vespasian and his two sons. In his Imperial salute, Valerius makes two claims regarding Vespasian: first, that Vespasian will earn even greater fame than did the Argo for his voyage to and conquest of Britain (*Arg.*1.7-9, *tuque o pelagi cui maior* *aperti fama, Caledonius postquam tua carbasa vexit Oceanus*);[32] and second, that after his apotheosis, Vespasian will serve as a reliable guide-star for seagoing vessels (1.17-19, *neque enim Tyriae Cynosura carinae certior aut Grais Helice servanda magistris tu si signa dabis*).

These claims are obviously appropriate to Valerius' poem, for they praise Vespasian in nautical terms, equating his achievements with those of the Argonauts themselves (like the Argonauts, Vespasian too will open up a sea-route for traffic), and describing how his astral apotheosis will benefit sailors. They thus establish the principle of reading the poem's events in terms of the Imperial house, and they create a pleasant enough conceit in the initial set piece of Imperial praise. Yet as the poem progresses and as Valerius examines the details of the Argo myth in more depth, we might question the benign equation of Vespasian and the Argonauts advanced at the outset. For the detailed narrative of the poem raises several negative consequences of the Argo's voyage, and raises as well some negative perspectives from which we are asked to view Rome's own origins.

The first specific link to the Roman world within the epic's narrative comes in *Argonautica* 1, when Jupiter responds to the joint complaints of Sol and Mars about the Argo expedition and the threats it poses to their interests--Sol is the father of Aeetes, and the Golden Fleece decorates a grove

---

[32] Vespasian served under Claudius in the expedition of AD 43.

sacred to Mars (1.509-573). In his speech, Jupiter first reminds his fellow gods that all is already fixed by fate (1.531-533), and then proceeds to describe the subsequent vision he has of history and of the shifting of power from Asia to Troy to Mycenaean Greece (1.537-554). After the primacy of the Mycenaeans, Jupiter says he will bestow his favor on other races (1.555-556, *gentesque mox alias fovebo*), testing them to see where he might entrust more lasting power:

> "arbiter ipse locos terrenaque summa movendo
> experiar quaenam populis longissima cunctis
> regna velim linquamque datas ubi certus habenas."
> (*Arg.* 1.558-560)

> " As judge in this matter, I myself will test
> different capitals by shifting the world's balance of
> power, finding out which kingdoms I might want to
> last the longest among all races, and where I might
> securely hand over all control once I have passed on the
> reins of power."

Valerius draws clearly here on the *Aeneid*: Jupiter's mention of *longissima regna* recall *Aeneid* 1 and his assurances there of the unlimited *imperium* reserved for Rome. Yet, unlike in the Vergilian scene, Valerius' Jupiter does not specify that Rome will be the final holder of divinely sanctioned *imperium*; he leaves his options entirely open. His words confirm the Argo's importance for later historical events but leave the reader in suspense as to whether or not Rome is the place where he will ultimately establish lasting power. It is entirely possible that, as far as Valerius is concerned, Jupiter's test is still ongoing and that no final decision has yet been made.[33]

Valerius makes the link between the Argo's voyage and Rome's rise to domination more explicitly in *Argonautica* 2, in an episode that had no place in Apollonius' epic, the confrontation between Hercules and Laomedon. After Hercules has saved Hesione and Laomedon has invited Hercules and the rest of the Argonauts to spend the night at Troy, Valerius remarks:

> dixerat haec; tacitusque dolos dirumque volutat
> corde nefas, clausum ut thalamis somnoque gravatum
> immolet et rapta ludat responsa pharetra:
> namque bis Herculeis deberi Pergama telis
> audierat. Priami sed quis iam avertere regnis
> fata queat? manet immotis nox Dorica lustris
> et genus Aeneadum et Troiae melioris honores.
> (*Arg*.2.567-573)

> Having said this much he fell silent; and he contemplates secret traps and deadly crime in his heart: Laomedon intends to cut Hercules down when he is shut in a bedroom and groggy with sleep, for once he has stolen the quiver he might cheat the oracle that told him how Troy was due to fall twice to the weapons of Hercules. As if anyone could steer fate away from the realms of Priam--the night of the Dorians awaits in the inevitable pass of time, as does the race of Aeneas and the glory of a better Troy.

Valerius' narrative strategy here is significant as well as characteristic of the epic as a whole: he has diverged from the

---

[33] Davis (1990), 64, sees a similar ambiguity in Jupiter's words here.

Apollonian *Argonautica* in a way that dramatically tightens his poem's connections with the Roman world: Laomedon's treachery, Hercules' revenge, the sack of Troy by the Greeks, and Rome's foundation--all are now linked in unbreakable sequence, and the actions of the Minyae bear directly on the emergence of the Roman state.

Valerius here takes advantage of an important Vergilian premise, defining Rome's origin in terms of its own people's ruin in the fall of Troy; and he emphasizes the continuity between the two cities in his reference to the race of the Aeneadae (2.573, *genus Aeneadum*)--a phrase that includes not only Aeneas and his immediate descendants, but Julius Caesar and Augustus as well. But whereas in the *Aeneid* Aeneas describes Troy's fall retrospectively and with a measure of optimism for the future, Valerius presents the fall of Troy as an inevitable event to come, stemming here from the tyrannical actions of its ruler Laomedon.

As far as the *Argonautica* is concerned, then, Troy is poised for its fall, and its successors are lined up in proper order, with Rome prominent on the list. Valerius has thus managed to collapse mythic time in a way similar to what we see in Catullus' Poem 64, though, instead of Peleus and Thetis, he uses Hercules to link the Argo legend to the fall of Troy and the growth of Roman domination.

The links noted thus far in this chapter that connect Valerius' *Argonautica* , Catullus' Poem 64, and Seneca's *Medea*, are important, for they counter any positive connection we might see between the voyage of the Argo and Rome's later development.[34] Like Catullus and Seneca, Valerius sees the Argo voyage as the source of many other myths; yet even more explicitly than Catullus Valerius suggests that the Argo voyage will usher into the world new types of loss and ruin. Thus Neptune addresses the Argo near the close of the first book, when he has calmed the first storm faced by the Minyae:

> "hanc mihi Pallas
> et soror hanc" inquit "mulcens mea pectora fletu
> abstulerint; veniant Phariae Tyriaeque carinae
> permissumque putent. quotiens mox rapta videbo
> vela notis plenasque malis clamoribus undas!
> non meus Orion aut saevus Pliade Taurus
> mortis causa novae. miseris tu gentibus, Argo,
> fata paras, nec iam merito tibi, Tiphy, quietum
> ulla parens volet Elysium manesque piorum."
> (*Arg.*1.642-650)

"Pallas and my sister may have stolen this ship from me, softening me up with their tears. So let Pharian and Tyrian ships set sail, and let them think that what they do is allowed. Soon I will see plenty of ships driven out of control by the North wind, and my oceans will be filled with the noises of disaster. The cause of this new form of death won't be my grandson Orion, or Taurus who turns ugly in the season of the Pleiades; you, Argo, are the one who prepares these deaths for unfortunate mortals; and as for you, Tiphys, though you might already have earned it, no mother will ever hope that you gain the peace of Elysium or a place among the shades of the just."

---

[34]Davis (1990) clearly traces the interrelationships between these works.

The message that Neptune delivers is clear: the voyage of the Argo will bring new types of suffering to mortals, and Neptune implicitly identifies the Argo as the source of a whole new type of deaths for mortals (1.648, *mortis causa novae*). His words here sharply undercut the happy praise of Vespasian in the poem's proem, as they spell out the negative costs rung up by the Argonauts on their trip. The statement that Vespasian might have been following in the wake of the Argo in his expedition to Britain takes on different meaning once Neptune defines the mythic voyage's costs. In *Argonautica* 1 and 2 Valerius acknowledges the importance of both Rome's evolution and the long-range consequences of the Argo expedition for his poem, and in the finished portion of the epic he returns once more to these two issues together, in a simile in *Argonautica* 7. It comes at the moment when Jason learns what deeds he must perform in order to receive the Golden Fleece from Aeetes; in his distress he is compared to an Ionian or Tyrrhenian sailor who, in sight of the Tiber's mouth, is driven off by a sudden storm and now faces shipwreck on the Syrtes instead of a safe haven at Rome (*Arg.*7.83-86).

    Valerius here articulates Jason's panic in terms familiar to his Roman audience--the references to the Tyrrhenian and Ionian seas (two seas that surround Italy) and to the Tiber all point to an era in which Rome has become a shipping center for the Mediterranean; Rome's river, the Tiber, represents the safe haven denied to this unlucky sailor. That Valerius paints Jason's panic and the sailor of the simile in such distinctly

Roman terms reminds us, as Jason is on the verge of his success at Colchis, of the later destruction promised by Neptune and of the fact that this destruction will continue down into Roman times, and even into Valerius' own day.

Valerius' *Argonautica* breaks off incomplete, and so we cannot say where he would have taken these lines of thought by the end of the poem; indeed, he might have revised a great deal in what we do have. It is clear enough from the surviving portions of the poem, however, that he aimed at involving Rome's own development in the progress of poem, and that this progress did not necessarily bode well either for Rome or for the initial equation in the poem between the ruling house and the Argo's own passengers.

b. The *Thebaid*

Rather than simply creating a series of fortuitous and pleasant coincidences between poem and society, Statius explicitly imparts a sharp relevance to his poem in its opening passages, and his poem offers a far angrier commentary on the connections between myth and reality than that seen in the *Argonautica*. He confronts this issue right in the opening lines of his poem, where he expresses his complete inability to isolate one era of the Theban myth for his poem--the connections between mythic eras are too completely interwoven. He finally settles on an arbitrarily chosen boundary:

> limes mihi carminis esto
> Oedipodae confusa domus, quando Itala nondum
> signa nec Arctoos ausim spirare triumphos
> bisque iugo Rhenum, bis adactum legibus Histrum
> et coniurato deiectos vertice Dacos
> aut defensa prius vix pubescentibus annis
> bella Iovis teque, o Latiae decus addite famae,
> quem nova mature subeuntem exorsa parentis
> aeternum sibi Roma cupit.
> (*Theb.*1.16-24)

> Let the house of Oedipus in all its chaos be the limit for
> my song, since I do not yet dare to breathe a word about
> Italian standards, or Northern triumphs and the Rhine
> twice bridged, or Histria twice subjected to our laws
> and the Dacians thrown down from their rebel peaks, or
> the battles of the Capitoline fought earlier when you
> were barely a young man; you who are a credit to
> Latium's fame, and whom Rome wants forever for
> herself, now that you have so quickly assumed control
> of your father's fresh achievements.

Statius' explanation of his choice of topic here is remarkable:[35] he suggests, first of all, that since he is unable yet to write of Domitian's wars against the Dacians and Germans, the wars and fratricide at Thebes offer a logical alternative for preliminary effort (1.17-18, *quando nondum ausim spirare*). The leap Statius requires his reader to make here is vast--since when is the story of Eteocles and Polynices an appropriate alternative to the celebration of Roman triumphs? Moreover, his description of his topic--*Oedipodae confusa domus*--set in such proximity to his address of Domitian, begs the reader to

---

[35] I follow here the analysis of Ahl (1986b), 2812-2822.

consider the parallels that exist in the family histories: Domitian's claim that Vespasian originally intended the brothers to share power;[36] Domitian's affair with Titus' daughter, Julia[37]--a *confusa domus* indeed. Statius insists on the impossibility of arbitrarily isolating one generation from another, suggesting that neither should one try to isolate Domitian's actions from earlier generations. Rather, given the causal force that *quando* carries in line 17 above, it is possible to construe a continuum back from Domitian's time to early mythic history, even as far back as the events at Thebes.

Statius lays down his subject's parameters here with geometric precision: the Theban mythic cycle presents a chain of events reaching far back into the past (1.7, *longa retro series*); the best one can do in defining this backward extent is to set an arbitrary boundary for one's account (1.6, *limes mihi carminis esto*). But the precision of these terms and the orderly, interlinked progression of ages that they imply are undercut by the implicit threat in these events to break out of their bounds and to defy easy confinement--*limes* itself suggests that there are forces outside that need to be kept out as well as forces within that need to be contained. When Statius says that he will sing of Domitian's achievements at a later date he compounds the images of disorder and transgression by introducing an element of madness into his poetics; he will, he says, only sing of Domitian when he is goaded by a Pierian

---

[36] Suetonius, *Dom.* 2.2.
[37] Suetonius, *Dom.* 22.

gadfly (1.32-33, *tempus erit, cum Pierio tua fortior oestro tua facta canam*).[38]

Statius' poem, then, stands as a paradox--a mythic world demanding segregation and clear boundaries, yet one that threatens always to burst out of confinement, and one that might require frenzied and illogical inspiration for its articulation. Even in establishing a starting point for his poem, then, Statius suggests that there is a paradoxical impossibility in the task. And this futility carries over into the rest of the epic, which attempts, on one level, to trace the causes and progress of the war between the two Theban brothers, but turns into a commentary on the impossibility of isolating such "causes". Indeed, the rest of the *Thebaid* charts the ways in which those mythic boundaries alluded to at the poem's outset (and several other boundaries as well) are transgressed. Rather than presenting a linear picture of cause and effect terminating with the mutual killings of Eteocles and Polynices, Statius confounds such logic and insists on its impossibility. For an example of this impossibility we might look to *Thebaid* 8, to the scene in which Amphiaraus rides down into the Underworld to his death. Amphiaraus was sent by Apollo to his death because Apollo feared that if he was killed in battle his corpse would be left unburied; but his live arrival in the realm of the dead

---

[38] Statius' wording here is strange--he and Juvenal are among the few Roman writers to use the word in a non-agricultural context, and both of them use it in passages involving Domitian (c.f. Juvenal, 4.123). It is possible that both are making a passing reference to Domitian's strange penchant for killing flies and to the joke of one Domitianic senator (Suetonius, *Dom.* 3.1).

(another boundary transgressed) prompts Hades to prevent the burial of all Argives who fall at Thebes--in other words, Apollo's fear of crimes that might appear on the Theban battlefield itself generates these very crimes.

It is into this confused tangle of causality that Statius brings his suggestions of the Roman world to come. He links his own vision of the Roman world with the myths of Thebes, suggesting that the Theban myths are a first step in his own poetic progress toward a poem about Domitian, and suggests as well some sort of continuum carrying through the mythic past to more "historical" times--in that it is impossible to isolate any one sequence of events from its predecessors or successors.

Immediately after Statius has argued for these connections between the remote past and his own time, he describes what was at stake in the struggle between the two brothers (*Theb.*1.144-170), and asks the reader to imagine the consequences of such a fight if other things were at stake. His questions here seal the link between his Theban narrative and the Roman world, for he instructs the reader to imagine vast territories (such as one finds under Roman control) and the combined wealth of the Phrygian and Tyrian empires (such wealth, in other words, as Rome enjoys) being fought over.[39]

Statius may go so far as to include a punning reference to Crassus and an oblique reference to Antony and Cleopatra in

---

[39] Ahl (1986b), 2826-2827.

this list of questions,[40] thereby introducing figures from Rome's own civil wars into the text. But in any case the end result of Statius' questions here is that the reader is encouraged to entertain throughout the *Thebaid* the question of what would happen if Eteocles and Polynices were to share the Principate instead of a primitive throne in Bronze Age Greece--what if this *were* a poem about the rivalry between Titus and Domitian. Indeed, at the end of this passage Statius introduces Eteocles for the first time, and one of the terms he uses to denote Eteocles' position of authority is *princeps* (1.169). This is the one and only time in Flavian epic that *princeps* is used of any ruling figure; that it occurs at the moment when Statius first establishes the link between Theban and Roman civil wars gives final reinforcement to the bonds between the two worlds.

Once Statius has established the precise parallel between the Theban world and his own Roman world, he generally leaves it unspoken and implicit in the rest of the poem, and the epic moves inexorably toward the final confrontation between the two brothers. But when Statius reaches their final duel he returns to more explicit meditations on his poem's relevance to Rome's own experiences

---

[40] The reference to Crassus would be in 1.144, *et nondum crasso laquearia fulva metallo*--though the reference is slight enough that I do not insist on it. The allusion to Antony and Cleopatra seems more obvious to me: 1.149, *nec cura mero committere gemmas*; c.f. Pliny's account of Cleopatra's extravagant gesture of dropping an extraordinary pearl into vinegar and then drinking it, at *NH* 9.58. 120-121. Mozley (1928), 351, seems to construe this phrase as a reference to studding a wine-cup with gems, though such a reading involves an unusual distortion of *merus*.

After Eteocles and Polynices have killed each other in *Thebaid* 11, Statius' own voice intrudes into the narrative on two occasions, both times reminding the reader of his poem's aptness to his own era. Statius' first interjection comes immediately after Polynices and Eteocles stab each other, and it comments darkly on who he thinks needs to learn from his poem:

> Ite truces animae funestaque Tartara leto
> polluite et cunctas Erebi consumite poenas!
> vosque malis hominum, Stygiae, iam parcite, divae:
> omnibus in terris scelus hoc omnique sub aevo
> viderit una dies, monstrumque infame futuris
> excidat, et soli memorent haec proelia reges.
> (*Theb.*11.574-579)

> Go, savage souls, foul the dead air of Tartarus with
> your death and exhaust all the punishments of Erebus.
> And you, Stygian goddesses, now spare us such human
> evils: let one day alone have witnessed such a crime for
> every land, for every age, and let this monstrous act be
> excised from future eras. May kings alone remind
> themselves of the wars at Thebes.

Statius' language here is violent--the crime of Eteocles and Polynices is a *monstrum* that needs to be cut out by its roots; and their souls are polluted, worthy of any punishments that Hades can offer. Statius suggests that kings in particular would be the most appropriate audience for his poem, as they have the most to learn from the fate of the Theban brothers.

These remarks, coming at the poem's horrible climax-- the mutual killing of twin brothers and rulers--draw an unpleasant connection between Statius' poem and figures of political authority. They epitomize, perhaps better than any other passage of Flavian epic, the idea that we need to read this poetry in terms of its implicit as well as explicit significations. Statius here uses the term *reges*, carefully steering clear of any open connection to the *princeps*; but the word is emphatically placed at the end of a verse, the final word of Statius' prayer, and it is a term rich in Roman connotations. Though Roman leaders of every age were desperate to avoid the title, the principate could not easily distance itself from it, as we already saw in Valerius' simile of *Argonautica* 6 which links *reges* to Roman civil war.

Statius' words imply an almost blanket condemnation of monarchs (for the lesson Eteocles and Polynices offer is too often ignored by them), and he has *already* implicated the *princeps* in his mythic representations of rulers, as we have seen, introducing Eteocles as *princeps* when we first meet him in *Thebaid* 1. Moreover, his remarks here suggest that the Stygian goddesses to whom he prays have *not* kept these ills away from mankind, and that the situation at Thebes is all too relevant to his own Roman audience.

c. The *Punica*

The *Punica* obviously has a different relationship with both the Flavian era and the lines of causality connecting its subject matter to its own day than those seen in the *Argonautica* and the *Thebaid*. For the *Punica* is an epic about Roman history itself--its subject matter *is* the people, the places, and the institutions upon which the principate and the contemporary world were built. It needs no separate strategies to link it with the Roman world, since Roman readers would see themselves and their past in every scene of the poem.

Yet the *Punica* contains many surprises for the reader who expects to find either a glorious evocation of Rome's past and the links of past glories to contemporary Rome or a linear representation of Rome's post-Hannibalic evolution. Instead, in presenting a vision of Rome's development it employs several narrative strategies that create a critical perspective on both the Flavian principate and its connections to the past.

Consider first the *Punica*'s explicit references to Rome's history after the Hannibalic wars. Silius regularly directs the reader's attention to these later periods of history, but he leaves an extremely large piece out of the historical puzzle, for he erases the Julio-Claudian house almost completely from his references to Rome's post-Hannibalic evolution: In *Punica* 3, Jupiter's prophecy leaps with dazzling speed from Scipio's victory in Carthage to the birth of the Flavian *gens* in Sabine territory (3.594-596); when Scipio visits the underworld in *Punica* 13 and is shown a series of Rome's future leaders, the Sibyl abruptly ends the parade with some surprising words of praise for Sulla and then a brief description of Pompey and Julius Caesar (13.861-868). Finally, at the very end of the epic, Silius' praise of Scipio contains several details that recall

Jupiter's praise of Domitian in *Punica* 3, and so the epic closes with an image of Scipio that anticipates Domitian himself (17.645-654).

This intentional lacuna creates a bizarre, teleological perspective in the poem, for it establishes the Flavian principate as a virtually direct consequence of the Punic wars: in the *Punica* the actions and events of the Hannibalic era have a direct impact on the Flavian world, and the poem suggests that these consequences are often grim. We see, in the course of the poem, several disturbing tendencies emerge in the Romans who fight against Hannibal: Rome relies more and more on the decisions and actions of individual leaders like Scipio Africanus and Gaius Claudius Nero, while its collective strength and counsel become resources less frequently utilized. In fighting a cruel and proverbially treacherous opponent, Rome gradually learns and adopts similar techniques--we see, for example, beheading as a distinctly Gallic and Punic practice in the epic's earlier books; but as the poem progresses, we find decapitation becoming a more Roman activity (the pattern receives its final articulation in *Punica* 15, when Claudius Nero beheads Hasdrubal, Hannibal's brother, and then carries the head to Hannibal's camp and tosses it over the wall). Finally, as Roman triumphs replace Punic ones in cities around Italy (Capua, most notably), Rome takes on the role of dominant invader, and Silius occasionally singles those who oppose

Roman occupation for the same praise that he bestowed on Hannibal's opponents.[41]

When Silius describes the praiseworthy actions of Republican commanders and leaders, he occasionally contrasts these actions explicitly to the less noble behavior of later generations, especially of his own day. Consider, for example, the following passage from *Punica* 14, at the close of Silius' account of the Roman capture of Syracuse under the command of Marcellus:

> Felices populi, si, quondam ut bella solebant,
> nunc quoque inexhaustas pax nostra relinqueret urbes!
> at, ni cura viri, qui nunc dedit otia mundo,
> effrenum arceret populandi cuncta furorem,
> nudassent avidae terrasque fretumque rapinae.
> (*Pun.*14.684-688)

> How fortunate people would be if our peace now also left their cities as thriving as once even wars were accustomed to do. But vicious greed would have stripped the land and sea bare, were it not for the man who has brought an era of peace to the world; his care has checked man's frenzied rush to despoil everything.

Silius, immediately before these lines, has been praising Marcellus for the restraint he exercised in capturing Sicily's most wealthy city, and he apparently sees in Marcellus' laudable actions an opportunity to praise the provincial policies of his own emperor, Domitian.

---

[41] e.g. a Capuan named Taurea, whose suicide in defiance of Fulvius at 13.369-380 will be examined in our fifth chapter.

And yet, the praise he offers is faint, at best. It is only by ignoring lines 684-685 that scholars can hold this up as a clear example of Silius' praise of Domitian.[42] Ostensibly Silius here praises Domitian's provincial policies; yet two details sharply undercut his compliment. First, Silius says that the peace the world enjoys under Domitian (14.685, *nostra pax*) is even more destructive than wars used to be (14.684, *quondam ut bella solebant*), hardly a ringing endorsement. Second, Domitian's protective measures alluded to by Silius in lines 686-688 must be ineffective, at least in the poet's eyes, if *nostra pax* is still exhausting the cities--and the emphatic *nunc quoque* of line 685 indicates that this is the case.

Rather, the peace guarded by Domitian contains the same destructive force seen in the notorious, Neronian *pax* of Lucan's *Pharsalia* 1,[43] and it rivals as well the provincial peace described by several individuals in Tacitus' works.[44] While Domitian may deserve praise for his attempts to check the rapacity of governors and of the rest of the provincial bureaucracy,[45] Silius' remarks here suggest that these measures are ultimately ineffective and that imperial peace has grave provincial consequences.

The *Punica* gives us a vision of a Rome that has learned many of the wrong lessons to be found in the Second Punic

---

[42] E.g. McDermott and Orentzel (1977), 31-32.
[43] *Phar.* 1.670, *cum domino pax ista venit.*
[44] E.g. *Ag.* 30.5, *auferre trucidare rapere falsis nominibus imperium atque ubi solitudinem faciunt pacem appellant.*
[45] For which see Jones (1979), 22-24, and (1992), 109-114..

War (e.g. cruelty and *dominatio*), and has not learned from many of the more positive models--or at least is unable to implement what they might learn from these better examples (e.g. Marcellus). It charts at every turn the myriad ways in which Rome was becoming like its opponent and was slowly turning into its own enemy.

This maxim was familiar to Romans of every generation, but Silius, coming where he does in the Latin literary tradition, is able to take particular advantage of it. For he is able to use the epics of Vergil and Lucan as historical bookends--he defines the moment at which Rome changed its evolutionary course from any of the positive potential seen in the *Aeneid* toward the disastrous collapse of Rome seen in the *Pharsalia*.[46]

The relationship that the *Punica* bears to the *Pharsalia* is especially important, as by Silius' day Lucan has already articulated in epic terms the idea that Rome became its own worst enemy once it had eliminated its foreign enemies. In looking back to the era in which Rome confronted its greatest external foe, Silius is able to anticipate the action of the *Pharsalia* even though he writes 20-30 years after Lucan. We can best appreciate this fact simply by looking at Silius' Hannibal for a moment. By Silius' time Hannibal had not only come to represent the greatest external threat ever faced by Rome; he had also been turned by Vergil and Lucan into an

---

[46] See Ahl (1986a), 2556, for this point.

earlier anticipation of Rome's greatest internal enemy, Julius Caesar, as both these poets describe Caesar's march on Italy as if it were the second coming of Hannibal,[47] and Lucan portrays the destruction of the Republic's civil wars as Hannibal's vengeance on Rome.[48]

When we confront Silius' Hannibal, then, we are facing a literary character who not only embodies all of the characteristics found in Livy's Hannibal and in the avenger of Dido's curse in *Aeneid* 4, but one who anticipates in great detail the Hannibalic Caesar seen in both *Aeneid* 6 and the entire *Pharsalia*. Ahl has shown how Silius' Hannibal encapsulates other epic figures as well,[49] Lucan's Pompey most notably; but these likenesses only reinforce our point--that Hannibal in the *Punica* represents both Punic and civil war. It is no coincidence, and not simply a case of historical accuracy, when Silius mentions in *Punica* 3, that Hannibal leads towards Italy warriors from Zama, Thapsus, Ilerda, and Munda (3.261, 359, 400). As Silius himself notes, these places will later be the sites of some of the bloodiest battles in Rome's history of civil

---

[47] Compare Anchises' description of Caesar at *Aen.* 6.830-831, *aggeribus socer Alpinis atque arce Menoeci / descendens* to Jupiter's description of Hannibalic Carthage at 10.12-13, *cum fera Karthago Romanis arcibus olim / exitium magnum atque Alpis immitet apertis*, with its similar representation of ruin coming down on Italy out of the Alps. In the *Pharsalia*, see the silent complaints of the people of Ariminium, a town at the feet of the Alps, who liken Caesar's onset to earlier Gallic and Punic invasions (*Phar.* 1.248-257).

[48] E.g. at the defeat of Curio in North Africa where Lucan says (*Phar.* 4.789-790) *ferat ista cruentus / Hannibal et Poeni tam dira piacula manes*.

[49] See Ahl (1986a), 2511-2519, for his analysis of Hannibal's character in the *Punica*.

war, a history that carried up into Silius' day with the battles of AD 69. Nor should we be surprised that, when Silius provides a catalogue of Roman cities and warriors before the battle of Cannae, he groups together a set of Italian cities that participated in the Roman civil wars of several eras, and describes them in terms that imply some antagonism and rivalry among them:

> Certavit Mutinae quassata Placentia bello,
> Mantua mittenda certavit pube Cremonae...
> (*Pun*.8.591-2)

Placentia, shaken by war, vied with Mutina, and
Mantua vied with Cremona in sending forth young men.
Silius here links three cities, Mutina, Placentia, and Cremona, whose names would trigger memories of both the Republican civil wars and the recent wars of 69 AD, together with one, Mantua, as famous for its greatest citizen, Vergil, as for its involvement in Republican wars.

Conclusions

Like Valerius and Statius, then, Silius uses several general techniques to gear his epic to his own world, and the devices used in all three poems have an important effect, for they create a poetic field well suited to the allusive and indirect techniques of *emphasis* and *schema*. A reader of these poems is regularly encouraged to weigh the epic material encountered against historical, social, and political realities of the Imperial era in general and the Flavian period in particular, and the epic narratives speak repeatedly to the issues of the day. Rather than being distant and isolated from their world--as many would still wish to see these poems--the Flavian epics create a dynamic that binds poetic material to its surrounding world at every turn.

Now that we have sketched out the general principles that create such a perspective in the Flavian epics, we can turn to the specific images that recur with impressive frequency in the course of each poem--civil war, tyranny, and suicide.

We should begin with the image of civil war, for it is, in Roman terms, the type of event that produces a monarchic or tyrannical system. In fact Pliny, in his *Panegyricus* to Trajan, uses this idea to disparage the Flavians and exalt Trajan himself, claiming that the Flavian house benefited from civil war in ascending to the Principate, while Trajan needed no route so sordid for his own ascendancy.[50] One wonders at Pliny's desperate scramble for reasons to praise his *princeps*-- he claims that, even if Trajan had to gain access to the throne by a revolt of the Praetorians it was worth it, as was Nerva's killing of the Roman conspirators against Domitian,[51] a claim that almost rivals Lucan's sarcastic praise for Nero[52]--but his

---

[50] Pliny, *Pan.* 5.1.

[51] *Pan.* 6.2, *si tamen haec sola erat ratio, quae te publicae salutis gubernaculis admoveret, prope est ut exclamem tanti fuisse...postremo coactus princeps quos nolebat occidere, ut daret principem, qui cogi non posset.*

[52] *Phar.* 1.33-37:
> quod si non aliam venturo fata Neroni
> invenere viam magnoque aeterna parantur

comments do reflect the fact that in the immediate post-Flavian world the connection between the Flavian principate and civil war was seen clearly enough. Let us, then, turn to the portraits of civil war that we find in the epics of the Flavian era.

---

                regna deis caelumque suo servire Tonanti
                non nisi saevorum potuit post bella gigantum,
                iam nihil, o superi querimur.
There are still some who would argue that these set pieces of flattery are sincere; see, e.g. Vessey (1973) for Statius, and both Grimal (1960) and Capaiuolo (1976), 188-194, for Lucan. Consensus seems to be building, however, for more double-edged readings of these praises; see Johnson (1988), 121-123, and Sullivan (1985), 144-148, for Lucan, and Ahl (1986b), 2812-2822, for Statius.

CHAPTER 3: FLAVIAN EPIC AND CIVIL WAR

No passage of Neronian poetry better prefigures the next generation's epic program than *Pharsalia* 4.402-581, where Lucan narrates the mutual suicide of several Romans trapped on a raft off the Illyrian coastline. Lucan describes how C. Antonius and a group of Caesar's troops are trapped by M. Octavius, one of Pompey's commanders, who has the help of Cilician sailors. When Antonius tries to slip through Octavius' blockade, one of the three rafts he has constructed is caught in a snare laid by the Cilicians. The commander of the raft, Vulteius, urges his men to kill each other rather than fall into the hands of Pompey's forces, and they proceed to do so with alacrity, starting with Vulteius himself:

> nec plura locuto
> viscera non unus iamdudum transigit ensis.
> conlaudat cunctos, sed eum, cui volnera prima
> debebat, grato moriens interficit ictu.
> concurrunt alii totumque in partibus unis
> bellorum fecere nefas. sic semine Cadmi
> emicuit Dircaea cohors ceciditque suorum
> volneribus, dirum Thebanis fratribus omen;
> Phasidos et campis insomni dente creati
> terrigenae missa magicis e cantibus ira
> cognato tantos inplerunt sanguine sulcos,
> ipsaque, inexpertis quod primum fecerat herbis,
> expavit Medea nefas.
>
> (*Phar*.4.544-556)

Without another word from Vulteius several swords pierce his body; he praises them all, but singles out the soldier who delivered the first wound for special honor: as Vulteius dies he kills this man with a welcome blow. Now the rest run together, and in a single place are seen all the crimes of war: so the Dircaean troops sprang from the seeds of Cadmus and fell wounded at the hands of their own brothers, a terrible foreshadowing for later Theban brothers. On the plains of Phasis too earthborn men, born from the teeth of the sleepless dragon, in a rage sent by magic spells filled all the furrows with familial blood, and Medea herself feared the crime she created with unfamiliar drugs.

In the mass suicide of Vulteius and his men Lucan creates a vision of civil war in miniature, and he makes their deaths an emblem for his entire epic, claiming that Antonius' men produced all the crimes of war by their action (4.548-549, *totumque in partibus unis bellorum fecere nefas*).[1] In the middle of a war already civil, Romans of the same side are driven to kill each other and to delight in both the killing and the dying. Overall, the *Pharsalia* exerts a powerful and manifold influence on the Flavian epics and their representations of civil war, as it molds the events of Roman civil war in epic terms and defines such wars as the destroyers of familial bonds, as suicidal events on a national scale, and as the producer of tyrannical regimes. But the particular similes that Lucan incorporates into this scene take on special resonance for readers of Flavian epic, for in them Lucan anticipates the two mythic traditions that will be explored in detail by Valerius and

---

[1] Ahl (1976), 117-121, discusses this passage in relation to the rest of the *Pharsalia*, providing a detailed bibliography on p.118, n.1.

Statius, and points to one mythic element in particular that they hold in common: the *spartae*, or *terrigenae*, the fratricidal warriors that figured in the founding of both Colchis and Thebes.

When we turn to the Flavian epics, Lucan's similes seem almost prophetic in their programmatic connection of civil war, Phasis, Thebes, and suicide. Not only do both Valerius and Statius steep their poems deeply in the images and dynamics of civil strife, but Silius does as well, repeatedly enfolding anticipatory allusions to Republican and Imperial civil wars within the context of his Hannibalic narrative.

As we noted in the opening chapter, there would be good reasons for the Flavian poets to be so concerned with the issue of civil war. They all lived through the chaos of AD 68-69--indeed, Silius was serving as *consul suffectus* when Nero committed suicide in June of 68 and he appears in Tacitus' *Histories* among the supporters of Vitellius.[2] In the course of Domitian's reign all three poets would have been familiar not only with any rumors about Titus' murder and with the attempted revolt of Saturninus, but also with the fact that Domitian's reign was threatening to end like Nero's--for he had no worthy successor near at hand and faced increasing erosion of support on many fronts. These poems, in short, might focus on civil war so consistently in anticipation of possible strife to

---

[2] Tacitus, *Hist.* 3.65.

come as well as in response to each author's experiences in the strife that followed Nero's principate.

There should be no doubt about the prevalence of civil war in these poems. The links between Statius' poem and civil war are self-evident, of course, but Statius also finds room in the *Thebaid* to incorporate visions of civil war in addition to its Theban manifestations: during Polynices' journey to Argos in *Thebaid* 1 we learn that Mycenae is experiencing its own fraternal strife between Atreus and Thyestes simultaneous to the action of this poem (*Theb.* 1.325);[3] in *Thebaid* 5 Hypsipyle narrates at length the intrafamilial strife that turned Lemnos into a desert island and sent her on her way to Nemea (5.29-498); later in the same book civil war threatens to break out in Nemea itself (5.690-710), and in the sixth book the Nemean games almost turn into deadly kindred combat on more than one occasion (6.731-738; 911-923). In all of these episodes we find typologies that are derived from Roman paradigms of civil war, both mythic and historical--*socer / gener* ties (like Caesar and Pompey, like Aeneas and Latinus); the mutual combat and murder of brothers (twins even), relatives, or allies; the presence of the Furies and Discordia.

Though Valerius is writing a poem less integrally linked with civil war than the *Thebaid* (Colchis, with its *terrigenae*, after all, is not the locus for the entire Argo myth), we find the same preoccupations running throughout the *Argonautica*;

---

[3] Statius remarks on the situation at Mycenae a second time at 4.305-308.

indeed, civil war breaks out, or threatens to do so, at almost every stop along the Argo's voyage--at Iolcus, where Jason and Aeson both entertain thoughts of leading a revolt against Pelias (1.71-73 and 1.761); at Lemnos (2.107-310); during their visit with Cyzicus (3.15-332);[4] and at Colchis (all of *Argonautica* 6). The Argonauts on board the Argo might well represent some allegorical vision of Roman statehood, but civil unrest is part of this allegory, and part of the Argonauts' identity as well: Cyzicus addresses them as "soldiers of Emathia" in *Argonautica* 2,[5] linking them directly to the most notorious site of Republican civil war,[6] and civil war appears in the Argo's wake so frequently that one can almost picture Discordia as a worthy bowsprit for the ship.

Most surprising is the presence of civil war in the *Punica*, though its mere presence is not the key issue; indeed it would be hard to imagine a historical epic written in the 90's AD not acknowledging the *major* type of turmoil to affect the Roman state between the Hannibalic era and its own day. What is most impressive is the degree to which the poem emphasizes these later periods of strife. Like Statius and Valerius, Silius creates episodes that involve Roman paradigms of civil war--at Saguntum and in his Cannae narrative, especially--and he also implements a highly innovative technique in his epic as he

---

[4] This is not, strictly speaking, a civil war; but we will subsequently discuss the degree to which Valerius endows it with the *topoi* of civil war.

[5] 2.639-640, "*o terris nunc primum cognita nostris / Emathiae manus....*"

[6] Obviously, the word *Emathiae* also links them to the opening line of the *Pharsalia, Bella per Emathios plus quam civilia campos.*

consistently chooses names for his Roman warriors that evoke Rome's later civil war experiences. We have already seen how Silius uses a warrior named Galba to create a fleeting vision of AD 69 on the battlefield at Cannae; in the course of the *Punica* we also encounter warriors named Bibulus, Brutus, Casca, Catilina, Cethegus, Cinna, Crassus, Curio, Labienus, Laenas, Marius, Metellus, Milo, Piso, Sulla, and Tullius--and many others as well--all of whose names evoke subsequent Roman eras and episodes of civil war. These names have a great effect on the fabric of the entire epic, for they create throughout the poem a steady set of resonances between the periods of Hannibalic war and those of civil war.[7]

In their treatments of civil war the Flavian poets are participating in the same discussion that occupied the attention of many other Roman writers.[8] But the specific literary and historical situations of the Flavian era give special force to the manner in which these poets approach the topic. Lucan had, after all, defined the Roman civil wars of the first century BC as the last gasp of *libertas* before the Principate took control, attributing to Figulus the following remark:

> "et superos quid prodest poscere finem?
> cum domino pax ista venit. duc, Roma, malorum
> continuam seriem clademque in tempora multa
> extrahe civili tantum iam libera bello."
> *(Phar.*1.669-672)

---

[7] See McGuire (1995) for a more detailed discussion of this point.
[8] The survey provided by Jal (1963), pages 231-359 in particular, testifies to the topic's powers of attraction in the first centuries BC and AD.

"Besides, what good is it to ask the gods to end this madness? That peace comes complete with lord and master. Rome, carry on this endless string of troubles and drag out your collapse for many ages, since you will only be free so long as civil war lasts."

For Figulus, Imperial peace means dominion and tyranny, and one of the few positive facts he can point out about the civil wars is that while they last Rome remains its own free self. He thus underscores the paradoxical significance civil war has throughout the *Pharsalia* for Rome: while it represents Rome's last vestiges of freedom, and the last era in which Rome enjoyed its own identity,[9] it also is a deadly force in its own right--a form of national suicide which will eradicate Rome's own identity[10]--and so its prolongation is only a prolongation of the Republic's death throes.

In the years following the wars of AD 69, when the Principate is gaining fuller control of the workings of the Roman state, the Flavian poets respond to both of these premises laid down by Lucan. They frequently set their scenes of civil war in close conjunction to tyrannical figures and to suicidal actions, and they focus repeatedly on civil war's

---

[9] C.f. *Phar.*7.442-445, where Lucan claims that after the civil wars Rome's government will be no different than that of the Arabs or the Medes; the only difference will be that Rome had once enjoyed freedom:

felices Arabes Medique Eoaque tellus,
quam sub perpetuis tenuerunt fata tyrannis.
ex populis qui regna ferunt sors ultima nostra est,
quos servire pudet.

[10] *Phar.*1.2-3, *populumque potentem / in sua victrici conversum viscera dextra.*.

capacities to obliterate more normal social, individual, and even linguistic traits. We can turn now to a more detailed examination of civil war's place in these poems, beginning with the objects and forces that inspire such struggles and then moving on to a discussion of the ways in which each Flavian writer marks civil war's corrosive and destructive powers.

Deadly prizes

In their narratives of civil war the Flavian poets all avail themselves of an identical vocabulary when they mention the prizes or symbols of power that lie at the heart of the immediate strife. The most vivid example of this comes in the opening verses of the *Thebaid*, when Statius defines the focus of his poem:

> nunc tendo chelyn satis arma referre
> Aonia et geminis sceptrum exitiale tyrannis
> nec furiis post fata modum flammasque rebellis
> seditione rogi tumulisque carentia regum
> funera et egestas alternis mortibus urbes...
> *(Theb.*1.33-37)

> Now I pitch my harp sufficiently to describe the battles of Aonian Thebes and the scepter deadly to twin tyrants; I will describe as well their unlimited rage after death, the flames that continued to fight back in the strife of their funeral pyre, the royal funerals that lacked even a tomb, and the cities that were wasted away by mutual deaths.

The deaths of the two brothers, the strife waged by their pyres, the unholy treatment of Polynices' corpse, and the loss of two cities' men, are all grouped here around a single symbol of power at Thebes--the *sceptrum exitiale* wielded by the ruler. Later in the poem this scepter will exhibit its deadly powers, for Polynices will be stabbed by the dying Eteocles in the act of calling for the scepter he thinks he has won,[11] and Creon begins to display the tyrannical traits that earn him his own speedy death at the moment that hostile Fortune hands the scepter over to him.[12]

The scepter that goes with the Theban throne is thus marked as possessing great talismanic and destructive force, and it is the source of much of the trouble at Thebes. But Statius is not alone in his fascination with such symbols of power or in his focus on the term *exitiale*; similar symbols and the same vocabulary appear at significant moments in the *Argonautica* and the *Punica*, lurking at the root of civil strife in both poems.

Valerius turns the Golden Fleece into such a symbol in *Argonautica* 5, when he describes the beginnings of the civil strife at Colchis. Aeetes is told that he must give up "the deadly fleece," *exitiale vellus* (5.261-262), and his refusal to do so helps to alienate his people, for it reveals how little he cares for anyone but himself.[13] The Golden Fleece will of course eventually bring destruction to Colchis at the hands of outside

---

[11] *Theb*.11.559-560, *huc aliquis propere sceptrum atque insigne comarum, / dum videt.*

[12] 11.649-651, *alio sceptrumque maligna / transtulerat Fortuna manu, Cadmique tenebat / iura Creon.*

[13] 5.264-265, *nec vulgi cura tyranno / dum sua sit modo tuta salus.*

forces; but Valerius calls it *exitiale* before the Argonauts have arrived, at the moment when it serves to trigger internal strife, for in refusing to relinquish it Aeetes provides his brother Perses with an opportunity to instigate a revolt against the king (5.263-267).

Silius assigns the epithet *exitiale* to a royal scepter in his narrative of the situation at Syracuse after the death of the king Hiero, most likely drawing on Statius' description of the Theban scepter. When Hiero's youthful and corruptible grandson succeeds to the throne, Silius says that Syracuse's own "deadly scepter" passed into the grandson's hands (*Punica* 14.86, *primaevo cessit sceptrum exitiale nepoti*), and he then proceeds to describe the young ruler's tyrannical actions, a plot that forms against him, his assassination, and the strife that is tearing Syracuse apart when Marcellus reaches the island in 214 BC (14.88-109).

These objects all have a power that is primarily divisive; they are the perfect instruments to promote strife, for they inspire rivalry, envy, and sedition, and their holders are frequently threatened, their deaths the object of their rivals' desires. In creating such tokens and in focusing consistently on the word *exitiale* the Flavian poets look back primarily to the Trojan Horse and to Helen in the *Aeneid*, both of whom earn the epithet *exitiale* for the ruin they bring to Troy.[14] But our

---

[14] For the horse see *Aen.*2.31, *pars stupet innuptae donum exitiale Minervae*; at 6.511-512, Deiphobus says of Helen, "*sed me fata mea et scelus exitiale Lacaenae / his mersere malis.*"

poets change the force of this term slightly: whereas Helen and the Trojan Horse are both welcomed into Troy from outside, and then bring upon Troy destruction at the hands of outside forces, the deadly objects we find in the Flavian epics all generate strife and devastation from within, creating in specific individuals a desire for power and a willingness to reach for that control at any cost.

The emphasis that both Statius and Silius place on scepters in particular also contributes to the picture they draw of power's capacity to corrupt and to create strife. We have already mentioned how Statius reintroduces the image of the scepter in describing Polynices' death and Creon's accession to power; in fact Statius invokes the image a second time in describing Creon's transformation into a tyrant, remarking at *Thebaid* 11.656, *pro blanda potestas et sceptri malesuadus amor*.

Silius too returns to the image of the scepter at a couple of crucial points in the *Punica*. The most significant instance comes in *Punica* 16, during a set of games put on by Scipio in Spain in honor of his dead father and uncle. After staging a chariot race and a running race, Scipio pits several men against each other in gladiatorial combat. Two combatants stand out among the gladiatorial entrants--twin brothers fighting for their throne:

> hos inter gemini (quid iam non regibus ausum?
> aut quod iam regnis restat scelus?) impia circo
> innumero fratres cavea damnante furorem

> pro sceptro armatis inierunt proelia dextris.
> (*Pun.*16.533-536)

> Among these warriors was a pair of twin brothers--What now has not been dared by those who rule? What crime now remains untried by kingships? In the vast ring with the crowd cursing their madness, they drew their swords and engaged in unholy combat for their nation's scepter.

In this passage Silius is drawing on an episode also recorded by Livy, but he has changed the details of this deadly fight in order to recall Statius' account in *Thebaid* 11 of the final battle between Eteocles and Polynices; indeed, what we have here is a rendition in miniature of the Theban conflict.[15] Silius has the Spanish twins match the Theban brothers in motive--they are fighting *pro sceptro*--and he immediately moves on to describe not only their mutual destruction but also the continued antagonism of their shades after death, for like the flames of Eteocles and Polynices on their funeral pyre in *Thebaid* 12, the flames of these twin princes refuse to mingle (*Punica* 16.537-548).

In addition to the strong narrative echoes of the *Thebaid* here, the language and poetics of these verses underscore the issues of monarchy and civil war that are at stake: the repetition of regal terminology (*regibus... regnis*), the emphatic placement of the words *furorem* and *dextris*,[16] and the extended

---

[15] Ahl (1986b), 2814-2816; Venini (1969), 778-783.

[16] C.f. the emphatic placement of *dextra* at *Phar.*1.3, *in sua victrici conversum viscera dextra*.

hyperbaton marking the phrase *impia proelia*, all draw the reader's attention to these themes. Moreover, the rhetorical questions, *quid iam non regibus ausum? aut quod iam regnis restat scelus*? (16.533-534), recall Statius' own comments at the moments of Eteocles' and Polynices' death (11.577-9, *scelus hoc...viderit una dies...soli memorent haec proelia reges*) and they look as well to Statius' comment when Eteocles first designed an ambush to kill Tydeus (*Thebaid* 2.487ff., *quid regnis non vile...o semper timidum scelus*). All three passages imply that this sort of action is both criminal and especially typical of kings. Such a suggestion is somewhat surprising at this stage of the *Punica*, for, lest we forget, these are *Scipio's* games here--he is the one who allows brother to fight against brother, though the crowd howls its protest (16.535, *cavea damnante furorem*), and who is guilty at least by association with this crime supposedly peculiar to kings.

There is one further link between Scipio and the word *sceptrum*, and it comes in the last lines of the epic, when Scipio has defeated Hannibal and has returned to Rome in triumph. At *Punica* 17.627 Silius says of him, *securus sceptri, repetit per caerula Romam*, and he then goes on to describe briefly the triumph awarded Scipio on his return (17.629-650), and to close the poem with his own salute to Scipio:

> Salve, invicte parens, non concessure Quirino
> laudibus ac meritis, non concessure Camillo.
> nec vero, cum te memorat de stirpe deorum,
> prolem Tarpei, mentitur Roma, Tonantis.
>   (*Pun*.17.651-654)

> Farewell, undefeated father; you won't yield place in
> your praise and achievements to Quirinus or Camillus.
> And when it records you as an offspring of the gods, as
> the child of the Tarpeian Thunderer, Rome does not lie.

Silius here likens the conqueror of Hannibal both to Romulus (a god, but also a brother killer) and to Camillus, and he claims his own belief in Scipio's divine parentage (17.651-654). But what are we to make of the phrase *securus sceptri* that describes Scipio at the outset of the passage (17.627)? Surely it contains a pun on Scipio's own name--a *scipio* is a rod or baton, and is often used of the staff carried by a *triumphator*;[17] *sceptrum* too is occasionally used in this triumphal sense.[18] Thus, *securus sceptri* might imply that Scipio is indeed "assured of a (triumphal) scepter," by virtue of both his name and his defeat of Hannibal. But the pun here cannot completely answer our question, for the word *sceptrum*, as we have seen already, has a decidedly negative force where it appears in the *Punica*--when used in the singular it denotes exclusively a king's scepter, and by extension his power.

The key to this puzzle might lie in the subsequent comparison Silius draws between Scipio and Camillus, for these two figures, in addition to commanding Roman forces in two of the Republic's greatest victories (Camillus against the Gauls in 390 BC and Scipio against Hannibal at Zama), also were the two most noteworthy consulars to go into exile from

---

[17] Livy, 5.41.9, uses the word to describe such an honorific staff.
[18] Juvenal 10.43, *da nunc et volucrem, sceptro quae surgit eburno.*

Rome. The tradition surrounding Scipio's exile remains murky, and the charges against him may well have been trumped up by an opposing faction in the Senate.[19] What is important here, though, is that his career after the African triumph does reflect the ever-increasing polarization in Roman politics during the second and first centuries BC, and that his own power could have led his opponents to try removing him from office. In his description of Scipio as *securus sceptri* and in his comparison of Scipio to Camillus, Silius marks Scipio's growing personal power and its impending consequences--the commander's self-imposed exile to Liternum.

In focusing on such symbols of power the Flavian poets thus shape their epics in such a way as to explore the attractions exercised by political power itself and the ways in which this power generates strife within a society. They then proceed to analyze the ways in which this strife takes shape and the effects that it has on different communities, creating episodes both incidental and global within which they can examine the dynamics of strife. In doing so they are no doubt responding to the events they themselves witnessed in the turbulence of AD 69, when Roman commanders from around the Mediterranean engaged in a deadly game of king-of-the-hill; but they are also setting their works into a long-standing literary tradition at Rome--primarily rhetorical and historical--that discusses and defines the different effects civil war had not only

---

[19] See Gruen (1984), 228-229, for a brief discussion and bibliographical note.

on Roman politics but on the military and on society in general. Indeed, the Flavian epics seem particularly concerned with civil war's capacity for destroying the more normal means of defining an individual--his personal, familial and social bonds-- and we can best discuss the massive presence of civil war in these poems by focusing on this aspect of its effects.

The breakdown of familial and national bonds that civil war initiates is a frequent theme in earlier Roman and Greek descriptions of such strife.[20] One of the most striking things about the Flavian epics, however, is the way in which this theme informs almost every conflict in the poems--even wars that are not precisely civil take on the attributes of civil war and become vehicles for further consideration of these effects.

Ties that no longer bind I: The Argonautica

We have already noted the several episodes in the *Argonautica* where the image of civil war surfaces, and we have seen the specific point at which Valerius links civil war in his epic to the Roman civil wars of AD 69--the simile in *Argonautica* 6 that compares an incident in the Colchian war to Roman legions and rulers (*reges*) fighting each other. It is also worth briefly considering how Valerius might have developed the civil war theme in episodes subsequent to the point at which

---

[20] Jal (1963), 393-417, has a thorough catalogue of the types of familial breakdown brought on by civil war.

his *Argonautica* breaks off. There are several episodes in Apollonius' account that Valerius could have developed further: The murder of Absyrtus by his sister Medea and his new brother-in-law Jason would offer one such opportunity; so too, one might well assume that had Valerius reached the Argonauts' expedition across the Libyan desert in his narrative, we would find in it several references to Cato's desert march in *Pharsalia* 9; and, had his poem included the Argo's return to Iolcus, he might have included a narrative of Medea's and Jason's revenge against Pelias--tricking Pelias' own daughters into butchering him.

Even in what Valerius did finish of his poem, however, there is ample discussion of civil war and its effects. In addition to the war in *Argonautica* 6 between Perses and Aeetes, the Lemnian massacre and the accidental war that the Argonauts wage with Cyzicus and the Doliones furnish the best opportunities for discussion of these issues; let us turn to each of these two episodes to see how Valerius uses the *topoi* of civil war to inform his narrative.

a. Lemnos

On Lemnos Valerius gives us a vision of strife within a community and within families, and he shapes his version of the Lemnos myth in such a way as to emphasize far more than

Apollonius did the eradication of family ties.[21] Apollonius briefly mentions the Lemnian women's killing of their husbands at the start of his Lemnian episode (1.609-610, 616-619), and he says that they did so because Aphrodite made the husbands prefer their Thracian female captives to their wives as a punishment for the neglect of her divinity by the Lemnian women (1.611-615). Valerius' account presents a much different picture: he begins by tracing the episode back to the long-standing strife existing between Venus and Vulcan (2.82-100), thus providing an Olympian precedent for the domestic schisms on Lemnos; and he presents the murder of the men as an action decided on before the men have even gotten off their boats--Fama and Venus conspire specifically to have the women kill their husbands, not to drive them mad with rejection.

Within this context Valerius then narrates the murderous night in horrifying detail (2.190-241), and the massacre stands as a model of strife and slaughter, charting the complete eradication of familial bonds:

> hoc soror, hoc coniunx, propiorque hoc nata parensque
> saeva valet, prensosque toris mactatque trahitque
> femineum genus, immanes quos sternere Bessi
> nec Geticae potuere manus aut aequoris irae.
> his cruor in thalamis et anhela in pectore fumant
> vulnera seque toris misero luctamine trunci
> devolvunt.

---

[21] See Vessey (1985) for an analysis of the Valerian episode's connections to the version of Apollonius.

(*Arg.* 2.229-235)

> Sisters and wives, and, closer to home, daughters
> and mothers, all thrive in this savage work; the entire
> race of women lays hold of the men in their beds, drags
> them out and cuts them down--the same men whom the
> huge Bessi, the Getic hordes, and the ocean's furies
> failed to subdue. Blood is running in the bedrooms;
> wheezing wounds smoke in the men's breasts; with
> pitiful effort torsos roll themselves off of their marriage
> beds onto the floor.

Of course, Valerius places a special emphasis on broken marriage ties here (perhaps in anticipation of the disastrous marriage between Jason and Medea that lies at the heart of the Argo myth); again and again he invokes images of the marriage bed (*torus*, 230, 234), the bedroom (*thalamus*, 215, 233), and the marriage relationship (*coniunx*, 226, 229, 237). But by the end of the night all kinship ties are broken, as Valerius notes the participation of mothers, sisters, wives, and daughters (2.229-230).

Our perception of this episode depends to a significant degree on the language and rhetoric drawn from Roman civil war literature. It is true that the Lemnian crime stands in part as a model of gender crime or sexual crime for Valerius, as it does for earlier writers.[22] But Valerius' place in the Roman literary and historical tradition also inform his Lemnian narrative--it is a very different thing to recount this story *after* Rome has experienced extended periods of civil war and proscriptions,

---

[22] Valerius claims that the crime belongs to the *femineum genus* at 2.231; c.f. Aeschylus' use of the Lemnian crime at *Choe.*631-638.

and after Roman poets and historians have articulated the connections between familial crimes and civil war.

In fact we can see traces here of poetic representations of familial degeneration;[23] of historical accounts of familial betrayals and murders during the proscriptions and civil wars;[24] and of rhetorical models that analyze the effects of civil war or tyranny on family dynamics.[25] Valerius reinforces these connections of his material to such literature by noting the presence of two usual attendants to scenes of civil war: he remarks specifically on the presence of *discordia* at Lemnos; and he repeatedly emphasizes the influence of *furor* on these events.[26] *Furor* and madness dominate the Lemnian massacre from the moment when Venus first incites the Lemnian women to rise up and murder their husbands. At that initial moment Valerius notes how the women's reason toppled (2.186-187, *ilicet arrectae mentes evictaque matrum corda sacer Veneris gemitus rapit*) and images of madness and fury resurface throughout the massacre (e.g. 2.226-228, 239).[27]

The full scope that Valerius gives to his narrative of the Lemnian massacre and Hypsipyle's heroism is especially striking given the fact that it intrudes so little on the encounter

---

[23] e.g. Catullus 64.397-408: Horace, *Carm*.3.6.17-32.
[24] e.g. Appian, *B.C.* 4.12.45, 4.13.51.
[25] e.g. Seneca, *Con.* 2.5, 3.2, 3.4, and 5.4.
[26] See Jal (1963), 417-425, for *furor*'s prominence in civil war contexts.
[27] 2.227-8, *tantum oculos pressere [manu] velut agmina cernant / Eumenidum ferrumve super Bellona coruscat*; 2.239-40, *ast aliae Thressas, labem causamque furorum, / diripiunt*.

between the Lemnian women and the Argonauts. By the time the Argonauts arrive, the massacre is long since passed; Hypsipyle, because she has concealed her rescue of her father, has become the island's ruler. Jason and his men are warmly welcomed (unlike in Apollonius' epic where the Lemnian women attack the Argo when it appears[28]); past crimes are hidden beneath an air of serenity; the Argonauts spend several months with the Lemnians (time enough for Jason to impregnate Hypsipyle, 2.424-425), before moving on to Troy and the realms of Cyzicus.

b. War with Cyzicus

The arrival of the Argonauts in the land of Cyzicus is marked by warmth, enthusiasm, and a spirit of alliance; but the episode in which they stay with Cyzicus and return unwittingly to fight the Doliones and kill Cyzicus himself is also fraught with mistaken identities and the *topoi* of civil war.

Confused identities surface in the first moments after the Argo's arrival, when Cyzicus admits to the Argonauts that he constantly fears an invasion of Pelasgian enemies. Jason reassures him that, were Pelasgians to appear, Cyzicus would see his guests take up arms and would never be troubled by attacks again (2.654-662),[29] but Jason fails to mention a key

---

[28] Apollonius, *Arg.*1.633-639.
[29] See especially 2.659-662, where Jason says, "*utinam nunc ira Pelasgos adferat...arma videbis hospita nec post hanc ultra tibi proelia noctem.*"

fact to Cyzicus: that the Argonauts *themselves* are Pelasgians, a detail that he later reveals at Colchis when first identifying himself and his men to Aeetes (5.474-6, *siquos Phrixus memorare Pelasgos...hi tibi...cernimur*).[30]

Jason's assurances to Cyzicus thus prove all too true a couple of nights after his arrival, for the (Pelasgian) Argonauts, driven back to Cyzicus' city at night by the wrath of Cybele while all the heroes are asleep (Cybele is described at 3.27 as *tantae non immemor irae,* a phrase that links her directly to Vergil's Juno), are mistaken for enemy invaders by the Doliones; they engage in battle and Jason himself unknowingly kills his new friend and ally Cyzicus, thus fulfilling his promise in an unexpected way.

Valerius here has taken an episode from the *Odyssey* (the return of Odysseus' boat to the island of Aeolus while Odysseus sleeps) and adapted it to involve the theme of civil war yet again into his poem. The war is not a civil war in the strict sense of the word, but Valerius brings the image of civil war before the reader at several moments in the battle. Cyzicus notes several similarities between his own people and the Argonauts (2.646-647, *vestra fides ritusque pares et mitia cultu his etiam mihi corda locis*), and Valerius describes an alliance made by the two leaders (3.14, *manibusque datis iunxere penates*). The war is then described in terms usually reserved for civil war: it is instigated by a Fury (3.18, *unde tubae*

---

[30] See also 5.116, where Valerius himself identifies the Argo as a *puppem Pelasgam.*

nocturnaque movit Erinys); it is called both *infanda proelia* (3.15) and *impia bella* (3.30) by Valerius, involving, as it does, allied troops (3.30, *socias manus*); and Valerius later uses the term *nefas* to describe the following dawn that reveals to the Argonauts the familiar architecture of Cyzicus' city (3.258, *notaeque (nefas) albescere turres*).

    Whereas the emphasis in the Lemnian episode was on familial and marital strife, Valerius focuses on the rupture of civic bonds in the Cyzicus affair; but his battle narrative again is strongly informed by the imagery of civil war. The most striking instance comes when, in the dark of night, Castor and Pollux--the obviously available twin brothers--almost do battle with each other:

> Accessere (nefas) tenebris fallacibus acti
> Tyndaridae in sese: Castor prius ibat in ictus
> nescius; ast illos nova lux subitusque diremit
> frontis apex.
>   (*Arg*.3.186-189)

> An unspeakable crime: in the deceptive shadows the
> sons of Tyndareus were driven to attack each other:
> Castor was the first to aim a blow in ignorance, but a
> strange light and sudden peak of fire on their brows
> separated them.

Whereas the light of day will later reveal a *nefas* unavoided, here Castor and Pollux barely escape a *nefas* of a different sort--fratricide--when they recognize each other by the luminous glow given to them at the outset of the trip by Jupiter (1.586ff); they move on to fight others. It is unclear, however, that their subsequent opponents, the Doliones, are any more appropriate, and Valerius underscores this fact by giving their victims some curious names--Itys and Thapsus most notably (3.189 and 191), both of whose names evoke images of familial and civil war. The Castor and Pollux encounter, though it proves a "near miss," exemplifies a technique we have seen before in these epics, for Valerius uses it to create a compounded scene of civil war. Within a general context of civil or unholy war he encloses an individual scene of more extreme strife, or *bellum plus quam civile*, to borrow Lucan's terminology.

After leaving Cyzicus' kingdom a second time, the Argo gradually nears Colchis, where the Argonauts will once again become immersed in civil wars. We have already mentioned the Colchian strife on a couple of occasions, noting both how it constitutes both a radical departure from earlier accounts of the voyage and how Valerius specifically creates a vision of Roman civil war within its context, when Scythian chariots begin to mow down their own men and Valerius compares the carnage to that seen in Roman civil wars.

If we were to explore the wars of *Argonautica* 6 in more detail, we would encounter language and scenes of civil war similar to what we have seen in the Lemnos and Cyzicus episodes; I have focused on these earlier narratives rather than on *Argonautica* 6, however, in order to underscore the different Valerian contexts in which we find the dynamics of civil war and to emphasize how recurrent the imagery is in the course of the poem.

The Lemnian massacre and the battle between the Argonauts and Cyzicus, so similar in their patterns, are especially important, for they show that this epic is centrally concerned with the breakdown of the normal fabric of family and society--in much the same way as Catullus linked this particular myth with these particular issues in his 64th poem. The Lemnian episode focuses on this issue within the family and on how these internal familial breakdowns affect external life.

The Cyzicus tale, on the other hand, looks primarily at external social relations--it maps the different types of confusion, and the various threats to individual identity that are generated by such interaction: the Argonauts, new allies, become Pelasgian invaders; Jason, Cyzicus' friend, becomes Cyzicus' killer; the twin brothers Castor and Pollux almost become each other's murderers.

Yet the connections that run from the Lemnian massacre to the battle with Cyzicus, and then to the civil war scenes at Colchis suggest further that there is an unbreakable cycle operating in the universe of the Argonauts. The same hysteria, self-destruction, and fury that precede their arrival at Lemnos appear again in their encounter with Cyzicus, and again, at least twice (in the civil war of Book 6 *and* the *terrigenae* of Book 7), at Colchis. Indeed, one of the reasons why Valerius does not need to go into so much detail about the earth born monsters whom Jason must defeat in *Argonautica* 7 is that we have just seen an entire book of the epic devoted to such fraternal strife--

the *terrigenae* are simply repeating the actions of Perses' and Aeetes' armies, or of Arminius' scythed chariots, of the Argonauts in their battle against Cyzicus, and of the Lemnians.

It is to this *cycle* of civil strife that Valerius adds a Roman patina, by his reference in *Argonautica* 6 to Roman legions and Roman kings. The idea that the continual cycle of civil war concerns Valerius more than any isolated outbreaks is especially significant in Roman terms: what began, really, with the Gracchi and resurfaced with Marius and Sulla, with Caesar and Pompey, and with Octavian and Antony, has come around again during Valerius' own lifetime, in AD 69. And like the dozens of heroic Argonauts who encounter a series of strife-ridden situations, the Roman leaders and people often seem helpless witnesses to, or participants in, these conflicts.[31]

Ties that no longer bind II: The Thebaid

The *Thebaid* takes its description of civil war's abilities to shatter societal and individual bonds at least one step further than the *Argonautica*, for in it Eteocles and Polynices display an ugly eagerness to reject and to trample their fraternal bonds, in much the same way that they trampled Oedipus' eyeballs earlier in the poem (*Thebaid* 1.238-239).[32] Oedipus himself--whose

---

[31] Masters' comments regarding the endlessness of Roman civil war and the problematic structure of *Phar.* 9-10 seem especially apt here; (1992), 247 ff.

[32] Henderson (1993) provides an especially powerful interpretation of the interrelationship of kinship, myth, and imagery in the epic.

inability to recognize his own familial ties brings destruction on his house--is no less eager to bring his sons to ruin: in his initial prayer to Tisiphone he specifically asks her to destroy all kinship ties (1.84-5, *i media in fratres, generis consortia ferro / dissiliant*).

Oedipus' wishes will be fully satisfied: though Polynices and Eteocles sometimes waver in their resolution, they are, for the most part, hell-bent on each other's destruction through the rest of the poem. We see more of Polynices in the course of the poem than we do of Eteocles, and his disregard for kindred relationships, and even for his own life, reaches bizarre proportions at times. In *Thebaid* 3, for example, when Tydeus returns from his embassy to Thebes having survived Eteocles' ambush, Polynices regrets not having gone himself on the mission to Thebes, as he denied Eteocles a chance to kill him and thus be guilty of a horrible crime (3.371, *infelix, fratri facinus tam grande negavi*). His words here are part of a dissembling speech designed to insure Argive support for his cause (3.381-382), but they nevertheless underscore his obsessive will to bring down Eteocles at any cost to himself or to his new Argive kin.

A second telling incident in *Thebaid* 6 reconfirms Polynices' willful disregard of these bonds. Late in the games put on in honor of Opheltes, we suddenly find him and Agreus (an Epidaurian) preparing to engage in a fight to the death with swords:

> sunt et qui nudo subeant concurrere ferro.
> iamque aderant instructi armis Epidaurius Agreus
> et nondum fatis Dircaeus agentibus exul.
> dux vetat Iasides: "manet ingens copia leti,
> o iuvenes! servate animos avidumque furorem
> sanguinis adversi. tuque o, quem propter avita
> iugera, dilectas cui desolavimus urbes,
> ne, precor, ante aciem ius tantum casibus esse
> fraternisque sinas--abigant hoc numina!--votis."
> (*Theb.*6.911-919)

> There are also some who would attempt a fight with naked swords: quickly presenting themselves with ready weapons are Agreus of Epidaurus and the Theban exile, though fate was not yet pressing at his heels. Adrastus, of the line of Iasus, forbids their duel: "Young men, plenty of death awaits us. Restrain your fighting spirit and your rage that is thirsty for an opponent's blood. And you in particular, on whose account we have abandoned our families' lands, and for whom we have emptied our beloved cities, I beg you not to grant so great a decision to chance or (may the gods prevent such a thing) to your brother's prayers before the battle itself."

Adrastus tells the two young men to preserve their desire for an opponent's blood for a later date, when there will be ample opportunity for slaughter; and he adroitly dodges the real issue here, which is that Polynices and Agreus are ready to shed *allied* blood.[33] Statius emphasizes their casual willingness to do so by setting this proposed duel shortly after Capaneus has

---

[33] Vessey (1973), 226, notes the Iliadic precedent for the scene (though he identifies the Homeric combatants as Odysseus and Ajax, instead of Diomedes and Ajax. The fact that there is an Iliadic precedent for sword combat during funeral games should not blind us to the different contexts of these two sets of games--in the *Thebaid* the combat between Polynices and Agreus is directly linked to the theme of the entire poem.

refused to box against a fellow Argive, lest he stain himself with kindred blood (6.735-737). Capaneus is the *Thebaid*'s archetypal hater of the gods, and yet even he has more concern for his fellow soldiers than Polynices.

Adrastus adds his own bizarre touch to the scene, as he strives for a positive and hortatory tone of voice (6.614-619), while his words testify to the perversity of this military effort: not only does he promise that "a huge opportunity for slaughter still awaits" both fighters--as if this were a point of reassurance--but he identifies Polynices as the individual for whose sake the Argives have abandoned their ancestral lands and beloved cities (6.916-917), a fact that might damn Polynices more than it honors him.

Adrastus' speech also reflects a second key point about the representations of this fraternal conflict in *Thebaid* 1-10 (the books leading up to the brothers' final battle), in that Statius uses it to mark this proposed duel in *Thebaid* 6 as an opportunity --should Polynices die at Agreus' hands--to avoid the whole war at Thebes and its climactic duel between Polynices and Eteocles. In fact this is the second time in *Thebaid* 6 alone that Statius marks such a missed opportunity to forestall the war, for earlier, during the chariot race, Polynices is tossed from his chariot, and when he avoids being trampled by his fellow competitors Statius remarks:

> quis mortis, Thebane, locus, nisi dura negasset
> Tisiphone, quantum poteras dimittere bellum?
> te Thebe fraterque palam, te plangeret Argos,

> te Nemea, tibi Lerna comas Larissaque supplex
> poneret, Archemori maior colerere sepulcro.
> *(Theb.*6.513-517)

> If only stern Tisiphone had not forbidden it,
> Polynices--what a moment for your death; how vast a
> war would you have canceled? Thebes and your own
> brother would have grieved openly for you; Argos too,
> and Nemea; Lerna and Larissa would have knelt and cut
> their hair for you. You would have been honored,
> greater in your burial than Archemorus.

The irony of Statius' lament here is twofold. In an immediate sense we are told that if Polynices had been run over by another chariot he would have been mourned by all those who will pay for his campaign against his brother--even Eteocles himself. But Statius also marks the ironic relationship in the *Thebaid* between poet and subject, for, as he does elsewhere, Statius here implies his own wish that the material of his epic had never come to pass.

These two opportunities to end Polynices' life in *Thebaid* 6 are just two of several chances to stop the war in its tracks that Statius marks in the course of the epic. The first comes in the poem's very first book, when Tydeus--in exile for killing his own brother--and Polynices take shelter from a storm on the same porch. Territorial creatures that they are, they immediately begin to fight over control of the porch, and are ready to face each other with drawn swords, when Adrastus intervenes for the first time in the poem (it is his porch, after all).[34] Statius points out that it might have been better if Adrastus had not interrupted and if Polynices had simply fallen at this stage, for then Polynices would have fallen at the hands of an enemy's sword and would have been mourned by his brother (1.428-430).

These missed opportunities continue throughout the epic: Maeon seems to have a chance to kill Eteocles in *Thebaid* 3, but kills himself instead (3.58-91);[35] Mars, ordered by Jupiter in *Thebaid* 3 to stir the Argives to war (3.229-233), needs further prompting in *Thebaid* 7 before the war gets under way (7.1-33); finally, in *Thebaid* 8, Tydeus throws a spear at Eteocles and almost ends the war at an early stage (8.684-687). But like all the earlier chances, this one fails, and in the end all the other people involved must suffer before the two brothers at last confront each other on the battlefield.

This negative impetus that Statius imparts to his poem reflects the changing power or place of epic in the Neronian and Flavian eras: in the *Thebaid*, we have very little sense that we are dealing with the *klea andron* of earlier epics; instead the poet foregrounds his poem's negative energy and expresses his own inability to halt his epic's progress. The *Thebaid* bears a broad structural resemblance to the *Iliad* or the *Aeneid* in that the final objective of each poem--the fights between Achilles and Hector, Aeneas and Turnus, and Eteocles and Polynices--is continually

---

[34] *Theb*.1.401-446. See Ahl (1986b), 2850-2858 for further discussion of the character of Adrastus.

[35] We will look at this episode in detail in Chapter 5.

being delayed. But the *Thebaid* differs significantly from its predecessors by consistently presenting the final battle between the twin brothers as something that would be better avoided. Statius' narrator, like some of his characters, devotes huge amounts of energy to forestalling the duel, but without success. The brothers' mutual hatred defies Statius' invocations and efforts to dodge the event as effectively as it opposes the attempts of their relatives and friends to intervene.

Eteocles and Polynices

The duel between Eteocles and Polynices finally comes to pass in *Thebaid* 11, and both of these tendencies--the brothers' willingness to reject their kinship and the narrative's implicit and paradoxical desire to avoid its own subject--inform Statius' account of the fight: He does not begin to narrate the battle proper until 11.499, filling the first 500 lines of the book with accounts of the several last ditch efforts to stop the battle and with the Furies' successful blockade of all these attempts. Adrastus (twice), Eteocles' comrades, Antigone, Jocasta, and Pietas all try to intercede and fail;[36] Tisiphone, Megaera, and Creon are able to foil these efforts and to sharpen the anger of the brothers to such a pitch that the fight finally takes place. Indeed Megaera is so successful in inspiring Polynices that before he even takes the field he longs to die himself in the

---

[36] Adrastus: 11.196-197 and 424-446; Eteocles' comrades: 11.257-262; Antigone: 11.354-387; Jocasta: 11.315-353; Pietas: 11.457-482.

blood of his brother, once he has stabbed him (11.153-154, *perfossi in sanguine fratris / exspirare cupit*); before the book is finished his wish will have come true.

These efforts, coming as they do in so concentrated a sequence of episodes, reinforce for a final time the message Statius has repeatedly transmitted on his way toward *Thebaid* 11: this is a battle better left unfought and perhaps untold (recall Statius' impending wish in *Thebaid* 11 that kings alone recall these events). Kinship figures into several of the appeals,[37] but arguments based on the ties of kinship will not persuade either of the brothers--Eteocles says at 11.306, *coeant in proelia fratres*, echoing Polynices' own statement at 11.168-169, *fratrem in suprema bella...voco*.

When Statius finally launches into his narrative of the fight itself, he emphasizes the destruction of these bonds in a different way, blurring all distinctions between the two brothers and turning them into a single and unified embodiment of hatred, rage, and violence:

>   coeunt sine more, sine arte,
> tantum animis iraque, atque ignescentia cernunt
> per galeas odia et voltus rimantur acerbo
> lumine: nil adeo mediae telluris, et enses
> inpliciti innexaeque manus, alternaque saevi
> murmura ceu lituos rapiunt aut signa tubarum...
> ...sic avidi incurrunt; necdum letalia miscent
> volnera, sed coeptus sanguis, facinusque peractum est.
> nec iam opus est Furiis; tantum mirantur et adstant
> laudantes, hominumque dolent plus posse furores.

---

[37] E.g. Jocasta at 11.346; Adrastus at 11.429-435.

> fratris uterque furens cupit adfectatque cruorem
> et nescit manare suum...
>
> (*Theb.*11.524-529, 535-540)

> They join without prelude or technique, with only emotion and rage; they each see the hatred blazing from the other helmet and they scan each other's face with angry looks. There is no longer any middle ground between them, their swords and hands are interlaced; in their fury they feed on each other's mutterings as if these were the call of the clarion or the trumpet...They race on, urgent, and though they don't yet deliver death-blows, there is the beginning of bloodshed, and what they are doing is definitely a crime. There is no longer any need for the Furies; they can only stand by in admiration, shouting their praises, and they ruefully admit that the madness of these men outstrips their own. Each brother is hot for his brother's blood, and tries to spill it, unaware that his own is flowing too.

The brothers here match each other in every movement and every manifestation of fury, acting and reacting in concert, surpassing the talents of the Furies themselves, who can only stand by and watch enviously. The language reinforces the theme of the breakdown of identities, for throughout this section of the duel it is impossible to distinguish one brother from the other: their weapons and arms are interwoven; each one has the same motive; neither one can even tell his own blood from his brother's (11.539-540).[38]

Statius returns to this point in *Thebaid* 12 when he describes the cremation of Polynices on Eteocles' pyre. Even

---

[38] This idea finds reinforcement in Vessey's observations, (1973) 277, regarding the way in which Statius inverted the Euripidean roles of Polynices and Eteocles in the duel.

in death the two carry on their fight, as their flames refuse to mingle, and though it is possible to distinguish one from the other on the pyre (e.g. at 12.430 Polynices is the *novus advena*), they are eternally to be identified in terms of each other, bound together as an oppositional pair:

> Ecce iterum fratres: primos ut contigit artus
> ignis edax, tremuere rogi et novus advena busto
> pellitur; exundant diviso vertice flammae
> alternosque apices abrupta luce coruscant.
> pallidus Eumenidum veluti commiserit ignes
> Orcus, uterque minax globus et conatur uterque
> longius...
>   (*Theb.*12.429-435)

> Once again, the brothers: when the hungry fire first touches his limbs, the pyres shake and the recent newcomer is driven from the fire; the flames burst forth in a twin peak and they glitter at their double tops with intermittent light. Just as if bloodless Orcus has added the torches of the Eumenides to the pyre, each ball of fire threatens the other and tries to reach higher.

In fact, the language of the entire epic often functions in a way that reinforces what we find here in the passages describing the brothers' deaths and post-mortem struggles, as it can create a linguistic reflection of the epic's strife-ridden themes. Double images abound in the poem; Statius makes frequent references to alternation, doubleness, repetition, and ambiguity. Consider the following passage in which Tisiphone first advances against Thebes:

> ut stetit, abrupta qua plurimus arce Cithaeron

occurrit caelo, fera sibila crine virenti
congeminat, signum terris, unde omnis Achaei
ora maris late Pelopeaque regna *resultant*.
audiit et *medius* caeli Parnassos et asper
Eurotas, *dubiamque iugo* fragor impulit Oeten
in latus, et *geminis* vix fluctibus obstitit Isthmos.
(*Theb*.1.114-120)

When Tisiphone stops at the place where vast
Cithaeron challenges the sky with its jagged height, as
a sign to these lands she redoubles the savage hissing
in her snaky hair, and the entire shoreline along the
Achaean sea and the lands of Pelops reverberate far and
wide. Parnassus, the mid-point on the way to heaven,
heard it as did the tumbling Eurotas; the crash drove
ambivalent Oete from its ridge onto its side, and the
Isthmus scarcely stands up against twin surges of its
waters.

Tisiphone redoubles the noise of her snakes' hissing; Oete is *dubiam*, uncertain or ambivalent; the Isthmus is described in terms of its own twin shoreline. Much of the passage is built on oppositional terms and Statius creates an elaborate tension between forces of alliance and separation. *Sociisque comes discordia regnis*, he remarks shortly hereafter (1.130): in Statius' world, discord is the natural consequence of alliance, and yet objects in opposition are inextricably bound together by their very struggle against each other.

Doubled language and images continue throughout the poem; Maeon's suicide in *Thebaid* 3 and the boxing and wrestling matches in *Thebaid* 6 contain especially concentrated clusters of such doubled images.[39] A final concentrated burst of doubling occurs in *Thebaid* 8:

> Inachidae *gemini, geminos* e sanguine Cadmi
> occultos galeis--saeva ignorantia belli--
> perculerant ferro; sed dum spolia omnia caesis
> eripiunt, *videre nefas, et maestus uterque*
> *respicit ad fratrem pariterque errasse queruntur.*
> (*Theb*.8.448-452)

> Twin sons of Inachus kill twins of Cadmus' race who are concealed by their helmets--yet another instance of war's ignorant brutality. They had run them through with their swords, but when they were stripping all the spoils from the corpses they saw their crime; each brother looks at the other in grief, and they complain that they have each made the same mistake.

Here twins from Argos kill twins from Thebes in battle, and do not realize what they have done until they strip the corpses. The language is forceful: Statius says that they recognize their act as a *nefas*--a term regularly reserved for acts of civil war, murder, and the like--as if to kill another set of twins is itself at only one remove from fratricide. The passage bears a striking resemblance to Valerius' description of the near battle between Castor and Pollux in *Argonautica* 3 (also termed a *nefas*);[40] and, like Valerius, Statius here creates an additional scene in miniature to underscore the fraternal crime of civil war.

While Statius restricts his narrative to events at Thebes, his poem ultimately focuses on the same cycles of mutual self-

---

[39] See *Theb*.3.33-113 and 6.731-911.
[40] See the discussion of *Arg*.3.186-189 above.

destruction that we saw in much of the *Argonautica*. Thus it is that shortly after the mutual slaughter of the two sons of Oedipus we see Creon ascend the throne, only to lose it (along with his life) almost immediately. The close of the poem, with no reference to who, or what sort of government, will succeed Creon, hints at the continuous cycle of madness and destruction at Thebes no less than did the opening of the epic (according to the Theban mythic tradition, after all, a second expedition against Thebes will come in the next generation). As in the *Argonautica*, this sense of cyclic strife is produced by several visions of civil war that are tangential to the fraternal war at the heart of the epic: even chance encounters on a stranger's porch can trigger bloody combat; and Thebes' *sceptrum exitiale* awaits yet another claimant at the close of the epic.

But Statius also adds a further dimension to his poem's representations of strife and civil war, for these themes inform the poetic language in a way we did not see in the *Argonautica*. Statius' language implicates incidental players and even the very landscape in the strife that lies at the core of his poem, eliminating barriers and boundaries not only between mythic eras but between the literary and the physical worlds--the words of his poem themselves become representations of opposition and conflict.

Ties that no longer bind III: The Punica

The battle of Cannae stands as the centerpiece of the *Punica*, occupying three whole books at the physical center of the epic, and reflecting the high point of Hannibal's fortunes as well as Rome's own low point. Silius' Cannae narrative provides the clearest adumbrations of the strife to which the Roman republican system of government was subjected in the post Hannibalic eras, a powerful affirmation of the idea that the Hannibalic war fostered the tendencies that led to Roman civil war. This idea finds its clearest articulation when Silius is describing the election of Terentius Varro, an unworthy demagogue who receives most of the blame for the disaster at Cannae, to the consulship:

> hunc Fabios inter sacrataque nomina Marti
> Scipiadas interque Iovi spolia alta ferentem
> Marcellum fastis labem suffragia caeca
> addiderant, Cannasque malum exitiale fovebat
> ambitus et Graio funestior aequore Campus.
> (*Pun*.8.253-257)

> The voters in their blindness had set this man (a disaster for the Fasti) in the ranks of names consecrated to the god of war, the Fabii, the Scipios, and Marcellus who dedicated his prestigious spoils to Jupiter; bribery and the Campus Martius, more deadly than any Greek lands to the South, produced the ruinous disaster of Cannae.

Silius here bemoans the fact that Varro has reached the same rank in Roman politics as Marcellus, the several Scipios, and the Fabii. Unlike the leadership of Fabius Maximus, whose efforts are praised to the stars by Silius at the opening of *Punica* 8, in part for the *concordia* they produced (8.8, *concors miles*), Varro's very election represents discord and strife. We have already seen how the Flavian poets use the word *exitiale* primarily in contexts involving civil strife. Silius' use of the term here certainly marks the dissension that prompted Varro's election and, I would argue, prefigures the strife that will eventually engulf the Republic.

Silius creates such a bifocal perspective in the Cannae episode by creating two types of confused, or double, identity. In the first place, he blurs the distinctions between Punic and Roman individuality in order to make the point that Varro and other Romans were so confused themselves about Rome's best interests that they ended up helping Hannibal more than Rome. Second, these confusions also tap explicitly into the imagery of Roman civil war, for during his Cannae narrative Silius steers his reader's attention to the events of Roman civil wars of the first century BC and AD by including in these books a prominent and obviously anachronistic set of Roman commanders, whose names evoke these later periods of civil war.

a. When is a Roman not a Roman?

Silius uses *Punica* 8 to lay the complex groundwork for his Cannae narrative, and the first half of the book describes the events on both the divine and mortal levels that precipitate this Roman disaster--the apparition of Anna Perenna, bringing instructions from Juno, to Hannibal, and the election of Gaius Terentius Varro to the consulship at Rome. *Punica* 8 opens with a glimpse of Hannibal deeply worried--Fabius Maximus' wise Roman leadership has given him reason to worry about his supply lines, governmental support at home, and his allies who are increasingly impatient for a final victory (*Punica* 8.11-24). The solutions to Hannibal's several problems come from Anna and Varro, and with both of them Silius emphasizes the fact that these are *Roman* figures acting on Hannibal's behalf.

In the case of Anna Perenna, we are of course faced with a figure of both Punic and Roman pedigree--Anna is Dido's sister who becomes an Italian deity after fleeing to Latium. But Silius' narrative of her flight to Latium (to escape her murderous brother Pygmalion) emphasizes her ties to Rome and her willingness to break these ties in order to help Hannibal. She herself notes these ties at the opening of the episode (8.43, *inter Latios Annae stet numen honores*), and Silius gears his entire "digression" about Anna to explaining how the Romans could have begun worshipping a Punic figure (8.46-7, *cur Sarrana dicent Oenotri numina templo / regnisque Aeneadum germana colatur Elissae*). The point of his narrative is quite clear: what is a *Roman* goddess doing fighting for the Carthaginians? The answer is equally obvious: Anna is in essence a double agent--though worshipped by the Romans, when asked by Juno she pledges her first loyalty to Dido and to

Dido's mandate (8.42, *mandataque magna sororis*), and she willingly delivers to Hannibal the message that he should proceed to Cannae, where he will find a second Flaminius and, presumably, a second Trasimene (8.218).

The importance of the Anna story for the rest of the Cannae narrative lies in the fact that her story reflects at the divine level the way in which Roman policy becomes confused at Cannae: figures whom one would assume to be acting on Rome's behalf prove to be subverting Rome's interests and helping Carthage. Her story thus sets the stage for the next step on the road to Cannae, the election of Varro to the consulship.

Varro's election marks a great split in Roman approaches to the war against Hannibal, and it ruins the concord that Fabius Maximus had so recently achieved. Varro, according to Silius, has none of the characteristics necessary for a consul serving in wartime; his only skill is his demagoguery. He gains his election by attacking the Fabian policy of delay and non-engagement,[41] a policy supported by his consular colleague, Aemilius Paulus.[42] But Varro is pitted not only against Paulus in his criticisms of Fabius. By Silius' time there is a long-standing epic tradition of praise for Fabius the

---

[41] See *Pun*.8.263-277. In the course of his tirade against Fabius Varro unwittingly voices support for Fabian policy: he says, at 8.273-274, "*mora sola triumpho / parvum iter est*," by which he seems to mean that a short march is the only delay between Rome and triumph; but his words come close to saying that delay alone offers a quick path to triumph.

[42] Fabius and Paulus discuss the problems Varro poses for Fabius' policy of non-engagement at 8.298-348.

Delayer's policy,[43] and so Varro is set in opposition to the likes of Vergil and Ennius as well.

The election of Paulus and Varro ushers in a period of strife and conflict, and Silius' descriptions of this strife are laden with the images of civil war. Varro takes on all the features of a non-military Marius, or a Catiline: a *novus homo* adept at manipulating the masses with his demagoguery:

> Dumque Arpos tendunt instincti pectora Poeni,
> subnixus rapto plebei muneris ostro
> saevit iam rostris Varro ingentique ruinae
> festinans aperire locum fata admovet urbi.
> atque illi sine luce genus surdumque parentum
> nomen, at immodice vibrabat in ore canoro
> lingua procax. hinc auctus opes largusque rapinae,
> infima dum vulgi fovet oblatratque senatum,
> tantum in quassata bellis caput extulit urbe,
> momentum ut rerum et fati foret arbiter unus,
> quo conservari Latium victore puderet.
> *(Pun.*8.242-252)

While the Carthaginians head toward Arpi, their spirits high, Varro rails from the Rostra, bolstered by the purple seized through the generosity of the *plebs*; in his rush to create an opportunity for massive destruction he brings his city closer to its end. Varro's family lacked any distinctions; one hears nothing of his parents' name. But no matter: he let his own tongue flap endlessly, droning on and on; he amassed some wealth in this way, and was generous with his own gains, courting the lowest classes of the mob and hounding the Senate, until he achieved such

---

[43] *Ann.*XII.i.363, *unus homo nobis cunctando restituit rem*; Vergil, *Aen.* 6.846, *unus qui nobis cunctando restituis rem.*

prominence in the war-torn city that he was the pivotal figure of the moment and the sole decider of Rome's fate, even though Latium would be ashamed to be saved by such a man's victory.

Varro's rage, his energy for destruction, his lack of birth, his liberality, and his tongue combine to endow him with all the earmarks of a Sallustian demagogue and to set him off from the figures of Fabius and Paulus. Varro goes so far as to promise, in his speech to the people, that a single day, the day on which he fights Hannibal, will end both the Hannibalic wars *and the rule of the Senate*.[44] Varro here presents himself as a champion of plebeian interests, and his promise is emblematic of times of internal strife in the annals of Republican Rome, from the early secessions of the *plebs* to the days of Caesar's campaigns against Pompey's Senatorial forces. Silius adds to this atmosphere of strife immediately after Varro's speech, when he compares Varro at his departure from Rome to an out of control charioteer:

>Haec postquam increpuit, portis arma incitus effert
>impellitque moras, veluti cum carcere rupto
>auriga indocilis totas effudit habenas
>et praeceps trepida pendens in verbera planta
>impar fertur equis; fumat male concitus axis,
>ac frena incerto fluitant discordia curru.
>   (*Pun.*8.278-283)

>After he has finished raging along these lines he spurs himself on, moving his army out of the city and attacking any delays. Just like an unseasoned charioteer

---

[44] 8.274-275, *quae prima dies ostenderit hostem, / et patrum regna et Poenorum bella resolvet.*

> in the early stages of a race, who lets go of the reins completely and is carried along by his horses, incapable of control he leans out over them headlong, with no sure balance; his axle begins to smoke as it can't sustain the pace and the reins flutter along behind the careening car.

Silius here carefully echoes the well known simile at the close of *Georgics* 1, in which Vergil compares the civil wars of his own day to a chariot out of control.[45] His simile suggests, on one level, that Varro is not skilled enough to handle the reins of power in war; he is an *auriga indocilis*. But the connection to civil war suggested by the clear echoes of Vergil's simile suggest further that Varro's policies are prompted more by his urge for discord than by any clear sense of how to conduct the war with Hannibal. As if to emphasize this, Silius modifies the Vergilian simile to include a reference to the reins of power as *discordia frena* (8.283).

Like Anna's assistance, Varro's actions help the cause of the Carthaginians, and the dissension created by Varro's election has created a situation in which Roman and Carthaginian policy have become confused--so much so that Silius repeatedly introduces the idea that Varro is as much a threat to Rome as Hannibal. Fabius first observes this in his

---

[45] G.1.510-514:

> vicinae ruptis inter se legibus urbes
> arma ferunt; saevit toto Mars impius orbe;
> ut cum carceribus sese effudere quadrigae,
> addunt in spatio, et frustra retinacula tendens
> fertur equis auriga neque audit currus habenas.

conversation with Paulus, where he warns Paulus that strife and a dangerous enemy await him in the Romans' own camp: *Ausonidum te proelia dira teque hostis castris gravior manet* (8.300-301). Paulus recognizes this fact, and comments, himself, to Fabius: *consul datus alter, opinor, Ausoniae est, alter Poenis* (8.332-333).

Roman affairs have been so destabilized, then, that the Romans should trust neither their divinities nor their leaders. But Silius has not finished delineating the ways in which Cannae breaks down the normal categories of identity for Rome, for he also includes familial bonds among those shattered by forces at play at Cannae, and in so doing he incorporates into his narrative more obvious *topoi* of civil war.

At the close of *Punica* 8 and the start of *Punica* 9, Silius recounts two omens immediately preceding the battle itself; both of them reaffirm not only Carthage's impending success but also the confusion that engulfs all Roman identities. In the first omen a Roman soldier is suddenly possessed by a prophetic frenzy. When he pictures the triumphs that might soon be celebrated at Carthage, he describes them in distinctly Roman terms, picturing Hannibal attended by consular axes, lictors, and fasces (8.671-673).[46] His vision reverses Carthage's and Rome's usual identities, endowing Hannibal and the

---

46   "gestat Agenoreus nostro de more secures
consulis, et sparsos lictor fert sanguine fasces.
in Libyam Ausonii portatur pompa triumphi."

Carthaginians with the rituals and identifying features of Roman consular triumphs.

Silius goes into much greater detail about the second portent which he describes at the outset of *Punica* 9, and with it he moves more clearly into the *topoi* of civil war. This second portent, occurring during the night before the battle of Cannae, involves an almost impossible concatenation of coincidences: a young Italian named Mancinus dies during a skirmish on the eve of the battle (9.12-14); his corpse is stripped during the night by none other than his own father, Satricus. Satricus, a Libyan slave since the first Punic War, is trying to escape from his Carthaginian master (who is fighting at Cannae), and he pauses in his flight to strip a corpse of its weaponry (9.66-94). *Meanwhile*, Mancinus' brother Solimus, also a Roman soldier, is trying to find Mancinus' corpse on the battlefield, and he finds a stranger (in fact, his father) stripping his brother's corpse. Vowing to return his brother's weapons to his home town and to his mother, Solimus fatally wounds his father, who still has time to identify himself to his son and to reveal both of their errors. Solimus stabs himself in grief, and dies after writing a warning to Varro in blood on his shield: *fuge proelia Varro* (9.95-177).

This story is not found in Livy's account of the battle of Cannae, and with his invention Silius stretches the reader's credulity to the limit, piling coincidence upon coincidence. Moreover, this final omen takes us into the narrative typologies of civil war, reflected in so many of the episode's details--father stripping son of weaponry, son killing father, son committing suicide rather than live beyond such a crime, Varro's own surprising claim that this omen is the work of the Furies (9.265). Moreover, the story continues the pattern of confusion between Punic and Roman that we have seen building through *Punica* 8, as becomes clear in the final conversation between Solimus and his dying father: Satricus offers his son some consolation by saying that he himself was an enemy in his son's eyes at the crucial moment, *iaceres in me cum fervidus hastam, Poenus eram* (9.129-130).

To sum up what we have seen thus far in *Punica* 8-9, Anna, Varro, and the final omens before the battle of Cannae, all blur the distinctions between friend and foe, and thus link Silius' narrative to the common Roman doctrine that Rome would become its own worst enemy once it had rid itself of external threats. The Cannae omens further push the scope of the epic toward the world of Roman civil war in their inclusion of standard tropes from civil war descriptions. At Cannae and elsewhere in his poem, however, Silius forges one further and highly specific link between his own narrative and the Roman civil wars of the first centuries BC and AD, in his extraordinary manipulation of Roman names. Let us turn now to a more detailed exploration of this technique.

b. When is the third century not the third century?

The most consistent technique used by Silius to keep the issue of civil war steadily before the reader's eyes is his use of suggestive and anachronistic names for his Roman and enemy warriors alike. As we noted earlier, Bibulus, Brutus, Casca, Catilina, Cethegus, Cilnius, Cimber, Cinna, Crassus, Curio, Galba, Labienus, Laenas, Lateranus, Maecenas, Marius, Metellus, Milo, Piso, Scaurus, Sulla, and Tullius, and many other anachronistic characters appear on the battlefields of the *Punica*. These names, powerful and evocative, create brief but frequent glimpses of civil war throughout the *Punica*;, nowhere is Silius' use of them more apparent than in *Punica* 8, in the catalogue of Roman forces that constitutes most of the second half of this book (8.356-616). The catalogue comes in the middle of *Punica* 8, after the Anna Perenna episode and after Silius' description of Varro's election. In it Silius creates a catalogue of Roman forces to rival the Latin forces mustered against Aeneas in *Aeneid* 7, as we find the same glorification of Italian identities and the same emphasis on rustic simplicity and enthusiasm that Vergil brought to his catalogue.[47]

But here in the midst of a catalogue so evocative of the past days of Latinus and Aeneas, we find a group of names

---

[47] The best discussion of Silius' catalogue in *Punica* 8 can be found in Venini (1978); she explores the catalogue's usefulness as a historical source for third-century Italy, and she provides an exhaustive catalogue of the towns mentioned by Silius and their appearance in other works of Latin literature.

suggestive of Roman commanders of the future--not only of the future, but of Roman eras of civil war. The commanders are: Scaurus, Scaevola, Sulla, Tullius, (Claudius) Nero, Curio, Piso, Galba, Scipio, Cethegus, and Brutus. To the best of our knowledge, only six of these names, Nero, Scipio, Galba, Piso, Scaevola, and Cethegus have any connection with the Second Punic War as a whole, and none of these six can be linked to the battle of Cannae in particular. Moreover, of these six, Silius has three (Galba, Piso, and Scaevola) die at Cannae, even though the historical figures of the same name were known to have been involved in events subsequent to Cannae-- according to Livy, at least.[48] In sum, eight of the eleven commanders named by Silius have no known connection to the events to which Silius assigns them.

In fact, only two of these commanders reflect known historical figures: Scipio and Claudius Nero.[49] Historical necessities won't allow Silius to distort too radically the roles of these two figures in the war--they were, after all, responsible for the two most decisive defeats of Carthaginian forces in the

---

[48] Galba: a P. Sulpicius Galba is elected consul in 210 BC (Livy 26.1.1) and appears regularly in Livy's narrative, Books 26-29. Piso: a Piso is elected praetor in 210 BC (25.41.12), and a C. Calpurnius is captured by Hannibal at Cannae and sent to negotiate on behalf of Roman prisoners (22.60-61). Q. Mucius Scaevola is elected praetor for 215 BC (23.24.4), and serves for several years in Sardinia, before dying in 209 BC (27.8.4). For the deaths of similarly named Romans in the *Punica* see *Pun.* 10.403-404.

[49] Too little is known about any Cethegi in the Second Punic War to say for sure whether or not Silius' Cethegus corresponds to or counters what we know of historical figures.

war. But the rest of the commanders are, as best we can tell, Silius' own invention, and as a group their names powerfully evoke the civil wars of the Republic and of AD 68-69. Tullius, Curio, Sulla, Cethegus, Brutus, and even Scipio, are names closely linked to the Republican civil wars; Nero, Galba, and Piso recall the strife of AD 69.[50]

These names take on even more force when we recall Livy's Cannae narrative. Livy provides no exhaustive list of Roman divisions and commanders; rather he asserts that Paulus and Varro commanded the Roman forces together with Servilius (*Livy,* 22.45.8). That is all. Silius gives us a list of 11 commanders. He does not include Paulus or Varro in the list, and, more important, *none* of the commanders in his list appear *anywhere* in Livy's Cannae narrative. Indeed, few of the commanders in this list appear very prominently, if at all, in the rest of *Silius' own* Cannae narrative --we are clearly faced here with a catalogue invented by Silius to stand *per se,* as an independent entity in the text.

These names possess great power in and of themselves to conjure up visions of civil war. But Silius does not simply rely on his names alone to maintain his focus on civil wars. He repeatedly shapes his descriptions of these commanders in ways that recall events and characteristics peculiar to the later bearers of these names: more simply put, the narrative

---

[50] The names Scaurus and Scaevola do not fit so obviously any pattern associated with civil war.

surrounding these names recalls the details of civil war as clearly as the names themselves do.

We have already seen how Silius' description of Galba at Cannae might stand as a vision of the emperor Galba's activities in the wars of AD 68-69; Silius includes a similar link to the more famous Galba of the Imperial era in his catalogue of *Punica* 8, placing his commander Galba next to a commander named Piso (8.446-494), letting the pairing of these names recall the importance of another Piso for the *princeps* Galba's brief reign and for his assassination itself. With other names, Scaurus and Cicero most notably, Silius makes direct references to later generations of the family; indeed, with Tullius he specifically points to Marcus Tullius Cicero and his conciliatory role in the struggles of the first century BC.[51]

Other names here also might have some specific allusions linked with them in the catalogue, though the references are not nearly so obvious. Thus Silius notes that the commander Cethegus praises the weaponry of his troops;[52] we know of a Cethegus who was in charge of stockpiled weapons

---

[51] For Scaurus see *Pun.*8.370-375, especially line 371, *sed iam signa dabat nascens in saecula virtus*. For Tullius, see *Pun.*8.408-413:
> indole pro quanta iuvenis quantumque daturus
> Ausoniae populis ventura in saecula civem!
> ille, super Gangen, super exauditus et Indos,
> implebit terras voce et furialia bella
> fulmine compescet linguae nec deinde relinquet
> par decus eloquio cuiquam sperare nepotum.

[52] *Pun.*8.562-587, especially 582-584.

in the Catilinarian conspiracy.[53] So too, Silius puts his Brutus in charge of the cities of Cremona, Placentia, Mutina, Ravenna, and Aquileia;[54] aside from these city names' own associations with later civil wars, we learn from Appian and Dio Cassius that Antony besieged Decimus Brutus at Mutina in 43 BC, and that Brutus then fled to Ravenna and Aquileia.[55]

Silius thus employs several different strategies in his Cannae catalogue to superimpose a vision of civil wars on his Hannibalic narrative: direct and indirect references to later eras and pointed juxtapositions of names all contribute to this technique of historical overlay. Nor does he restrict his manipulation of Roman (and non-Roman) names to his catalogue in *Punica* 8. We find equally suggestive names throughout the *Punica*, usually occurring in swift battle narratives, at points where Silius notes both victors and victims in a particular fray. Thus in *Punica* 7 we find within a space of 35 lines Bibulus, Casca, Sulla, Crassus, Metellus, Brutus, Torquatus, and Furnius (*Punica* 7.617-651). Torquatus and Brutus, it is true, call to mind Rome's early Republican history as powerfully as its later history, but the primary thrust of these names as a group is toward the first century BC, when bearers of all these names participated in the events of Roman civil war.

As I suggested earlier, the primary effect of all these anachronistic names is to remind the reader of Rome's future

---

[53] Cicero, *Catil.* 3.3.8 and 3.5.10.
[54] *Pun.*8.591-592.
[55] Dio, 56.35-38; Appian, *B.C.* 3.74-98.

development at every step of the Hannibalic War. To propose a modern analogy, it is as if a late-20th century American reader of a historical novel about George Washington's crossing of the Delaware were to encounter John Dean, Donald Segretti, J Edgar Hoover, Arthur Bremmer, James Watt, Lee Harvey Oswald, Gary Hart, Bebe Rebozo, Charles Colson, Jim Wright, G. Gordon Liddy, and Mayor Richard C. Daley as oarsmen.

But one must explore these historical overlays a bit more closely, for the *Punica* draws causal as well as chronological connections between the two major eras that it evokes. In charting the progress of the Second Punic War, Silius traces the ways in which Roman policy against Hannibal evolved, both in the early days of the war and in the slow Roman recovery after Cannae. He emphasizes, among other points, the collective nature of Rome's strength and of its concerns in the early stages of the war, implying, perhaps, a contrast with Carthage's dependence on one charismatic and fierce general.[56] But as the war progresses Silius shows the reader a Rome increasingly dependent on the risky, and often brutal, attacks of its own generals.[57] While these tactics to a large degree brought Rome its victory over Hannibal, they also

---

[56] *Pun*.1.3-6:
>   da, Musa, decus memorare laborum
>   antiquae Hesperiae, quantosque ad bella crearit
>   *et quot Roma viros*, sacri cum perfida pacti
>   gens Cadmea super regno certamina movit....

[57] Ahl (1986b), 2540-2542 and 2555.

help us make deeper sense of our anachronistic names. For the names point to the historical period during which Rome found itself totally at the mercy of its military strongmen, and so they suggest the ultimate consequences of the changing Roman policy against Hannibal. Unlike other Roman moralists and historians who pinpointed the origins of Roman decline to the post-Hannibalic eras,[58] Silius seems to argue that it is in the very act of fighting Hannibal that Rome set itself on the path to civil war, for it is in the fight itself that the city began to rely to greater degrees on individual generals (especially Scipio Africanus and Claudius Nero) for its survival. It is also in the fight against Hannibal that Roman generals began to create a new type of name for themselves; Scipio provides the best example of this shift to more self-interested leadership in *Punica* 16, where he argues for his proposed expedition to Africa, and notes the *titulus*, or honorific name, that such an expedition would earn (16.665-668, *senectus intremit...ne finem longis tandem peperisse ruinis sit noster titulus*). As Silius later notes, Scipio is honored with the name Africanus when he defeats Hannibal (17.626, *devictae referens primus cognomina terrae*).

Silius' manipulation of names endows his epic with several powerful dynamics. First, this technique points to a key way in which the *Punica* reflects the same concerns as the *Argonautica* and the *Thebaid*. For the names of the *Punica*, while they steadily direct the reader to the civil wars in Rome's

---

[58] See, for example, Sallust, *Cat.*10.1 and *Jug.* 41.2-3, as well as the remarks of Earl (1961), 41-59.

future, also throw personal identity and individuality within the poem into confusion. And it is this confusion between friend and foe, between external and internal enemy that lies at the heart of the Flavian poets' narrations of civil war.

A case in point: Gaius Claudius Nero. Silius' Nero has an impeccable set of attestations in Livy's accounts of the war, and Silius does not generally alter the facts regarding Nero's involvement, with one notable exception: he clearly identifies Nero as the killer and beheader of Hannibal's brother Hasdrubal at the battle of the Metaurus (15.805-807); Nero himself subsequently parades Hasdrubal's head in front of Hannibal's camp (15.811-816).[59]. In historical terms this is a glaring alteration, for if Nero, a consul, *had* killed Hasdrubal, the enemy's commander, Nero would have been entitled to the *spolia opima*, a honor we know was not accorded him.

But Silius is writing in the aftermath of the emperor Nero's reign, and when he details so carefully a scene in which a Roman commander named Nero abuses the head of a slain enemy, we see the distinctions between the third century BC commander and the first century AD emperor begin to blur uncomfortably. If we can rely on Tacitus for this point, the emperor Nero, like several of his predecessors and successors, took great delight in demanding and receiving heads of his murdered opponents.[60]

---

[59] Another alteration of the Livian tradition, for which see Livy, 27.51.
[60] See Tacitus, *Ann.* 14.57.6 and 14.59.4, for Nero's witticisms on receiving the heads of Faustus Cornelius Sulla and Rubellius Plautus.

The compounded identities that Silius thus creates in his epic also bring to the epic a narrative dynamic similar to that which we found in the *Thebaid*, where the language of the poem reinforces the theme of civil war. Like Statius' constant emphasis on doubled and paired images, Silius' anachronistic names appear throughout his epic, stretching the chronological boundaries of his poem, and repeatedly weaving the issue of civil war into the poetic fabric of his text.

Conclusions

All three poets take great advantage of their epics' capacities to represent the patterns and actions of Roman civil war, and in so doing they reflect the degree to which civil war remained a concern in literary and intellectual circles in the post-Neronian Roman world. The nature of their concern is reflected in part in the vocabulary that attends these moments of civil strife, for in their representations of the *topoi* of civil war we frequently find the Flavian poets invoking the term *nefas* to mark the actions that they describe. This word, frequent enough in the *Aeneid*, and invoked by Lucan with dazzling regularity, remains a key term in each of the Flavian epics, and its presence underscores the paradoxical relationship these poems have to much of their material, as it marks episodes and actions that might be better left unaccomplished or undescribed.

In their use of the term *nefas* the Flavian poets owe much to their immediate predecessor, Lucan, for while Vergil might use the term to mark images of civil war in the *Aeneid*,[61] he also uses it in more innocent contexts--for example, to describe the flames that appear in Lavinia's hair.[62] Lucan, however, links the term directly to the civil wars of his poem, defining them in the opening lines as a *commune nefas*,[63] and returning to the term repeatedly in the course of his epic.[64]

Lucan thus establishes a particular connection between the word *nefas* and civil war, and the Flavian epics, maintain this association. Valerius uses the term twice to define the crimes committed on Lemnos,[65] and four times in his descriptions of the unholy war fought by the Argonauts with their ally Cyzicus;[66] Silius uses it to mark the suicide of the

---

[61] Most notably Cleopatra's presence at the battle of Actium on Aeneas' shield at *Aen*.8.688, *sequiturque (nefas) Aegyptia coniunx.*

[62] *Aen*.7.72-73, *et iuxta genitorem astat Lavinia virgo, / visa, nefas, longis comprendere crinibus ignem.* C.f. Aeneas' use of the term at *Aen*. 2.719, where he tells his father that it would be *nefas* for him to handle the *penates* before purifying himself.

[63] *Phar*.1.4-7:

                                      et rupto foedere regni
            certatum totis concussi viribus orbis
            in commune nefas, infestisque obvia signis
            signa, pares aquilas et pila minantia pilis.

[64] He uses the word *nefas* 47 times in the *Pharsalia*. See Ahl (1976), 120 and 239-240, for brief discussions of two of the contexts in which it appears: the suicide of Vulteius and his men (4.548-549, *totumque in partibus unis / bellorum fecere nefas*), and Cato's definition of civil war as a *summum nefas* at 2.286.

[65] *Arg*.2.101 and 210.

[66] *Arg*.3.186, 258, 284, and 301.

Saguntines,[67] the Anna episode in *Punica* 8,[68] and the deaths of Satricus and his sons in *Punica* 9;[69] and finally, Statius gives the word programmatic force in the *Thebaid*, invoking it a total of 53 times.

We have already seen in this chapter how Statius endows his poem with a sort of negative momentum, pausing at several points to express his own despair with the direction his narrative must take--and his despair is especially ironic in light of the fact that he has consciously chosen his topic in preference to writing about his *princeps* Domitian. We might see some of the same negative impetus in the use all three of these poets make of the word *nefas*--for each of them, in narrating moments of civil and familial strife and patterns of action quite familiar to their Roman audience, is attempting to articulate things better left unsaid.

---

[67] *Pun.*2.618--we will discuss in chapter five the ways in which the suicide of the Saguntines involves visions of civil war.
[68] *Pun.*8.102 and 177.
[69] *Pun.*9.125.

CHAPTER 4: FACING THE TYRANT

(a) ...non enim ante medium diem distentus solitaria cena spectator adnotatorque convivis tuis immines...
(Pliny, *Pan.* 49.6)

...Of course, Trajan, you would not arrive at your dinner parties stuffed with your own lonely midday feast, nor would you loom over a party watching and taking note...

(b) Ceterum ex iracundia nihil supererat secretum, ut silentium eius non timeres: honestius putabat offendere quam odisse...
...Hunc rerum cursum, quamquam nulla verborum iactantia epistulis Agricolae auctum, ut erat Domitiano moris, fronte laetus, pectore anxius excepit.
(Tacitus, *Ag.* 22.4, 39.1)

Moreover, if he was angry, he made no secret of it, so that you never had to fear his silences: he thought it more honorable to give offense than to indulge in hatred...
...Although Agricola had not enhanced his account with any boastful descriptions, when Domitian received news of these events, he did so, as was his custom, with a cheerful expression on his face, but deep anxiety in his heart.

(c) tum iuvenem tranquilla tuens nec fronte timendus occupat et fictis dat vultum et pondera dictis...
...talibus hortatur iuvenem, propiorque iubenti conticuit, cautis Scythico concurrere ponto Cyaneas tantoque silet possessa dracone

> vellera, multifidas regis quem filia linguas
> vibrantem ex adytis cantu dapibusque vocabat
> et dabat ex taetro liventia mella veneno.
> mox taciti patuere doli nec vellera curae
> esse viro, sed sese odiis immania cogi
> in freta.
>
> (*Arg.*1.38-39, 58-66)

> Looking at the youth with a placid and reassuring gaze he addresses him and adds expression and force to his deceptive words...He encourages Jason with such words, but when he verges on direct commands, he falls silent, saying nothing of the Cyanean rocks that collide in the Scythian sea; nothing of the fact that the Fleece is kept by a huge serpent. This snake is always flickering its tongue in its deep cave, but the daughter of the king used to charm it out with magic chants and foods, giving it honeyed cakes dripping in black poison. Soon the silent tricks of Pelias are exposed and it is clear that he is not concerned with the Fleece; but Jason feels himself forced out into the vast ocean by hatred.

When read in conjunction with posthumous descriptions of Domitian, the Flavian epics pose a tantalizing riddle. Not only do all three poems present a consistent picture of tyranny--tyrants boiling with rage, plotting deadly crimes, and masking both emotion and intent behind silent and reassuring facades--but their composite portrait of tyranny constitutes a perfect model for subsequent descriptions of Domitian himself--an emperor consumed by paranoia, silent and watchful, ready to eliminate any distinguished men whom he considers a threat. And hence the riddle: How much of Domitian is in any of these characterizations--poetic or historical? Do Tacitus and Pliny (and Suetonius too)[1] provide us with accurate characterizations of Domitian which we can then read back into our interpretations of tyranny in the Flavian epics, or do the Flavian epics present a stereotype of tyranny that subsequently influences the next generation's portrait of the last Flavian emperor?

Certainly the Flavian poets are influenced by the long-evolving rhetorical and poetic tradition regarding tyrants and tyranny.[2] The rhetoric of the first century BC, itself relying on earlier Greek philosophical and rhetorical models of tyrants, established in Roman terms a strong and consistent image of tyranny that influenced the Roman poets of subsequent generations, one that especially takes hold in the poetry of Ovid. The essential elements in this stereotype are *vis*, *crudelitas*, *superbia*, and *libido* (both for power and for sexual victims). The poetic tyrant usually displays most, if not all, of these features, and his face is usually as accurate a barometer of these characteristics as his behavior.[3]

But in the course of the first century AD this stereotype changes--in response, no doubt, both to the individual, diverse rulers who grace the Palatine and to the increasing fixedness of the Principate as an institution. As a result, the models of

---

[1] In addition to the passages cited above, the chief passages are to be found in Tacitus, *Ag*.39-45, and Pliny, *Pan*.5, 11-12, 16, 33, 48-49, and 53; see also Suetonius, *Dom. passim.*
[2] See Dunkle (1967) and (1971).
[3] Evans (1969), especially pages 46-67.

tyranny that we find in the Neronian and Flavian eras differ markedly from the models of the Augustan era. In the Flavian epics, especially, we find a cadre of tyrants in many ways more subtle than their literary predecessors: their sexual appetites (so often the marker of those who lust for power, both in Ovid and in Neronian literature) seem to be held completely in check, and they are generally far more adept both at masking their deadly intentions and at manipulating silence in insidious ways.[4]

That Domitian is *in part* responsible for this shift in the tyrannical stereotype seems plausible, for the Flavian poets again and again emphasize the importance of concealed emotions and silences in the tyrannical persona--characteristics most suggestive in Roman Imperial history of Domitian and one of his Imperial predecessors, Tiberius.[5] Tacitus and Suetonius both note the ways in which Tiberius used silence as a tool, and they comment as well on his talent for masking his anger and his murderous plans.[6] As the excerpts above from Tacitus and the younger Pliny allege, Domitian too often concealed deadly intents, and often let his ambiguous silences signal disapproval

---

[4] It is true that Seneca's tragedies also note a tyrant's abilities to manipulate silence and various facades--see for example Atreus in the *Thyestes*. My point, however, is that the Flavian epics place far more consistent a stress on these tyrannical features.

[5] These features are not necessarily the exclusive domain of Tiberius and Domitian--compare Nero's manipulation of silence and false expressions at Tacitus, *Ann.* 13.15-16, during his murder of Britannicus. But they do serve as primary definitive characteristics for these two emperors, whereas one does not immediately associate Nero, or Claudius, or Caligula with the manipulation of silence.

[6] Tacitus *Ann.* 1.13 and 1.77; Suetonius, *Tib.* 22 and 32.

and stir fear.[7] The similarity between these two rulers may, in fact, have been more than coincidental: Suetonius records the remarkable fact that Domitian's sole reading material, after the early years of his reign, was the official memoirs and notebooks of Tiberius.[8] Perhaps he borrowed a few leaves from these pages.[9]

Silence lies at the heart of the Flavian portraits of tyranny as much as it serves to identify the contemporary *princeps*, and this fact provides us with an intriguing, though indirect testimony to the reliability of later historical and rhetorical representations of Domitian. We can never know for certain how close the similarity actually was between Domitian and this stereotype, but all indicators point to a fair degree of correspondence. Indeed, the fact that we cannot precisely distinguish the point at which biographical facts yield to rhetorical stereotypes in historical accounts of Domitian, and the fact that the Flavian poets never explicitly equate Domitian with their tyrants,[10] both underscore the rhetorical demands of *emphasis* and *schema* at play here: the allusions to Domitian in these poems are made *aperte*, as opposed to *palam*--the critical

---

[7] See also Tacitus, *Ag.* 42.4, *Domitiani vero natura praeceps in iram, et quo obscurior eo inrevocabilior.*
[8] Suetonius, *Dom.* 20.
[9] See Jones (1992) 3-5, for significant familial links between Vespasian's family and the Tiberian court.
[10] Though Statius does seem to come as close as one can when he identifies Eteocles as *princeps* at *Theb.*1.169.

meaning must not be stated explicitly, rather it lies exposed in the text in a potential state, left for the audience to discover.[11]

The capacity of these portraits to allude to the Flavian *princeps* is protected not only by the indirect nature of their commentary but also by the programmatic praises of the emperor included in each poem. These set pieces of praise that come at the opening of the *Argonautica* and *Thebaid* and in the third book of the *Punica* provide the Flavian poets with some obvious cover for any more critical analyses of monarchy or tyranny that they make. But they do not negate the power that the tyrannical portraits might possess. Again, the remarks of Maternus and his guests discussed in an earlier chapter are pertinent here, for they argue strongly against any presumption that these tyrannical representations might lack any force of their own. Both Maternus' remarks in Tacitus' *Dialogus* about the dangers inherent in representing mythic tyrants and Roman tyrannicides, and Quintilian's comments about the feasibility of speaking *in tyrannum* reflect a different attitude toward literary and rhetorical representations of tyranny in the first century AD and show how such tyrannical representations were anticipated and were interpreted in connection with the contemporary *princeps*.[12]

---

[11] Again, see Ahl (1986), 192-196, for a fuller discussion of this; see also Quintilian 9.2.55 and 9.2.67 for the distinction between *palam* and *aperte*.
[12] G. Williams (1978), 205 n.31, claims that a certain *animus nocendi* distinguishes Maternus from the poets of his day, presuming that the poets would not have any reason or wish to criticize their *princeps*, rather than

To a certain extent, then, these poems can be seen to target the Principate and Domitian in their representations of tyranny, and, as one might expect in figured speech, they do so by indirect means.[13] But the representations of tyranny that we find in these poems do not stand as simple anti-Domitianic tracts; the behavior of these tyrants is not simply analyzed in terms of its own pure wickedness. Rather, the tyrants and their (Domitianic) characteristics are examined in terms of their effects on others--on other individuals and on society as a whole. We see the tyrants as they interact with other characters, and the poets explore the validity and utility of different types of response to the *tyrannus*. Ultimately, I would argue, the poets all acknowledge the ineffectiveness of most individual responses to tyranny. As should become clear both in the present chapter and in the following chapter on suicide, the nature of the tyrant's position and character in these poems is such that it channels the responses of those who oppose him into directions that in the end prove self-defeating.[14] In order to get a better sense of this argument's

---

allowing Tacitus and Quintilian to stand as evidence for how literature in general was interpreted.

[13] One of the most detailed readings of Flavian epic and its contemporary political relevance can be found in Dominik (1994a), especially pages 130-180.

[14] The lines of analysis that I trace in regard to this issue are based to some extent on New Historicist readings of Renaissance literatures. I do not mean to turn the Flavian poets into New Historicist theoreticians, but the Flavian representations of tyranny and of responses to tyranny do share several characteristics with Renaissance models of political behavior as defined by New

place in these poems, let us look first in more detail at the nature of these tyrants and the types of response to them that the Flavian poets portray, before moving on to an exploration of the ways that the tyrants defy any effective response.

Tyrannical types

On a general level, the simple fact that these tyrants constitute the most consistent vision (though not the only one) of the political world in the *Argonautica* and the *Thebaid*--and appear frequently enough in the *Punica* as well--is significant in its own right. These poets, in the course of their epics have the opportunity to create a myriad of different political types; and, in fact, we do encounter some non-tyrannical figures in each poem--Adrastus and Theseus in the *Thebaid*; Cyzicus, Lycus, and Jason himself in the *Argonautica*; the several positive Roman figures in the *Punica*. Yet the consistency of the tyrants' characterizations is as striking as any differentiations among them or any contrasts with the fewer, more positively portrayed rulers. Pelias, Laomedon, Cyzicus, and Aeetes in the *Argonautica*; Eteocles, Polynices, and Creon in the *Thebaid*; even Hasdrubal, Hieronymus, and Hannibal himself in the *Punica*; all have much of their character cut from the same cloth.

Historicism. For an excellent introduction to New Historicism, and for a full bibliography, see Veeser (ed.) (1989), especially the article by Graff, "Co-optation," 168-181.

As we mentioned above, this model is first set in Roman terms in the political rhetoric of the first century BC, and it quickly seems to inform poetic representations of tyranny, helping shape such figures as Tereus in Ovid's *Metamorphoses*. His Tereus incorporates virtually all of the standard rhetorical typologies about the tyrant, and emphasizes other aspects as well that will remain part of the stereotype: the fear that plagues the *tyrannus*, and the false expressions he uses to mask his true intentions.[15]

All three of the Flavian epics follow this same model of tyrannical representation, but they give it greater prominence in their poems than Ovid does: whereas Ovid returns only sparingly to similar patterns of characterization in his *Metamorphoses*, in the Flavian epics virtually every one of the tyrants listed above reflects the same set of characteristics-- violent instincts and feelings of pride, arrogance and cruelty, vast capacity for rage, and the ability to rule by fear. All are equally adept as well at concealing their violent plans behind pleasant expressions and words. We might, for an example, examine in more detail the passage from the *Argonautica* cited at the opening of this chapter (*Arg*.1.22-66), for it involves almost all of these attributes.

---

[15] For Tereus see *Met*.6.411-675. He is identified as a *tyrannus* at 6.549; his *libido* is noted at 6.458 and 562; his *vis* at 6.525; his *ira* at 6.549; he is *saevus* at 6.581; *ferus* at 6. 549 and 557; fearful at 6.549-550, and adept at dissimulation at 6.466-474.

This passage comes immediately (and perhaps pointedly) after Valerius' salute of the Imperial family, and in it the poet establishes several of the key components common to many of his fellow rulers in Flavian epic. Pelias, specifically labeled a tyrant (1.29), faces a difficult problem here at the beginning of the epic: he has learned from a prophecy that his brother's son, Jason, could ruin his iron-fisted rule of Iolcus (1.23, *iam gravis et longus populis metus*) and could even cause his death (1.27-28, *hunc nam fore regi exitio*); he is troubled as well by Jason's reputation and excellence (1.30, *instat fama viri virtusque haud laeta tyranno*). He needs to get rid of Jason, but Hercules has already single-handedly created a shortage of hero-threatening monsters in Greece (1.33-36). The life of a tyrant is never easy, but Pelias makes do with his own innovative plan of sending Jason overseas to test the ocean's wrath (1.37, *ira maris vastique placent discrimina ponti*), and once he has decided on this plan he summons Jason and masks his lethal intentions behind a placid demeanor (1.38-39). The only aspect of Pelias' character not fully apparent in this opening portrait is his anger; it will emerge soon enough, however, the clearest instance occurring at the moment when he rages at home after learning that his son Acastus has accompanied Jason.[16]

---

[16] *Arg.* 1.722-725:

>dixit et extemplo furiis iraque minaci
>terribilis, "sunt hic etiam tua vulnera, praedo,
>sunt lacrimae carusque parens." simul aedibus altis
>itque reditque fremens rerumque asperrima versat.

All or most of these characteristics are as readily visible in the other tyrants of the *Argonautica*, as well as those of the *Thebaid* and the *Punica*. Laomedon, Amycus, Aeetes, Eteocles, Hannibal, and Hieronymus are all identified as *tyranni*;[17] they all are capable of violent and even criminal action.[18] Valerius further emphasizes Laomedon's and Aeetes' abilities at concealing their violent intentions; Eteocles and Creon in the *Thebaid*, and Hannibal in the *Punica*, will be no less adept at concealment and trickery.[19] Most of these tyrants will also be plagued by paranoia and fear, and the restlessness of their minds forms another significant link to Pelias.[20]

As we noted earlier, however, there is a further point that is stressed in these tyrannical portraits--the tyrant's powerful control of silence--and again the initial description of Pelias provides an excellent example. Not only does he summon false and cunning speech to cloak sinister intentions (1.39, *fictis dat vultum et pondera dictis*); he also uses silence itself as a deadly tool, breaking off his speech at key points (1.58, *conticuit*), remaining silent about the dangers at Colchis

---

[17] Laomedon, *Arg*.2.577; Amycus, 4.751; Aeetes, 5.264 and *passim*; Eteocles, *Theb*.3.82; Hannibal, *Pun*.1.239; Hieronymus, 14.114.

[18] Pelias, *Arg*.1.725; Laomedon, 2.567-569; Amycus, 4.181-186; Aeetes, 5.519-522; Eteocles, *Theb*.3.387-388; Creon, 12.687-688; Hannibal, *Pun*.1.266-267; Hasdrubal 1.146-150; Hieronymus, 14.91-97; tyrants in general, 13.601-602; we might also note that *crimina* are specifically attributed to Caesar and Pompey both at *Pun*.13.867.

[19] For Laomedon, *Arg*.2.556 and 567-568; for Aeetes, 5.533; for Eteocles, *Theb*.2.487; for Creon, 12.687-688; for Hannibal, *Pun*.1.188 and *passim*.

[20] E.g. Laomedon at *Arg*.2.552-553; Aeetes, 5.533; Eteocles, *Theb*.3.1-32.

(1.59, *silet*), and cloaking his entire plan in silence (1.63, *taciti...doli*). Pelias' verbal silence is thus pointedly endowed with a power of its own, providing in immediate terms as effective a shield for his true intentions as his reassuring face.

Silence appears no less consistently as a weapon in the arsenals of the other tyrants of Flavian epic. When Hercules approaches Laomedon at Troy, the ruler's mind spins with different silent plots against the Tirynthian hero (*Arg*.2.567-568, *tacitosque dolos dirumque volutat corde nefas*). Aeetes is compared to a silent wave during his first encounter with Jason (5.521-522, *ceu tumet...unda silens*), and shortly thereafter we see him filled with silent rage (5.567, *tacita maestissimus ira*). When Eteocles hears Tydeus' angry demands early in the *Thebaid*, we are told that his "fiery temper rages beneath his silent breast" (*Theb*. 2.410-411, *illi tacito sub pectore dudum ignea corda fremunt*). Eteocles also sends silent weapons out to attack Tydeus in a nighttime ambush (2.487-8, *legatum insidiis tacitoque invadere ferro...cupit*). So too, when Creon admits his inferiority to Oedipus in *Thebaid* 11, he only does so silently (11.666-7, *seseque minorem confessus tacite*). Finally, Silius goes so far as to quote *Argonautica* 2.567-568 (*tacitosque dolos dirumque volutat corde nefas*) in *Punica* 8 when Dido appears to Anna and needs to convince her of the danger Lavinia poses to her (*Punica* 8.176-177, "*iam tacitas suspecta Lavinia fraudes / molitur dirumque nefas sub corde volutat*"). Though Lavinia is no tyrant herself, Dido uses this tyrannical imagery to arouse Anna's fears and to prompt her to flee from Aeneas' palace.

The silences these characters employ are often linked to another masking device--a cheerful or placid facial expression which, like silence, conceals violent emotions and intentions. Valerius marks this feature, already seen in the initial description of Pelias (1.38-39, *tum iuvenem tranquilla tuens nec fronte timendus / occupat et fictis dat vultum et pondera dictis*) with special consistency: we find Laomedon just as eager as Pelias to arrange his features in a reassuring manner (2.556, *patrio fatur male laetus amore*); and Aeetes adopts a similar mask on more than one occasion (5.533, *fingit placidis fera pectora dictis*).[21] Similar faces appear in the *Thebaid* and the *Punica*: in *Thebaid* 12 the new tyrant Creon adopts a cheerful countenance when meeting a messenger from Theseus (12.688, *fictumque ac triste renidens*),[22] and in *Punica* 11, Hannibal dons a pleasant mask in which to tour the city, immediately after ferociously abusing a Capuan rebel named Decius (11.260-261, *spectandis urbis tectis templisque serenos / laetus circumfert oculos et singula discit*).

These cheerful facades and the control of silence endow the tyrants of Flavian epic with a different sort of power than that found in the tyrants of earlier literature. Silence and

---

[21] Cf. 5.570, also of Aeetes, *interea laeto patitur convivia vultu*.
[22] This is a phrase that Tacitus will echo closely at *Ann.* 4.60.9; for general points of correspondence between Tacitus and Neronian and Flavian writers, see Burck (1981), 251-277.

pleasant demeanors, both possibly innocent attributes in and of themselves, now become potentially threatening, and the tyrants become more subtle, more difficult to decipher. Such a representation of the tyrants' methods not only reflects the types of behavior attributed to emperors like Domitian and Tiberius--whose good cheer and silence often masked anger and deadly intentions--but it also takes into account the consistently positive representations the emperors offer of themselves in the first century AD, in their portraiture, in their inscriptions, and in their building programs. By the time the Flavian poets are composing their epics, several emperors--all of whom adopt the same name, Caesar--have filled the city of Rome with impressive marble-faced structures, with honorific inscriptions, and with idealized portraits of themselves and their families. These glossy and omnipresent forms of self-promotion create a public facade behind which the individual identities of the *principes* are obscured, a facade that the Flavian poets transfer to the personal level when they note the verbal and facial facades employed by their tyrants.

It is in light of this split between the Caesars' public facades and their individual personalities that we might best appreciate the split in these poems between the programmatic praises of the Flavian *gens* and the more frequent and darker visions of authoritarian power that the poems place so consistently in the foreground. The praise passages in all three poems focus on the public achievements of the Flavian house--the military triumphs, the reconstruction of public temples and institution of Imperial cults, and the like--emphasizing the *decus*, the grace and honor, that these achievements bring to Rome.[23] But it is with the tyrannical characters within the epics that we find the poets offering their most acute analyses of a ruler's personal character as well as of the dynamics of power and authority. In creating their different portraits of authority they draw on the several characteristics that we have thus far noted; but these portraits also point to the different ways in which a tyrant's masks fail to conceal his true nature, and before turning to a discussion of the various responses to tyranny that these poems present, we should look more closely at the flaws that our poets note in the tyrannical facades.

Cracks in the facade

Just as in historical terms the facts of each emperor's reign provide a necessary corrective to the superficial sheen of the ongoing Principate by providing detailed and specific truths about each *princeps*, we also find in the Flavian epics poetic representations of the ways one can see through the silences and masks employed by the tyrants. The tyrants, despite their constant attempts to disguise their true nature, become paradoxical figures in these poems--their silences and placid masks are at odds with their several, more violent attributes, and their lust for power casts them as strangely eroticized

---

[23] *Arg.* 1.7-21; *Theb.* 1.17-33; *Pun.* 3.593-629.

figures, whose erotic impulses have become misdirected and depersonalized. These contradictory elements in the tyrannical portraits create the "seams" or "fissures" where one can "see through" the tyrant's masks, and they testify to the tyrant's own paradoxical situation--the very measures he must take to reinforce his own security further undermine that security.

The poets expose these contradictions repeatedly in their characterizations of the various tyrants, pitting violent expressions and motives and threatening language against more placid faces and words, emphasizing the tyrant's constant struggle for self-control. Consider Valerius' description of Aeetes, when Jason is first asking for the Golden Fleece:

> Talibus orantem vultu gravis ille minaci
> iamdudum premit et furiis ignescit opertis.
> ceu tumet atque imo sub gurgite concipit Austros
> unda silens, trahit ex alto sic barbarus iras.
> et nunc ausa viri, nunc heu sua prodita Grais
> regna fremit, quin et facili sibi mente receptum
> iam Phrixum dolet et Scythiae periisse timores;
> nunc quassat caput ac iuvenis spes ridet inanes...
> interea quoniam belli pugnaeque propinquae
> cura prior, fingit placidis fera pectora dictis
> reddit et haec...
> (*Arg.*5.519-526, 532-534)

> While Jason is making these pleas, Aeson presses
> close upon him with a threatening expression and blazes
> with inner rage. Just like a silent wave that swells up
> from the deepest surge and draws strength from the
> Southern winds, so the foreign ruler summons up anger
> from deep inside. One moment he is howling about
> Jason's boldness; and then about his own kingdom
> betrayed to the Greeks--he regrets the fact that he

received Phrixus so tolerantly and that he relaxed his fears about Scythia; then another moment he shakes his head, laughing at Jason's ridiculous hopes... Meanwhile, since he is preoccupied with war and an impending battle, he masks his ruthless intent behind deceiving words and makes the following speech...

Aeetes struggles valiantly to control his own reactions here, but before he gives his placid reply to Jason's speech his face and voice betray a series of quite different reactions--reactions that apparently go unnoticed by Jason, for when Jason sends Castor back to the ship to report on his meeting with Aeetes, Castor simply says *nec ferus Aeetes, ut fama* (5.553). A closer observer, or closer reader, can spot the conflicting elements in Aeetes' behavior: on his way to a reassuring reply he runs through a bizarre sequence of expressions, looming over Jason with threatening looks (5.519), shouting about the Greeks and Phrixus (5.523-525), shaking his head and laughing at Jason's request (5.526).

The other tyrannical descriptions in these poems provide similar contradictory markers of the tyrant's true nature and its constant struggle with the facades imposed on it, for all of these portraits are riddled with contradictory and oxymoronic characteristics, even at the most detailed level: in *Argonautica* 2, Laomedon is not simply happy when he faces the Greek heroes, he is *male laetus*; in *Punica* 6 Hannibal does not simply laugh at some temple reliefs at Liternum, he laughs *infesto vultu*; Creon, when he receives a messenger from Theseus in

Thebaid 12, smiles *triste*, while Eteocles, in *Thebaid* 1, passes laws against the law (*iura...trans legem...dabat*).

For all the tyrants' attempt to mask their tyrannical features, they can never fully succeed in their concealment-- their inner turmoil and violent urges constantly threaten to break out, and their innocent looks are often contradicted by more standard tyrannical physiognomics--their faces convey apoplectic rage and menacing looks as frequently as they evince placid serenity, and the epics frequently note the internal anxiety plaguing these tyrants, which they also try to mask with a cheerful expression.[24]

These contradictory aspects of the tyrants also reach down to deeper and more literary levels. The language of silence that surrounds these rulers, and indeed the language of mental turmoil itself, is a language more appropriate to Roman erotic poetry than to these epic realms, and its presence here obviously marks the eroticization of power that is often noted in connection with tyranny. But its intrusion into the Flavian descriptions of tyrants is surprising nevertheless, for the tyrants of Flavian epic are singular in that they do not manifest any of the usual and definitive sexual impulses of the stereotypical tyrant.

The erotic pedigree of some of the language surrounding these tyrants is nevertheless clear. We find that the

---

[24] For rage and menacing looks, see *Arg*.1.700-703 of Pelias; 2.554-555 of Laomedon; 5.268 of Aeetes; and *Theb*.2.410-414 of Eteocles. For their anxieties, see above, note 18.

placid masks and words of Pelias, Aeetes, Laomedon, and Creon, recall the soothing and placid features of both Amor and Nemesis in Ovid's *Amores*.[25] The terrifying brow that Pelias conceals in *Argonautica* 1 (*Arg.* 1.38, *nec fronte timendus*) echoes a similar phrase in the *Amores* describing calves not yet threatening in aspect.[26] The silent breasts (*tacito pectore*) of Dido in the *Punica* and Eteocles in the *Thebaid* find precedent in the silent hearts of Laodamia and Acontius of Ovid's *Heroides*.[27] The tyrants' mental anguish as well shares a common vocabulary with the mental distress brought on by love: Aeetes with his sickened heart (*aegro corde*) is cast in the mold of Tibullus with his sickened mind;[28] the mental restlessness seen so frequently in the Flavian epic tyrants, and connoted by such terms as *volutare* and *versare*, has strong precedent in the lyric poetry of the Augustan era as well.[29]

This erotic language serves two purposes in the Flavian epics. First, it suggests that the tyrants of Flavian poetry have refined their methods to a certain degree and have become more difficult to perceive or identify. Indeed, this Protean ability to appear in the guise of more innocent, more private, figures enhances the power of the tyrant. He is described in language already familiar to the Roman reader, and so the threat that he

---

[25] *Am.*1.6.1, *blandus vultus offers*, *Am.*2.4.59, *placido vultu Nemesis videat*.
[26] *Am.*3.13.15, *nondum fronte metuenda*.
[27] *Ep.* 13.89 and 20.201.
[28] Tibullus, 3.4.19, *aegra mente*.
[29] *versare*: Propertius 3.17.12; Ovid, *Am.*1.2.8, *Ars* 3.718, *Ep.*12.211.
volutare: Propertius 2.29.36.

poses is masked not only by the innocent facade that he is able to project, but by the private, innocent language that frequently surrounds him as well. But, as we noted earlier in this section, this language also acknowledges the presence of desire and lust in political realms, and in so doing it points to the perversions of power and ambition that define the tyrannies of these poems. The situation of these poems in the Roman epic tradition is significant, for they are all written after Lucan's *Pharsalia* has defined the strongly eroticized relationship between Pompey and the city of Rome. Pompey's ambitions might have been as self-centered as Caesar's own, but Lucan clearly shows how his ambitions stem from a profound love for Rome itself, putting a positive emphasis on the erotic elements in the relation between ruler and people.[30]

This relationship between the individual figure of authority and his people changes drastically in the Flavian epics. There is no place for a Pompeian love of one's people or ones nation; power and the scepter that symbolizes it become the sole objectives of desire. This concept finds its most obvious articulations in the *Thebaid*, where Statius frequently describes power's attractions in amatory terms. Tydeus attributes a love of power to Eteocles during their confrontation in *Thebaid* 2--terming it a *dulcis amor regni*, and defining *potestas* as something *blandum* (2.399). Statius himself adopts the same vocabulary in *Thebaid* 11, when Creon ascends to the

---

[30] Ahl (1976), 150-189.

throne; in lamenting Creon's violent transformation into a tyrant he exclaims, *pro blanda potestas / et sceptri malesuadus amor* (11.655-656).

Both Statius and Valerius also mark absence of love in the relationship between the tyrant and his people. Statius again uses his initial description of Eteocles on the throne to establish this idea. He states that the *vulgus* immediately becomes disenchanted with Eteocles on his accession and that the people transfer their love to the brother who is out of power: *tacitumque a principe vulgus / dissidet et, qui mos populis, venturus amatur* (1.169-170). Valerius includes a similar remark in his *Argonautica* when he describes the reaction of the Bebrycians on the death of their ruler, Amycus. Unlike earlier descriptions of the death of Amycus, in which his people then fight the Argonauts on his behalf, in Valerius' version of the story, the Bebrycians promptly take flight when Pollux has killed their ruler, since they had no love for their fallen king (*Arg*.4.315-316, *nullus adempti / regis amor*).

Like the silences that surround these rulers the language of love and desire forms part of the tyrants' facades in these poems, but it also helps to unmask the tyrants, as it reveals the misdirected nature of their desires and marks the total absence of love on the part of the subjects for their rulers.

Facing the tyrant

The tyrant's tools and all the contradictions they entail thus receive frequent consideration in these poems; but there is more to the tyrants' role in the epics than the basic representation of their attributes. The tyrants define a broader political context in the Flavian epics, as the poets explore in some detail the different types of approach and discourse available to those who come face to face with tyranny. This is true of the *Punica* as well as of the two mythic epics, for in the shifts of power that Silius charts during the Second Punic War we see Carthaginians and Romans alike gaining positions of dominance and imposing on their opponents measures that verge on the tyrannical.

The options available to those set in opposition to the tyrant range from quiet submission to attempts to incite state-wide revolt. But while different confrontations might help to reveal the true essence of tyranny, they do little to bring an end to such a system. The Flavian epics thus set themselves in a decidedly pessimistic position: they endorse the efforts of those who resist tyranny, but they reaffirm, however unwillingly, the impossibility of completely or effectively subverting such a political system.

In examining the exchanges between tyrants and subjects all three poets focus primarily on individual confrontations with tyranny as opposed to the response of the masses or of entire states. Such a focus makes for more vivid representations of the tyrant-subject relationship, and finds its rhetorical precedent in the rhetorical exercises of the Imperial era, where specific situations are set up within which to explore social, ethical, legal, and political problems. But this focus on the individual is also due in part to the prevailing characterization of the broader political unit--the populace as a whole--in these poems. The general population, while often cited as an accurate barometer of a tyrant's unpopularity, is rarely represented as an effective participant in political affairs. All three poets repeatedly describe the general population as a shifty and insubstantial force (the most common epithets for the *populus* or *vulgus* are *levis* and *mutabilis*) which usually steers clear of any serious confrontations.

Thus we see Jason and Aeson each reject the option of inciting the Iolchian population to revolt in *Argonautica* 1 (*Arg*.1.71, *populum levem*; 1.761, *mutabile vulgus*), and we see Perses fail in his revolt against Aeetes at Colchis, when he tries to take advantage of the population's fickleness and dislike of their king (5.270, *vulgi levitate*, and 5.267, *sequitur duce turba reperto*). In the *Thebaid* the Theban populace is equally dissatisfied, and equally ineffective, while Italian city and town citizenries in the *Punica*--including the people of Rome itself--are often confused, crazed, or unjust.[31]

---

[31] Silius' characterization of the Roman assembly at the election of Varro provides a good example: at 8.255 he describes their election of Varro as *suffragia caeca*; at 8. 286-287, when describing Paulus' unwillingness to act in any way against their vote for Varro, he remarks *sed mobilis ira est / turbati vulgi*.

Though general populations might be indecisive and capricious, all three of these poets validate the importance of its voice in the political arena, marking either the ways in which members of the *populus* try to speak out, or the ways in which the citizenry has been silenced. We find in *Thebaid* 1 an anonymous critic of Eteocles, who condemns Eteocles and the concept of an alternating monarchy in language remarkably close to Statius' own remarks as narrator of the epic.[32] Later, when an old man named Aletes speaks out against Eteocles after the massacre of 49 Thebans by Tydeus, Statius expresses his surprise that someone (one whose name we even know) would dare to speak so freely:

> haec senior, multumque nefas Eteoclis acervat
> crudelem infandumque vocans poenasque daturum.
> unde ea libertas? iuxta illi finis et aetas
> tota retro, seraeque decus velit addere morti.
> *(Thebaid* 3.214-217)

> The old man voiced this much, piling up the crimes of
> Eteocles, calling him unspeakably cruel and sure to pay
> a price. Where did he get this sense of freedom? In
> fact his end was near, his entire life behind him, and
> so he wished to add some dignity, no matter how late,
> to his own death.

The point Statius makes with his representations of the criticisms voiced by everyday citizens in the *Thebaid* is that freedom to speak becomes a surprising and remarkable event under a tyranny.[33] The only reason that Statius gives for

---

[32] Ahl (1986b), 2828-2830.
[33] Ahl (1986b), 2830-2832.

Aletes' willingness to speak out is a cynical one: he is near death anyway; his words will bring added *decus* to an already imminent end.[34]

While Statius at several points gives voice to the average citizen, marking its significance as well as its powerlessness, Valerius focuses more on the lack of a people's voice in his poem. The populations that the Argonauts encounter on their way to Colchis remain faceless masses, cowed by their tyrants into quiet obedience. When the Argo reaches Troy, for example, and Laomedon is in the process of antagonizing Hercules, Valerius comments on the reaction of Laomedon's fellow Trojans to their tyrant's arrogance: *promissa infida tyranni / iam Phryges et miserae flebant discrimina Troiae* (2.577-578).

The silence of the masses in the *Argonautica* is even more apparent at a later stop on the voyage, in Bebrycia. Amycus is not subtle in his approach to tyranny--he rules by brute force alone and his people are entirely submissive. Valerius comments on their silent fears when Amycus first approaches the Argonauts (4.200-201, *quem nec sua turba tuendo / it taciti secura metus*), and he marks their submission even more clearly in the aftermath of Amycus' death at the hands of Pollux. Earlier accounts of the Argo voyage state that when Amycus was killed by Pollux, the Bebrycians

---

[34] Cf. Seneca, *Phaed.*139, *fortem facit vicina libertas senem.*

immediately attacked the Argonauts in an attempt to avenge their king;[35] Valerius, however, radically changes this detail:

> Bebrycas extemplo spargit fuga: nullus adempti
> regis amor; montem celeres silvamque capessunt.
> haec sors, haec Amycum tandem manus arcuit ausis
> effera servantem Ponti loca vimque iuventae
> continuam et magni sperantem tempora patris.
> (*Arg*.4.315-319)

> The Bebrycians immediately scatter in flight. They had no love for their fallen king, and they swiftly seek the mountains and forests. Fortune and the fist of Pollux thus put an end to Amycus' crimes, as he presided over the wild realms of Pontus, hoping for a prolonged youth and the life span of his great father.

Once Pollux has killed Amycus, the Bebrycians all immediately scatter, without a word of objection, to the surrounding hills and the forests. Valerius, in a dramatic reversal of earlier accounts, has turned the Bebrycians from ardent loyalists into a frightened and speechless mob, apparently no more willing to face their ruler's killer than they were to face the tyrant himself.

Valerius and Statius, then, both devote some attention to the citizen body in general, commenting on the ways in which tyranny can silence a population or turn speech into a dangerous activity. In these representations they create a reciprocal relationship between tyrants and subjects, for in their silence the masses mirror the silences of the tyrants themselves. On both

---

[35] Apollonius, *Arg*.2.98-129; Apollodorus 1.1.

sides this silence acts as a mask, concealing dissent,[36] but the silent facades of the *plebs* are not so potent as those wielded by the tyrants, serving rather to preserve their submissive status.

In the encounters in these poems between more prominent characters and ruling figures we find all three poets analyzing the dynamics of different types of speech in the face of tyranny, but, while the different modes of speech adopted by the individual might serve to expose the tyrant's true nature, they generally fail to achieve any positive benefit for the individual or any immediate change in the tyrant-subject relationship.

Jason's experiences in the *Argonautica* offer a good case in point, as he adopts different tactics and modes of speech in facing different tyrants. Pelias' initial demands leave Jason virtually helpless; as we noted earlier, he contemplates but rejects the option of attempting to lead a revolt,[37] and he ends up accepting Pelias' orders, placing his trust in Juno and Pallas. It is worth noting one ploy that Jason does resort to before leaving Iolcus: he tricks Pelias by convincing Pelias' son Acastus to join the voyage. He thus avails himself of Pelias' own tactics, and when Acastus comes on board on the day of departure Jason delights in his trickery (1.485, *ductor ovans laetusque dolis*). But this tyrant-like deception backfires on

---

[36] Cf., for example, Statius' description of the Theban *vulgus* when Eteocles first ascends the throne at *Theb*.1.169-170, *tacitumque a principe vulgus / dissidet*.
[37] *Arg*.1.71-76.

Jason,[38] for when Pelias learns his son has departed he becomes so enraged that he moves against Jason's own parents and causes their deaths (1.700-850).

Jason tries a different approach when he reaches Colchis; his opening speech to Aeetes is conciliatory and he sets Pelias up as a model of the unjust tyrant (5.483-489), offering the Colchian ruler a chance to distinguish himself from his Iolchian counterpart (5.492-494). Unfortunately for Jason, he speaks to a carbon copy of Pelias himself; Aeetes listens to Jason's request with a ferocious expression (5.519, *vultu gravis ille minaci*), and then disguises his silent fury (5.521-522, *ceu tumet...unda silens*) behind reassuring words (5.533, *fingit placidis fera pectora dictis*). A different approach yields identical results: Jason submits to the tyrant's will, allowing his fellow Argonauts to serve as mercenaries in Aeetes' civil war, and then facing with Medea's secret help the individual trials that Aeetes sets for him.

By the beginning of *Argonautica* 7 Jason understands his true situation, and in one of his few revealing moments he lashes out against tyrants in general:

> quo versa fides? quos vestra volutant
> iussa dolos? alium hic Pelian, alia aequora cerno.
> quin agite hoc omnes odiisque urgete tyranni
> imperiisque caput.
>
> (*Arg.*7.91-94)

---

[38] As he himself subsequently fears--see *Arg.* 1.693ff.

> What happened to your good faith? What tricks are rolled up inside these orders? I've only found another Pelias here, and more voyages in store. All you tyrants might as well take action against me together, and bear down on me with your hatreds and commands.

In their bitter reference to all tyrants Jason's words stand as a poignant Valerian companion to Statius' expressed wish that kings alone read the *Thebaid*, and they mark as well the cyclic quality of Valerius' poem--in its finished portions there is a maddening succession of similar rulers threatening and scheming against both Jason and his fellow Argonauts. But his words also point to one of the sources of a tyrant's power, for in calling the wrath and harsh commands of all tyrants down on his own head Jason marks the way in which a tyrant's tactics isolate the individual opponent and fragment any collective strength.

Like Valerius, Statius is primarily concerned with individual confrontations with tyranny--in the course of the epic we find at least three weighty encounters in the Theban throne-room, between Eteocles and Tydeus, Eteocles and Maeon, and Creon and Phegeus. Like Valerius too, Statius creates a cyclic pattern in these scenes of confrontation--Phegeus' embassy to Creon repeats several of the details from Tydeus' embassy to Eteocles, from the sacred olive branch carried by the envoy to the hostile response of the tyrant and the utter futility of the entire conversation.

But where Valerius explores Jason's attempts at different types of rhetoric in his meetings with different tyrants, these episodes in the *Thebaid* reflect different concerns involved in the question of speech and tyranny. In the first place, Statius devotes far more attention to the visual appearance of the tyrant's throne-room, marking the several barriers and trappings of the court that isolate the tyrant from those who approach him. Eteocles is perched high on a throne, fenced in by weaponry when Tydeus appears (2.385, *sublimem solio saeptumque horrentibus armis*). Later, when Maeon, sole survivor of the disastrous ambush ordered by Eteocles, returns, he is made to wait outside the reception hall, and when he finally enters he finds Eteocles protected by the same sort of retinue that Tydeus encountered.[39] Phegeus finds no lofty throne or retinue when he faces Creon at the end of the epic, but neither does he enter into a situation conducive to negotiation or dialogue--he bursts in on a bizarre spectacle, appearing on the scene just as Antigone and Argia are defiantly stretching out their necks, awaiting Creon's execution order (12.677-682). For all of the crude simplicity that Statius claims attended the Theban throne, it certainly possesses a full share of bureaucratic red-tape and royal pomp. One can be kept waiting outside, as Maeon is; inside, the high-set throne and the bodyguards set the tyrant off from his visitors, and odd instances of tyrannical

---

[39] *Theb*.3.58, *ut primum invisi cupido data copia regis.*

savagery occasionally form the backdrop to an official audience.

These details take us back to the dilemma we posed at the outset of this chapter, for descriptions of Domitian and his own audiences follow similar lines to the picture Statius gives us of the Theban throne room.[40] But, again, Statius takes his material beyond a simple (though suggestive) Imperial parallel, for his representations of the figures who confront the different Theban tyrants are themselves surprisingly uniform and problematic in their own right.

All three of these individuals possess some privileged status when they face Eteocles or Creon: Tydeus and Phegeus are ambassadors, whose olive branch and protected status Statius emphasizes; Maeon is an augur, favored by Apollo. Of the three, Maeon comes the closest to receiving Statius' own approval (though we will discuss the limits of the poet's endorsement in the next chapter when we examine Maeon's suicide in more detail); but in facing the different Theban tyrants all of these characters resort to a blunt and threatening rhetoric that is especially counter-productive. Consider Phegeus' appearance before Creon in *Thebaid* 12:

---

[40] Cf. Pliny, *Pan*.48.3-4:
> nec salutationes tuas fuga et vastitas sequitur: remoramur, resistimus ut in communi domo, quam nuper illa immanisssima belva plurimo terrore munierat, cum velut quodam specu inclusa nunc propinquorum sanguinem lamberet, nunc se ad clarissimorum civium strages caedesque proferret. observabantur foribus horror et minae et par metus admissis et exclusis.

>   ...dicta ferens Theseia Phegeus
> adstitit. ille quidem ramis insontis olivae
> pacificus, sed bella ciet bellumque minatur,
> grande fremens, nimiumque memor mandantis et ipsum
> iam prope, iam medios operire cohortibus agros
> ingeminans. stetit ambiguo Thebanus in aestu
> curarum, nutantque minae, et prior ira tepescit.
> tunc firmat sese, fictumque ac triste renidens...
>
> (*Theb*.12.681-688)

> Phegeus arrives bringing word from Theseus. He
> has the appearance of a peace-maker--so the innocent
> olive branches attest--but he is intent on war, and
> threatens it at the top of his voice. He is quite mindful
> of who has sent him, and he mutters darkly that
> Theseus is already near, and covers much of the land
> with his cohorts. The Theban stops, caught in the
> doubtful surge of his own worries; his threats slacken,
> and his earlier rage cools, but then he catches himself
> and gives a phony and rueful smile...

Phegeus' words, Statius claims, are loud and menacing, much as Tydeus' speech to Eteocles mixed harsh words with justifiable complaints.[41] Like Tydeus too, Phegeus carries an olive branch as a mark of his protected ambassadorial status, and yet his words, belligerent as they are, fall far short of his diplomatic status and put him right on Creon's level. In fact the speeches of all three of these characters to Eteocles and Creon are models of how *not* to speak to a tyrant--they serve only to exacerbate the tyrant's rage, and all three meetings end with violent and deadly results.

---

[41] *Theb*.2.392, *iustis miscens tamen aspera coepit* ;cf 2.452-453 and 2.464- 466.

The inappropriateness of Phegeus and Tydeus to their ambassadorial roles is important in its own right for it reflects a focus unique to the *Thebaid*--a focus on the institutions of power as distinct from individual figures of power. There is in much of the *Thebaid* an automatic pattern of behavior induced by different offices--back in *Thebaid* 1 Eteocles was addressed by Statius as *saeve* and the *plebs* silently dissented, before Eteocles had even had a chance to act as ruler of Thebes (1.165- 170). The tyrant, in short, is automatically perceived as savage, the *plebs* is automatically disgruntled.

With Tydeus and Phegeus we find a different sort of standard behavior, but one that adds its own negative dynamic to the struggles for power at Thebes: these envoys, acting on behalf of Polynices and Theseus, only exacerbate the situations in which they intervene, increasing the tyrant's fury with their bitter words and threats. Tydeus, with his sharp language and imperious tone, prompts Eteocles to send out an ambush to attack him; Phegeus (like Tydeus) carries an olive branch, symbolic of peaceful intentions, but loudly promises further wars for Thebes,[42] eliciting an immediate and disdainful reply from Creon (12.689-692). The fixedness of both the tyrants' positions and the envoys' modes of approach reinforce the system of power that is bringing such ruin on Thebes.

The *Punica* incorporates similar confrontational scenes involving tyrannical types and defiant opponents into its more

---

[42] 12.682-684, *ille quidem ramis insontis olivae / pacificus, sed bella ciet bellumque minatur, / grande fremens.*

historical framework, and it does so with pointed effect, first representing the Carthaginians in the tyrant's role, but then setting Roman conquerors in the same position. The episodes that focus most precisely on these issues come in *Punica* 1, with the encounter between the Carthaginian commander Hasdrubal and two Spaniards, and in *Punica* 11 and 13, where two different Capuans confront in turn a Carthaginian and a Roman conqueror. As was the case with Maeon in the *Thebaid*, we must delay our analysis of the Capuan episodes involving Hannibal and Fulvius and their Capuan opponents until our next chapter, since these encounters focus on the issue of suicide. The initial episode of *Punica* 1 involving Hasdrubal and the two Spaniards, however, is sufficiently representative of the ways in which Silius portrays confrontations between tyrants and their opponents.

This episode takes place early in *Punica* 1, after the death of Hannibal's father, Hamilcar, and before Hannibal himself has taken command of the Punic forces in Spain. Hamilcar's son-in-law, Hasdrubal, is in control, a commander, according to Livy, distinguished primarily by the peaceful and friendly relations he established with many Spanish communities,[43] but who, nevertheless, is assassinated by a Spanish slave. Silius describes this assassination, but in doing so he completely reverses Livy's positive characterization of

---

[43] Livy, 21.2.5-6, *Is plura consilio quam vi gerens, hospitiis magis regulorum conciliandisque per amicitiam principum novis gentibus quam bello aut armis rem Carthaginiensem auxit. Ceterum nihilo ei pax tutior fuit.*

Hasdrubal,[44] and turns him into a consummately tyrannical figure:

> tristia corda ducis, simul immedicabilis ira,
> et fructus regni feritas erat. asper amore
> sanguinis, et metui demens credebat honorem
> nec nota docilis poena satiare furores...
> (*Pun.*1.147-150)

> The ruler's heart was black, his anger incurable, and savagery was the only product of his reign. He had a fierce love of blood, and in his madness he believed that being feared was a great honor; nor was he willing to slake his anger with the usual torments...

As an example of Hasdrubal's ferocity Silius then cites his execution of a Spanish king named Tagus, and explains the subsequent assassination of Hasdrubal by one of Tagus' slaves as a response to the execution by a loyal servant. Livy, it is true, has a similar explanation for Hasdrubal's death,[45] and his account leaves unreconciled Hasdrubal's pacifistic and friendly tenure and his execution of this one individual. But Silius' reversal of the Livian tradition regarding Hasdrubal transforms the force of the episode in his poem, for the execution of an outstanding and popular ruler, Tagus,[46] becomes emblematic of Hasdrubal's tyrannical nature, and the slave's subsequent

---

[44] Silius seems to be expanding here on a vague and negative description of Hasdrubal attributed to Fabius Pictor by Polybius; see Polybius 3.8.
[45] Hasdrubal executes a Spaniard of no clear rank and is then assassinated by the man's loyal slave, Livy, 21.2.6.
[46] Tagus is described at *Pun.*1.151 as *ore excellentem et spectatum fortibus ausis*, and his military talents are detailed at 1.155-164.

assassination of his master's killer becomes a powerful blow against tyranny delivered by a heroic member of the oppressed classes.

The slave is subsequently tortured and put to death, and though Livy too describes the slave's remarkable endurance to his torments, Silius' changes in the episode transform the slave's endurance into a further example of resistance to tyranny:

> ferum visu dictuque, per artem
> saevitiae extent, quantum tormenta iubebant,
> creverunt artus, atque omni sanguine rupto
> ossa liquefactis fumarunt fervida membris.
> mens intacta manet. superat ridetque dolores
> spectanti similis fessosque labore ministros
> increpitat dominique crucem clamore reposcit.
> (*Pun.*1.175-181)

> The savage scene was horrifying to see, and even to describe: once his limbs were stretched out by the torturers' artistry, they swelled in response to the demands of each torment, and bones began to smoke while blood vessels burst and limbs melted. But his mind remains untouched. As if he were an onlooker himself he surmounts his own pains, laughing them aside, and he berates his torturers as they grow tired from their labors, and with a howl he demands a cross like his master's.

The slave's body is completely destroyed in ways that confound normal distinctions between flesh and blood--his blood is shattered (1.177, *sanguine rupto*) and his flesh is liquefied (1.178, *liquefactis...membris*)--but his mind remains unaffected.

This description, with its exaltation of the slave's mental endurance, has been justifiably cited for its reflection of a particularly Stoic sensibility,[47] but there is an unpleasant aspect to the slave's behavior here as well which still needs to be recognized. The slave is insatiable for more punishment, laughing at and abusing his tormentors, demanding a crucifixion like his master's. His behavior is excessive in its own right, reflecting a fanatical devotion to his martyrdom, and it sets him on a level equal to the tyrant whom he opposes. His laughter calls to mind the scornful and tyrannical laughter of Aeetes in *Argonautica* 5 (5.526, *spes ridet inanes*); his abusiveness too links him to more obviously tyrannical figures (Eteocles at *Theb*.3.32; Polynices at 11.547--*increpat* in both instances). One might even say that his thirst for his own blood--implicit in his demands for further punishments--matches the blood-lust that Silius attributes to Hasdrubal only thirty lines earlier (1.148-149, *asper amore / sanguinis*).

The encounter between this slave and his Carthaginian oppressors involves the same sort of pattern that we saw in the *Argonautica*'s and the *Thebaid*'s representations of confrontational behavior, in that it attributes to the oppressed party some of the very characteristics that mark and condemn the oppressor himself. The secrecy with which the slave first acts (1.166-167, *clam corripit ensem / dilectum domino*), the violence of the assassination itself (1.167-168, *pernixque*

---

[47] Colish (1985), 285.

irrumpit in aulam / atque immite ferit geminato vulnere pectus), and the ferocity with which he meets his own punishment, all match the tyrant's own methods and character in the same way that Tydeus and Phegeus match the Theban tyrants threat for threat, and Jason meets Pelias' trickery with tricks of his own. Indeed, even the fickle and silent *plebs* seen in the *Argonautica* and the *Thebaid* mirror their rulers in their silences.

These reciprocal patterns of behavior (which will become even clearer when we examine in the next chapter the episodes of suicide in the Flavian epics) point us toward the paradoxical problem that lies at the heart of the Flavian representations of authority and opposition. For the opponents of tyranny that we see in these poems are forced to act in a world defined by the tyrant, and their responses to tyranny are limited and circumscribed in such a way that they repeatedly take on tyrannical features at the moment of their own response. The language that defines opposition in these poems mirrors the language describing oppressive authority itself, and though we might admire the outspokenness of an Aletes or the *mens intacta* of the Spanish slave, their positive attributes are undercut, or co-opted, by other attributes that lock them and their fellow opponents into the tyrant's world.

CHAPTER 5: SUICIDE--THE OPPOSITION SELF-DESTRUCTS

The issues that we have been examining thus far in these poems--the place of the poet and of epic in the Flavian world, the *infanda proelia* of civil war and the interrelationship of tyrants and subjects--find their fullest articulation in the acts of suicide that punctuate each poem at significant moments. As was noted in the introductory chapter, all three of the Flavian epic poets devote a significant measure of attention to acts of suicide, and in doing so they focus on several aspects of suicide that involve both political and poetic issues, three of which are of particular importance:

1. Suicide is represented in these poems first and foremost as a political act--an act of defiance and self-liberation committed in the face of oppression and tyranny. In the *Argonautica*, Aeson and Alcimede commit suicide in order to foil the tyrant Pelias' plot against them; in the *Thebaid*, Maeon commits suicide in order to demonstrate his defiance of the tyrant Eteocles, while Dymas does so when captured and menaced by a Theban patrol; in the *Punica*, the Saguntines commit mass suicide in order to avoid Carthaginian domination, while different Capuans do so to avoid both Carthaginian and Roman domination. There are, it is true, some suicides in these epics that do not have such a political motivation--Menoeceus in the *Thebaid* provides the most obvious example, and there are

also suicides in the *Punica* that have no political force. The emphasis in all three poems remains nonetheless on the politically motivated suicides and it is these that will receive our closest attention.

2. While the three Flavian epics focus on suicide's political aspects, and while they voice their basic approval of the defiance that these suicides signify, they also weave into their descriptions of these acts several elements that call into question suicide's ultimate validity as an act of defiance. Suicide, after all, as eloquent an act as it might be, is an act of self destruction, and so, at the same time as it defines the absolute opposition to tyranny of the person who carries it out, it also terminates this opposition.

Moreover, like the Spanish slave seen in the last chapter who attacks Hasdrubal and is tortured himself in turn, these suicidal figures act in a world defined and circumscribed by tyranny; their actions against the tyrant demand their own assimilation to the tyrant, for they must adopt the same ferocity and hatred that guide the tyrant's own behavior, and they are reduced to committing acts of extreme violence on their own persons. All three of the poets clearly mark this reciprocity that binds their tyrannical and suicidal characters, and in so doing they place the act of suicide into a less noble class of activity than some of their philosophical predecessors might have: an act that is ideally the act of the *sapiens* for Seneca becomes in the Flavian epics the primary preserve of fanatical and excessively ferocious opponents to tyranny.[1]

3. Finally, in a telling departure from their epic predecessors, all three of these poets use these acts of suicide as the prime occasion for expressions of their own poetry's commemorative power--by linking their creative efforts so forcefully and consistently with suicide they identify their poetry more fully than did the poets of earlier generations in terms of self-destructive, self-silencing actions. Suicide and the consequent exclamations of the poet's approval thus reflect the increasing sense of despair that burdens the poets of the Flavian period in an era of increasing Imperial control; like Mayakovsky's poetry in the Stalinist period--which struggles to speak even as it throttles itself--these poets, even as they adopt the most full-throated of Roman poetic genres, identify themselves and their own poetic voice with figures who have been silenced, who in fact have silenced themselves.

Suicide does, of course, have several specifically Roman resonances that inform the treatment it receives in these poems; as many scholars have noted, there was a particular affinity between the Romans and suicide, and it was a common Roman solution--frequently debated, but often enough carried out--to political, military, and private problems. As Grisé and Griffin have both recently demonstrated, by the time the Flavian epics are being composed, suicide has gained a particular

---

[1] For Seneca's discussions of suicide, see *Ep*.70 and 77 in particular; see also Griffin (1976), 367-388, for a general discussion of Seneca's views on suicide.

esteem and notoriety at Rome, thanks to both the philosophical debates of the day and the suicide of numerous prominent Romans.[2] All of these social factors sit behind the Flavian poets' treatment of the issue; indeed, our poets can be seen to be engaging in the same debate that frequently preoccupied such writers as Seneca, Lucan, the elder Pliny, the younger Pliny, Martial, and Tacitus--the debate that focused on whether or not this increasingly popular act of self-destruction was in fact worth the effort and loss that it entailed.

The debate first gains momentum at Rome in the decades after the suicide of Cato and the fall of the Republic, but it was no doubt resuscitated in the aftermath of Seneca's suicide in AD 65. The chief issues in the debate are, of course, the extent of one's independence under an authoritarian regime and the value of suicide when and if that independence is too greatly curtailed. Though such debates survive primarily in Stoic discussions and were no doubt often argued in Stoic terms, it would be misleading to see these epic suicide scenes as mechanical applications of some common Stoic orthodoxy (if such a thing existed).[3] Rather, as we shall see by the end of

---

[2] As we noted in the opening chapter, Grisé (1982) provides the most thorough survey of suicide in Roman history and literature; Griffin (1986) analyzes the aura suicide gained in Imperial Rome. See also Dutoit (1936), J. Bayet (1951), W. Rutz (1960), and van Hooff (1990).

[3] For a basic introduction to Stoic doctrine and suicide in addition to Griffin (1976), see Rist (1969), 233-255. For a reading of Maeon's suicide in the *Thebaid* within the context of Roman Stoicism, see Vessey (1973), 107-116; also see Vessey (1974) for an analysis of the Saguntines' mass suicide and its reflections of Stoic thought.

this chapter, the Flavian poets clearly diverge on many points from Stoic teachings about suicide, and their presentations of suicide seem to reflect misgivings about the justification of any suicide, whether done for defiant or altruistic reasons. Such a stance is especially ironic in the case of Silius--who eventually ends his own life by starvation and becomes one of the younger Pliny's heroic suicides--but the *Punica*, in fact, presents suicide in no more positive a light than do the *Argonautica* and the *Thebaid*.

Let us turn, then, to the poems and the suicide scenes themselves to see how these various issues come into play in these episodes.

The Argonautica

>adstitit et nigro fumantia pocula tabo
>contigit ipsa gravi Furiarum maxima dextra;
>illi avide exceptum pateris hausere cruorem.
>Fit fragor; inrumpunt foribus qui saeva ferebant
>imperia et strictos iussis regalibus enses.
>in media iam morte senes suffectaque leto
>lumina et undanti revomentes peste cruorem
>conspiciunt; primoque rudem sub lumine rerum
>te, puer, et visa pallentem morte parentum
>diripiunt adduntque tuis. procul horruit Aeson
>excedens memoremque tulit sub nubibus umbram.
>   (*Arg*.1.816-826)

>The greatest of the Furies herself is in attendance
>at Aeson's house, and her right hand weighs heavily on
>the cup that foams dark with venom. Jason's parents
>eagerly take up the vessel and drain it of its blood. All

of a sudden, an uproar blares outside; Pelias' troops break down the doors, swords drawn, on their way to deliver their king's deadly orders. Too late--they see the old couple already sinking in death, their eyes glazed, choking on the blood as the poison surges through them. You were there, Promachus; inexperienced, and only in the first stages of life, yet already a pallid witness to your parents' suicide. The troops snatch you up and tear your limbs apart, adding your death to your parents'. As he departs, Aeson shudders, and he takes the mindful shade to the cloudy realms below.

Valerius closes *Argonautica* 1 with an extended description of an event that finds no place in Apollonius' epic and is only a minor development in other accounts of the story: the suicide of Jason's parents, Aeson and Alcimede.[4] His account of their deaths would certainly strike a familiar chord with the Roman readers of his own era, as it incorporates details common to several suicides of the Imperial era; and his narrative presents Aeson and Alcimede in a generally favorable way. Their suicide is as appropriate an act of suicide as we will find in these epics, and of the three poets, Valerius casts suicide in the most positive light. But Valerius' endorsement of the act is not total--he devotes a significant measure of attention to Promachus, the younger child of Aeson and Alcimede who is left to be murdered by Pelias' troops--and his identification of his own poetic powers with the self-destruction that suicide entails establishes a pattern that Valerius' fellow poets will

---

[4] For other descriptions of the deaths of Jason's parents and brother, see Apollodorus 1.9.27 and Diodorus Siculus 4.50; Ovid, *Met.*7.163ff., has Aeson survive even after Jason's return to Iolcus.

follow, one that marks all three poems with a self-conscious air of futility and pessimism.

This episode opens at *Argonautica* 1.693, when Jason, on board the Argo, begins to worry that he has insulted Pelias, king of Iolcus, by taking Pelias' son Acastus along, and that by his departure he has deprived his parents and brother of his protection. His fears are quickly realized: back in Iolcus Pelias rages at Jason's trick of taking Acastus along, and seeking revenge against Jason he decides to kill Jason's parents (1.700-729). Valerius then shifts the scene to Jason's home where Alcimede and Aeson are sacrificing to the underworld in hopes of receiving some reassuring prophecy about Jason from the shades. Aeson's father, Cretheus, appears to them, but in addition to reassuring them about Jason he tells them that Pelias is plotting against them and urges them to commit suicide (1.730-751). Aeson and Alcimede obey and prepare for their deaths; after sacrificing to Jupiter and the gods of the underworld, they share a cup of poison and die (1.816-818).

But their deaths do not conclude the episode; in fact, at this point it takes a remarkable turn. Aeson has not included his son Promachus in his suicide plans, but rather hopes that the youth will live on and preserve the memory of his parents' noble death (1.771-773). His hopes are dashed, however, for as he and his wife die, Pelias' troops burst in, and finding their plans to murder the parents foiled they take out their anger on the son, brutally slaughtering him and adding his death to those of his parents (1.819-826). At this point Valerius closes the scene, describing the arrival of the shades of Aeson and Alcimede in Elysium and the happy life that they find there (1.827-850).

Valerius has altered the tradition of the death of Jason's family in striking fashion here. Not only has he unified the deaths of Jason's parents, but he has also revised the chronology of the story, setting this scene far earlier than in previous accounts of the Argo myth.[5] As important as the suicide scene itself is what immediately ensues in Valerius' account: Pelias' troops burst into the house only to find their murderous intentions anticipated and thwarted. Their only satisfaction comes in the murder of Promachus. While this detail does find a precedent in earlier version of the myth, Valerius certainly develops it to a fuller and more dramatic scope.[6]

The effects of these narrative shifts are important, for by joining the deaths of Aeson and Alcimede, and by having them anticipate their ruler's sentence of death, Valerius has recreated a death scene all too familiar to the Romans in the first century of the Principate and recorded in such historical accounts of the period as Tacitus' *Annals*.[7] His narrative mirrors several of the

---

[5] Apollodorus, 1.9.27, places the suicide at the end of his account of the voyage, saying that Aeson survived until news of Jason's safe return reached Iolcus.

[6] Apollodorus, *loc. cit.* Diodorus 4.50.

[7] See, especially, the suicide of Asiaticus at *Ann.*11.3; that of Seneca at *Ann.*15.61-64; that of Petronius at *Ann.*16.18-19; that of Thrasea Paetus at *Ann.*16.33-35.

historical suicides in many of its details--the monarch's death sentence itself, the decision of the wife to join her husband in death, the arrival of palace magistrates or troops at the home of the condemned and the sharp contrast at this point between the private setting for the suicide and the more public and official presence of the ruler's agents. Valerius, in one respect, even considers possibilities unavailable to Tacitus' suicidal heroes, for Aeson contemplates (but rejects) the prospect of leading a revolt of senators against his king (1.761); the Senate in Tacitus' *Annals* is generally too submissive to contemplate such an act.

Aeson and Alcimede, in short, can be seen as Valerius' exemplars of noble action in the face of tyrannical, almost Imperial, oppression. Yet, to see a simple opposition between Pelias and Jason's parents ignores several details in this episode which raise questions about the value of suicide. He poses such questions primarily in his emphasis on Promachus' role in the episode.

Promachus, ironically, serves as one of Aeson's prime justifications for his own suicide: when Aeson is considering different responses to Pelias' actions, he looks upon his son and decides by his own death to provide the boy with a model of courage and bravery:

> est etiam ante oculos aevi rudis altera proles,
> ingentes animos et fortia discere facta
> quem velit atque olim leti meminisse paterni.
>   (*Arg*.1.771-773)

> Even now his other son, still an inexperienced youth,
> appears before his eyes. Aeson would like him to learn
> prodigious courage and brave action, and he would
> also like him to retain a memory of his father's death.

Aeson hopes here that Promachus will in his life preserve a memory of his father's noble death. But instead his and Alcimede's suicide leaves the boy unprotected, an easy prey for the violent urges of Pelias' troops. Valerius' description of Promachus' own death exposes the irony of Aeson's hopes:

> primoque rudem sub limine rerum
> te, puer, et visa pallentem morte parentum
> diripiunt adduntque tuis. procul horruit Aeson
> excedens memoremque tulit sub nubibus umbram.
> *(Arg.*1.823-826)

> You were there, Promachus; inexperienced, and only
> in the first stages of life, yet already a pallid witness
> to your parents' suicide. The troops snatch you up and
> tear your limbs apart, adding your death to your
> parents'. As he departs, Aeson shudders, and he
> takes the mindful shade to the cloudy realms below.

These lines in general equate Aeson and his family with some of the *Aeneid*'s most noteworthy dead, recalling especially the departure of Camilla's and Turnus' shades to the underworld.[8] But the words *memoremque...umbram* in particular powerfully underscore the futility of Aeson's plan. In fact, these words are ambiguous--for whose shade is this that Aeson carries to the underworld? It might be Aeson's own shade, in which case

---

[8] *Aen.*11.831 and 12.952, *vitaque cum gemitu fugit indignata sub umbras.*

memorem might refer to the father's mindfulness both of Pelias' cruelty and of his own inability to protect his son. But it might just as well be Promachus' shade, for *memorem* recalls Aeson's original hope that the son would remember his father's death (1.773, *meminisse*); and in this case the word *memorem* is even more ironic, for Promachus might recall not only the cruelty of Pelias' troops but also his parents' desertion of him.

It is left, instead, to the poet himself, Valerius, to try to preserve a memory of this event, and Valerius asserts his own presence in the scene with his direct address of Promachus at 1.824-825 (*te, puer, et visa pallentem morte parentum / diripiunt adduntque tuis*). Indeed, with his direct address of Promachus and his emphasis on the boy's youth Valerius adds a strong Vergilian color to the scene, recalling such youthful and innocent victims from the *Aeneid* as Euryalus and Pallas, who suffer in part from their own inexperience. The term *pallentem*, moreover, has its own Vergilian associations with suicide, for Vergil uses it to describe Cleopatra as she contemplates her imminent suicide,[9] and uses a cognate, *pallida*, to describe Dido in *Aeneid* 4.[10]

As these Vergilian echoes might suggest, the tradition of epic poetry--and Vergil's epic in particular--weighs heavily on this Valerian episode from start to finish: the world of Aeson and Alcimede has much in common with Dido's world in

---

[9] *Aen.*8.709, *pallentem morte futura*.
[10] *Aen.*4.644, *pallida morte futura*.

Aeneid 4,[11] and after their deaths they pass on into a decidedly Vergilian underworld. Valerius' repeated allusions to the *Aeneid* stand as an assertion of the poet's primacy--his own narrative gains added power by the references it can make to earlier Roman epic--and Valerius sets himself as the chief guardian of memory in this scene, when suicide and the tyrant's onslaught leave no immediate survivors.

But before this scene is concluded, Valerius calls into question poetry's own place in such a world. He does so when he describes the arrival of Aeson and Alcimede in Elysium, where, he remarks,

>   sol totumque per annum
> durat aprica dies thiasique chorique virorum
> carminaque et quorum populis iam nulla cupido.
>   (*Arg.*1.843-845)

> sunshine and balmy days continue year round, the men enjoy dances and choral songs and pursuits no longer desired by people today.

Here again, we encounter a Vergilian conceit, for like the inhabitants of the Elysian Fields in *Aeneid* 6, the shades here enjoy an idyllic life of play and song.[12] But there is a

---

[11] In addition to the verbal link between Promachus and Dido, the scene in which Aeson and Alcimede sacrifice to the Underworld and summon Cretheus' shade (1.730-751) bears a general similarity to Dido's sacrifices and visions in *Aen.*4.450-473.

[12] *Aen.*6.642-644:
> pars in gramineis exercent membra palestris,
> contendunt ludo et fulva luctantur harena;
> pars pedibus plaudunt choreas et carmina dicunt.

Cf. also Tibullus 1.3.57ff.

significant shift in Valerius' picture of Elysium, for with the words *et quorum populis iam nulla cupido* he implies that *carmina* can be classed with other things for which there is no longer an interest in his own world; like the suicides themselves, poetry increasingly belongs to Elysian realms of the dead.

In the *Argonautica*, then, suicide is presented as a plausible yet flawed response to tyrannical pressures. There is nothing of the fanatical martyr about Aeson or Alcimide, and their plight is cast in such a way as to engender a sympathetic response in the Roman reader. But Valerius questions the value of their act nonetheless: Aeson's chief motive for suicide is the positive example he can set for Promachus and the memory Promachus can preserve of his father's defiant end; Aeson's pathetic hopes only blind him to the reality of Promachus' situation once his parents will have left him. Valerius also calls into question the poet's own role as recorder of such events-- for with Promachus' death Valerius assumes the duties of remembrance, and yet his assumption of this obligation binds his narrative to acts of self-obliteration, and, as he implies at the close of the book, his poetic discipline might be verging on an extinction of its own.

The Thebaid

The *Thebaid* offers a bleaker vision of suicide than that seen in the *Argonautica*. It is true that Menoeceus' suicide--

which he commits in order to protect his city--is carried out with an impressive measure of piety and sanctity,[13] but even it brings significant problems in its wake: Capaneus is prompted to assail the walls of Thebes and the gods of Olympus at the spot of Menoeceus' suicide,[14] and the memory of his son's self-sacrifice transforms Creon into the tyrant who drives Oedipus out of Thebes and invites a second, more destructive attack on the city by Theseus.[15]

Nor does Menoeceus' suicide stand alone in the *Thebaid*; it is preceded by two other episodes of suicide that both explore suicide's value as an act of political defiance--the suicide of Dymas earlier in *Thebaid* 10 (which we have already discussed in some detail in Chapter 1) and the suicide of Maeon in *Thebaid* 3. Both of these episodes cast suicide in a more pessimistic light, marking suicide's capacity to silence, the ways in which the suicidal character takes on the traits of the tyrant against whom he acts, the violence of suicide, and the problematic nature of Statius' own poetic endorsements of suicide.

---

[13] See Vessey (1973), 116-131.
[14] *Theb.*10.845-846:
"hac" ait, "in Thebas, hac me iubet ardua virtus
ire, Menoeceo qua lubrica sanguine turris."
[15] *Theb.*11.264-267:
urit fera corda Menoeceus;
nulla patri requies, illum quaeritque tenetque;
illum sanguineos proflantem pectore rivos
aspicit et saeva semper de turre cadentem.

Most of these elements are apparent in the Dymas episode that we discussed in the opening chapter. The violence of the act is conveyed in the excessive power of the blow Dymas delivers to his own breast (10.435-436). Statius marks suicide's eloquence and its capacity to silence by having Dymas' suicidal sword-thrust stand as his first response to Amphion's questions--Dymas only speaks after his sword has struck home (10.435-441). Finally, Statius' salute to Hopleus and Dymas acknowledges the degree to which Statius identifies his poetry with such suicidal acts--Hopleus and Dymas delight in their deaths (10.444, *letoque fruuntur*) and Statius' poem will consecrate them both (10.445, *vos quoque sacrati*), perhaps even make them the equals of Vergil's Nisus and Euryalus (10.447-448).

These suicides of Dymas and Menoeceus stand as two of the most significant events in *Thebaid* 10, offering a last glimpse of honorably motivated but ineffective self-sacrifice before Statius turns to Capaneus' ferocious assault of Thebes' walls at the end of the book and to Polynices' and Eteocles' mutual annihilation in *Thebaid* 11. Part of their effect, however, derives from the first suicide of the *Thebaid*, that of Maeon back in *Thebaid* 3. The Maeon episode sets suicide into its most purely political context, as Maeon, a priest of Apollo, confronts the tyrant Eteocles in his throne room while the ruler's bodyguards look on; and it defines more fully than either of the subsequent suicides at Thebes the complex interrelationships between poet, suicide, and tyrant.

The suicide scene begins in the aftermath of the battle fought between Tydeus and Eteocles' band of ambushers which resulted in the annihilation of all Tydeus' opponents, save Maeon; at the close of *Thebaid* 2 Tydeus had spared him, sending him back as a messenger to Eteocles to promise war and revenge (*Thebaid* 2.697-703).

At *Theb*.3.33ff, dawn breaks, and early rising Thebans can see Maeon approach the city. His grief is obvious, and the fact that he returns alone prompts the anxious Thebans to begin mourning lost relatives (3.33-58). Maeon goes immediately to Eteocles' palace to wait for an audience with the king; when Eteocles grants the audience, Maeon violently rebukes him, to the point that the king's two bodyguards are on the verge of assaulting him. Before they can lay hands on him, however, Maeon falls on his sword:

> inde ultro Phlegyas et non cunctator iniqui
> Labdacus--hos regni ferrum penes--ire manuque
> proturbare parant. sed iam nudaverat ensem
> magnanimus vates, et nunc trucis ora tyranni,
> nunc ferrum aspectans: "numquam tibi sanguinis huius
> ius erit aut magno feries imperdita Tydeo
> pectora; vado equidem exsultans ereptaque fata
> insequor et comites feror exspectatus ad umbras.
> te superis fratrique--' et iam media orsa loquentis
> absciderat plenum capulo latus; ille dolori
> pugnat et ingentem nisu duplicatus in ictum
> conruit, extremisque animae singultibus errans
> alternus nunc ore venit, nunc vulnere sanguis.
> excussae procerum mentes, turbataque mussant
> concilia; ast illum coniunx fidique parentes
> servantem vultus et torvum in morte peracta,

non longum reducem laetati, in tecta ferebant.
sed ducis infandi rabidae non hactenus irae
stare queunt; vetat igne rapi, pacemque sepulcri
impius ignaris nequiquam manibus arcet.
(Theb.3.79-98)

Phlegyas and his partner Labdacus (quick himself in crime) prepare to move in on Maeon and even drive him out by force; the king's security lies in their hands. But the high minded prophet has already bared his sword; he speaks, looking now at his savage tyrant's face, now at his own sword: 'You'll never have power over my life, no more than you'll ever strike against the unbroken might of great Tydeus; I'm glad indeed to leave this life, to regain the death just denied me...my company is expected down below. As for you, the gods above and your brother will--...' In mid-speech he sinks the sword hilt-deep in his side. That one fights against the pain and falls over the blade, doubled up with effort. He gasps his last, as blood spills now from his mouth, now from his wound. Eteocles' court is dumbstruck; his advisers mutter among themselves in dismay. Maeon's loyal family, having had no time to enjoy his return, now carries him home; even in death he keeps his face determined and fierce. Eteocles is in a slavering rage, an unspeakable fury; he can't control it any more. He forbids Maeon's cremation, and in vain he bars his unfeeling shade from peaceful interment.

This passage raises several issues pertinent to our discussion here, first of which is the brief prospect Statius gives us here that Maeon might actually try to assassinate Eteocles. Maeon's initial speech (3.59-77) is alarming enough to stir Eteocles' bodyguards into action, and when he bares his sword, Statius has him pause suggestively, looking first at Eteocles' face and then at the sword he holds (3.81-82); even his words at 3.83-

87 might equally apply to one who knows that death at the hands of Phlegyas and Labdacus awaits the assassin of Eteocles. After Maeon strikes it is still not precisely clear that we are witnessing a suicide, as opposed to an assassination--the *ille* of line 88 remains ambiguous for several lines, until it is repeated in line 93.[16]

This ambiguity over who is the recipient of Maeon's sword stroke brings us to an important point about this scene, for in it Statius suggests an equation between suicide and assassination, implying that they are the chief alternatives facing anyone who wishes to act independently under tyranny. Each act does possess its own power, as Eteocles' reaction to the suicide confirms, for rather than feeling relief at escaping Maeon's attack, or dismay at such an incident taking place in his throne room, he instead becomes enraged (*rabidae...irae*, v.96)--so much so that he forbids burial to Maeon. Eteocles clearly appreciates the symbolic value of suicide and the threat martyrdom poses to a tyrant, and yet, his edict against Maeon here has the same effect as Creon's later edict forbidding burial to Polynices--it only reinforces his own tyrannical status.

As Maeon's words indicate (3.83-84, *numquam tibi sanguinis huius / ius erit*), independence is a key issue here, and Statius himself will praise Maeon for defining a route to freedom (3.101-102, *quaque ampla veniret / libertas, sancire viam*) but it is unclear that one can draw any reassurance from

---

[16] Ahl (1986b), 2889.

this sort of freedom. After Maeon's death when we see the old man Aletes complaining about Eteocles (a passage discussed in the previous chapter), Statius points out that he feels free to speak only because he is near death anyway (3.216-7, *unde ea libertas...*). Nor does Maeon himself display any outward signs of the freedom he might have achieved--in fact he preserves in death an expression as ferocious as Eteocles' own.[17] There is in this scene an uncomfortably thin line between positive and negative act, between oppressor and oppressed, as Maeon, at the moment of his suicide becomes his own oppressor, fiercely inflicting final punishment on his own body.

Finally, Maeon's last words and Statius' subsequent praise of him raise the issues of speech and expression, and the poet's own involvement in this area. Maeon's act attests to the power of suicide to silence, for his sword stroke cuts him off in mid-speech, before he can make clear what he foresees for Eteocles and his brother.[18] That he silences himself at the moment of his prophecy to Eteocles adds an ironic turn to Statius' words of praise for the seer, for Statius will claim that Apollo did not teach Maeon in vain--a problematical statement, given Maeon's inability to foresee the results of the ambush or to finish this warning to Eteocles.

---

[17] Cf. Statius' description of Eteocles at 3.82, *trucis ora tyranni*, to his description of Maeon at 3.94, *servantem vultus et torvum in morte peracta*.

[18] 3.87-88, "*te superis fratrique--*" *et iam media orsa loquentis / absciderat plenum capulo latus*.

Statius' own voice and his poetry's commemorative power also come to bear on the scene, as he assures Maeon that he will attempt by his *carmen* to provide Maeon with a reputation commensurate with his courageous deeds (3.102-103, *quo carmine dignam, / quo satis ore tuis famam virtutibus addam*). As he does with Dymas later in the epic, Statius here understates his poem's capacity to meet such a challenge, as he wonders what kind of song might actually provide Maeon with deserved fame.

These self-deprecatory comments add a further element to the futility that these scenes embody; and a sense of futility is especially appropriate to the Maeon episode: for, as the suggestions in this scene of a potential assassination reflect, what we are essentially faced with in the Maeon-Eteocles confrontation is a chance for someone to stop the conflict between Eteocles and Polynices before it ever really gets started. The ambiguity of Statius' lament for Maeon--praising him for achievements that are never, in fact, realized (both the path he paves for *libertas* and his own prophetic powers)--in part reflects the fact that Maeon missed his chance.

As we discussed in the third chapter, this idea is certainly in keeping with the rest of Statius' epic. The *Thebaid* charts the ever widening spiral of causality that wraps countless bystanders and innocent victims into the conflict between two brothers, from Adrastus to Archemorus to the Amazon women seen in *Thebaid* 12. In tracing this expanding network, Statius frequently marks the moments at which logical action or even chance might have eliminated one of the brothers before their dispute brought ruin to so many others.

To sum up, Maeon's self-destruction reflects many of suicide's ambivalent facets: suicide can help to expose a tyrant's true nature, and it is an individual's final opportunity to assert self-control in the face of tyrannical oppression or execution; but in its own commission suicide can also impart equal measures of brutality and fury to the one who attempts it, and it permanently silences the voices of opposition infrequently heard under a tyranny.

The Punica

We turn at last to the suicide scenes that confront us in Silius' *Punica*, of which there are many: we have already encountered the suicide of an Italian youth at Cannae, whose killing of himself and his own father is emblematic of the confused identities and kindred strife that permeate Silius' Cannae narrative;[19] we could cite other instances of suicide as well in the epic's battle scenes: for example, the younger Scipio tries to kill himself twice in *Punica* 4 on seeing his father wounded;[20] and Paulus rides into battle intent on dying, when

---

[19] *Pun.*9.66-177.
[20] *Pun.*4.457-459, *bis conatus erat praecurrere fata parentis / conversa in semet dextra bis transtulerat iras / in Poenos Mavors.* Here Silius clearly echoes *Aen.*6.32-33, *bis conatus erat casus effingere in auro, / bis patriae cecidere manus,* linking his description of Scipio's attempted suicide to a passage that

he sees that the battle of Cannae is lost.[21] There are, however, a series of suicides in the course of the *Punica* that are given more detailed treatment by Silius, and we will focus our discussion primarily on these episodes: the mass suicide of the Saguntines which stands at the end of *Punica* 2, and a set of suicides that take place at Capua in *Punica* 13.

The movement from Saguntine to Capuan suicide is significant, for whereas suicide is initially held up as a model of self-sacrificing loyalty to Roman causes and rejection of Carthaginian oppression, the Capuan suicides of *Punica* 13--the final vision we will have of suicide in the poem--come in response to Roman domination and oppression. Silius' narration of suicide can thus be seen to follow the same pattern that we have noted regarding other types of action in his poem (beheading, for example), as he uses a specific type of action to characterize the Carthaginians as brutal and oppressive (here, in the case of Saguntum, their violent treatment of captured cities and peoples); but he then shows the Romans adopting and practicing the same type of activity.

Silius' treatment of suicide in these episodes also takes us again and again to the same issues that suicide raises in the *Thebaid* and the *Argonautica*. Like them the *Punica* foregrounds suicide to a degree that we simply do not find in

---

focuses on the problems of artistic creation and commemoration; he also inverts the pattern established in the Icarus/Daedalus myth, for Scipio here is attempting to die before his father.

[21] See *Pun.*10.276-308 for Paulus' final speech and death.

earlier generations of Roman epic, and like Valerius and Statius Silius can use these suicidal moments for assertions of his own poetic voice and power. As we see in the *Thebaid* as well, the *Punica*'s representations of suicide suggest some grave misgivings about suicide's value--it is, in the first place, a representation in miniature of the strife associated with civil war. Equally important, the Silian suicides possess the same sort of ugliness and brutality that we saw in Statius' suicide scenes--like Statius, Silius too shows how suicide can force its practitioners to take on tyrannical attributes in their moment of self-destruction.

With these points in mind, let us turn first to Silius' narrative of Saguntum's end in *Punica* 2 before moving on to his description of the fall of Capua in *Punica* 13.

a. Saguntum in the Punica

In 219 BC Hannibal broke camp at New Carthage and proceeded to lay siege to Saguntum, a small city on Spain's south coast. Within eight months the city was sacked; its attack by Hannibal precipitated a sixteen-year struggle between Carthage and Rome, and determined the hierarchy of power in the Mediterranean for centuries to follow.

Polybius and Livy are our prime source for the events at Saguntum, and though the two writers do not entirely concur on whether the sack of Saguntum was the ultimate cause of the Second Punic War, they do agree that it marked the war's beginning.[22] Still, whatever Saguntum's causal impact on the Second Punic War, neither historian provides more than a brief account of the siege itself. Polybius treats Hannibal's attack in one chapter (3.17), focusing less on the siege itself than on the booty gained from the town's capture and on how the capture stabilized Hannibal's position, both with his troops and with his supporters back home. Livy gives this episode little more attention, including in his nine-chapter account (21.7-16) details of the siege itself, of negotiations between Hannibal and the Saguntines, and of debate at Carthage over Hannibal's activity. These historical accounts certainly give the incident its full due: though the capture of Saguntum was a key factor both in establishing Hannibal's authority and in ushering in the Second Punic War, the details of the siege would not seem to merit a greater place in either historian's narrative.

What, then, are we to make of Saguntum's role in the *Punica*? Events that demanded a single chapter of Polybius' narrative and nine chapters in Livy's account occupy most of the *Punica*'s first two *books*, nearly an eighth of the entire epic! Silius turns to Saguntum at *Punica* 1.271, and for the rest of the first two books he rivets his reader's attention to Saguntum and to the effects of its siege on Rome and Carthage.

No single explanation will account for the amount of space Silius devotes to Saguntum; as the initial episode in an intricate epic it must lay the groundwork for several themes and

---

[22] Polybius 3.6; Livy, 21.5-6.

movements--historical, narratological, and philosophical--that will develop over the course of the poem. Nevertheless, one of the most important elements in Silius' account, and one that contributes much to the explanation of Saguntum's prominence in the epic, is the suicide of the Saguntines that closes *Punica* 2.[23]

Saguntum's expanded role in the *Punica* has a basic thematic impact on the entire epic. By stressing its importance in the Second Punic War, Silius is able to detail, at the outset of his poem, an achievement of Hannibal's not to be found elsewhere in the subsequent fifteen books of the *Punica*--the successful siege and capture of a fortified city. In epic terms this is significant, for it indicates that we will follow Hannibal from victory to defeat instead of from defeat to victory, the usual heroic sequence.[24]

But the entire Saguntum episode produces another, even greater, thematic effect: Silius makes it clear at the start of his account that he is presenting a picture of Hannibal victorious that will contrast sharply with his later unsuccessful attacks on Rome itself. In other words, Saguntum, ultimately, will serve as Hannibal's substitute for Rome, and Silius emphasizes this

---

[23] Other readers of the *Punica* have read the Saguntum episode along moral and ethical lines. von Albrecht (1964), 47-55, argues that the Saguntum episode first establishes Fides as one of the chief "heroes" of the epic. Vessey (1974), 37, sees the Saguntines as having gained "universal status through their heroism" and reads the episode as "an instrument of philosophical and moral revelation."

[24] See Kissell (1979), 209-222, for a detailed analysis of the *Punica*'s structure.

idea throughout his narrative of Saguntum's capture. He maintains this emphasis in two ways. First, he constantly refers to Saguntum in terms of Rome, either comparing its siege to a siege of Rome itself or portraying Saguntum as a stepping stone to Rome.[25] Second, he repeatedly uses epithets evocative of Italy and suggestive of Saguntum's kinship with Rome to describe the Saguntines, most notably *Rutuli* and *Daunii*.[26]

Not only does the emphasis on Rome underscore the lack of success Hannibal will meet when he reaches Rome itself, but it also turns Saguntum itself into another Rome in poetic terms: by comparing Saguntum so consistently to Rome and by applying such suggestive epithets to the Saguntines, Silius encourages the reader to look for traces of *Romanitas* in Saguntum itself.

It is instructive to compare Silius' version of their mass suicide with Livy's. Livy presents three main elements in the destruction of the Saguntine people: some throw themselves onto a bonfire in the town square; others burn themselves up in their houses; Hannibal and his troops fight and kill numerous others who are more inclined to die in combat (*AUC* 21.14.1-4). Suicide does play an important role in Livy's description, but it is limited both in its scope and in its type: some Saguntines choose to die by fire, others prefer to die fighting

---

[25] E.g. at 1.268-272, 338-340, and 384-390.

[26] See Livy, 21.7.2 for the presence of settlers from Ardea at Saguntum. For the epithet *Rutuli* in the *Punica* see 1.377, 437, 584, 658; 2.541, 567, 604. For *Daunii* see 1.440, 665; 2.244, 557.

the Carthaginians. Silius presents an entirely different picture of this last scene. In his account he turns to divine mechanisms and to a narrative of events that has virtually no corroboration in the other accounts of Hannibal's siege, as he dramatically alters the nature and scope of the suicide. His account begins at *Punica* 2.475. Hercules, a patron of Saguntum, recognizes that the Saguntines are close to their end, and so he sends the goddess Fides down to their aid. Fides states that she can only ensure that the Saguntines die with praise and honor (*extendam leti decus*, 2.511). Fides is apparently thwarted, however, when Juno sends Tisiphone down to counteract her mission by filling the minds of the Saguntines with madness and an urge for suicide (2.539-542).

Tisiphone appears to the Saguntines as Tiburna,[27] urging that the Saguntines all put each other to the sword (2.561-579). The Saguntines vigorously respond to Tisiphone's suggestion, and for the next 116 lines Silius details their suicide. The divine machinery is important, as it underscores the self-conscious artifice of the entire episode; nevertheless, it should not obscure the basic action of these lines--the Saguntines, over a prolonged stretch of *Punica* 2, indulge in the atrocity of mass suicide.

The suicide of the Saguntines does not act as a mirror of tyranny like other suicides in the *Thebaid* and the *Punica*; rather, like the Lemnian massacre in *Argonautica* 2, it reflects

---

[27] Here, as with the epithets *Rutuli* and *Daunii* used of the Saguntines, it is worth noting the Roman name.

all of the standard patterns associated with civil strife. Silius repeatedly invokes these *topoi* of Roman civil strife in his description of Saguntum's end, *topoi* that we might especially recognize from Lucan's *Pharsalia*. Consider the following passage from the suicide scene of *Punica* 2:

> Invitas maculant cognato sanguine dextras
> miranturque nefas aversa mente peractum
> et facto sceleri illacrimant. hic, turbidus ira
> et rabie cladum perpessaeque ultima vitae,
> obliquos versat materna per ubera visus;
> hic, raptam librans dilectae in colla securim
> coniugis, increpitat sese mediumque furorem
> proiecta damnat stupefactus membra bipenni.
> nec tamen evasisse datur; nam verbera Erinnys
> incutit atque atros insibilat ore tumores.
> sic thalami fugit omnis amor, dulcesque marito
> effluxere tori, et subiere oblivia taedae.
> ille iacit, totis connisus viribus, aegrum
> in flammas corpus, densum qua turbine nigro
> exundat fumum piceus caligine vertex.
> at medios inter coetus pietate sinistra
> infelix Tymbrene, furis, Poenoque parentis
> dum properas auferre necem, reddentia formam
> ora tuam laceras temerasque simillima membra.
> vos etiam primo gemini cecidistis in aevo,
> Eurymedon fratrem, et fratrem mentite Lycorma,
> cuncta pares;...
>
> *(Pun.*2.617-38)

> The Saguntines' hands shrink from their task, but they stain them anyway with the blood of their relatives; they are amazed at the crimes they commit against their own will, and once they have acted they weep. One man is filled with rage and madness at the slaughter and at the fact that his life had now experienced the most extreme trials; and so he pierces his own mother's

> breast with his gaze. Another snatches up an ax and
> aims for the neck of his loving wife; in mid rage he is
> amazed and he screams curses at himself as he chops
> her to pieces. But there is no respite; the Fury plies her
> whips and hisses dank poisons from her mouth.
> Wedded love? Conjugal bliss?? All gone; as if there
> has been no wedding at all, all is forgotten. Now a man
> takes his last leap and lands in the middle of the fire,
> where the pine pitch pours forth black-tipped, heavy
> smoke. Tymbrene too rages in the crowd with her own
> misguided familial loyalty. In her hurry to deny the
> Carthaginians the death of her parent she tears away at a
> face and body much like her own. Eurymedon and
> Lycormas, twins alike in all respects, you too fell, cut
> down in the bloom of youth, brother duping brother.

Here we see son about to kill mother, husband killing wife, man killing self, son killing father, and twin killing twin. The list goes on, and when Silius finally concludes this catalogue of murder forty lines later he writes: *semiambusta iacet nullo discrimine passim / infelix obitus, permixto funere, turba* (2.681-682).

The scene is grim enough with all of its familial slaughter;[28] it is more unnerving to realize how closely Silius here echoes passages from *Lucan's Pharsalia*. Take this example from *Pharsalia* 2, where Lucan describes the killing that went on during Sulla's proscriptions:

> Non uni cuncta dabantur,
> sed fecit sibi quisque nefas; semel omnia victor
> iusserat. infandum domini per viscera ferrum
> exegit famulus; nati maduere paterno

---

[28] Vessey (1974), 34n, claims that Silius "has kept the details of the massacre within decent limits." I find the amount of detail here too extensive to dismiss.

> sanguine; certatum est, cui cervix caesa parentis
> cederet; in fratrum ceciderunt praemia fratres.
> busta repleta fuga, permixtaque viva sepultis
> corpora, nec populum latebrae cepere ferarum.
> hic laqueo fauces elisaque guttura fregit,
> hic se praecipiti iaculatus pondere dura
> dissiluit percussus humo, mortesque cruento
> victori rapuere suas.
> *(Phar.* 2.146-57)

> They all didn't choose the same crime; each found his
> own. But the winner had ordered all to go at once.
> A slave drove his sword through his master's ribs.
> Sons soaked themselves in their fathers' blood and
> raced each other to cut their fathers' throats. Brothers
> reaped the bounty of their brothers' deaths. Pyres were
> lit on the run; live bodies stuffed into the tombs of the
> dead; animal dens couldn't fit all who tried to hide there.
> One man tightened the noose around his throat and
> snapped his own neck, another weighted himself down
> and then launched himself headlong to the ground...All
> to steal their deaths from the bloodstained conqueror.

Silius echoes this passage from the *Pharsalia* in terms of the killings described, in the motive for some of the actions (*Poenoque parentis dum properas auferre necem* vs. *mortesque cruento victori rapuere suas*), and in the confusion among the dead (*permixto funere* vs. *permixtaque viva sepultis corpora*). Such precise echoes are extremely important for our reading of *Punica* 2, for they define a close relationship between Silius' Punic wars and the civil wars still to come in historical terms, but already charted in epic terms by Lucan.[29]

---

[29] Nor is it surprising that Lucan and Silius both echo here Catullus 64.405-406; for he too is discussing civil strife and its effects on Rome of his own day.

Silius' account of the Saguntines' suicide thus contains strong, extended allusions to kindred strife and civil war, but these allusions have been ignored by those who read the Saguntum episode in positive terms. More optimistic interpretations of this episode are based primarily on the framework that Silius builds around the suicide scene, in which he asserts the nobility of the Saguntines' actions and his own support for them.[30] He opens the frame at the very moment when the Saguntines are about to inaugurate their mutual and collective slaughter:

> Inde opus aggressi, toto quod nobile mundo
> aeternum invictis infelix gloria servat.
> *(Pun.*2.611-612)

> They then set to a task which throughout the world,
> forever, illustrious and ill-fated, glory preserves as
> an example for unconquered people.

Here at the passage's outset, Silius makes a claim for the universal and eternal glory that the Saguntines deserve. The description of their actions that follows, however, renders questionable any assertion of their honor. For all the Saguntines' loyalty, the horrors of the next one hundred lines hardly merit the term *nobile*. Indeed, what we see instead is a frightening perversion of *nobilitas* and *decus*, and Silius presses this point home throughout the passage, both by the

---

[30] Vessey (1974), 34-35.

length of the description itself and by repeatedly pairing up images of *pietas* with those of *dira scelera*.[31]

At the end of his catalogue Silius closes the frame for the passage by returning to the same themes:

> tum demum ad manes, perfecto munere, Erinnys
> Iunoni laudata redit magnamque superba
> exultat rapiens secum sub Tartara turbam.
> at vos, sidereae, quas nulla aequaverit aetas,
> ite, decus terrarum, animae, venerabile vulgus,
> Elysium et castas sedes decorate piorum.
> (*Pun.*2.693-698)

> The Fury has finally finished her errand, and now
> returns to the shades below having earned Juno's
> praise; she is proud, quite pleased with herself, as
> she drags a huge throng of Saguntines in her wake. But
> you, starry souls whom no age will match, pride of the
> earth, peerless mob, go straight to Elysium and drape
> yourselves in the seats reserved for the pure of heart.

Here in lines 696-698 Silius again presents the Saguntines' suicide as an honorable action. And he follows the example of Valerius and Statius, as he shows us the souls traveling down to Elysium, and addresses them with a brief apostrophe. Indeed, he goes even further, for the position of the words *sidereae, terrarum*, and *Elysium*, with their well ordered progression through the three realms of the universe at the start of successive lines, gives an impression of total cosmic harmony at the close of *Punica* 2.

---

[31] E.g. 2.632-635, where he describes the *pietas sinistra* of Tymbrenus, or 2.650-652, where he refers to the *laudanda monstra* taking place throughout the city.

Beneath this harmonious surface, however, lie significant inconsistencies. Lines 693-695, for example, contain a similar interrelationship of heaven (Juno), earth (the Saguntines), and the underworld (Erinys, Tartara), with precisely the opposite implication--the intercession of Juno and Tisiphone at Saguntum and the entire final scene at Saguntum demonstrate the complete disorder operating at heavenly, earthly, and infernal levels.

Moreover, Tisiphone's final action in *Punica* 2, the accompaniment of the Saguntine souls down to Hades, stands in sharp contradiction to Fides' promise that *she* herself would lead the Saguntine souls down to the underworld (2.510-512). Fides, however, is nowhere to be seen on the trip down to Hades. Rather, Tisiphone serves as the sole conductor, and her presence, recalling the presence of the Fury at the suicide of Aeson and Alcimede in *Argonautica* 1, reminds the reader of the almost mad fanaticism required for suicide.

Third, Silius' direct address of the Saguntines (2.696-98) contains its own jarring set of references and images. Line 696, *at vos, sidereae, quas nulla aequaverit aetas* is a line that can be read in two ways within this context: does Silius mean that the Saguntines will never be matched in their starriness? or that no age will match them in the deeds just described? We cannot judge whether any age did match the sidereal capacities of the Saguntines, but we do know of an era that matched the Saguntines in the deeds they have just completed--the last century of the Roman republic. Silius too recognizes the similarity, for as we have seen his descriptions of the Saguntines' suicide recall Lucan's descriptions of murder and proscription in the civil wars of the *Pharsalia*.

Like Valerius and Statius, whose salutes of their suicidal characters reflect the futility that underlies any glorification of such a self-destructive act, Silius uses his frame for the Saguntines' suicide, in which he praises their action, to suggest its ambivalent status. While their suicide stands as a remarkable example of loyalty and good faith, it also anticipates (in purely historical terms) the sort of crimes most regularly associated with Roman civil strife in the first centuries BC and AD. Silius' own voice thus takes on a sadly ironic tone in his framing of the suicide scene, attempting to praise the Saguntines in immediate terms for their actions, but acknowledging the broader perspective within which the Saguntines' suicide takes on a more negative force.

What then emerges in the Saguntum episode? We see a detailed exploration of the siege of Saguntum, out of all proportion to its historical importance; we see as well the first episode of the *Punica* climaxing in a long and drawn out description of the Saguntines' mutual suicide/slaughter. The suicide scene is framed by a pair of passages in which Silius tries to insist on the nobility of the Saguntines, but the actual content of the suicide passage itself argues against such an optimistic evaluation of their actions, as do some paradoxical statements within the frame itself. The specter of Rome's own civil war experiences--still in the future as far as the *Punica* is concerned--undercuts any attempts at optimism.

This is, I think, the final thrust of the Saguntum episode: in his echoes of the *Pharsalia* here at the close of *Punica* 2, Silius has Saguntum foreshadow much of what the rest of his epic will develop in detail. At the moment of the Saguntines' death Silius turns his gaze ahead to the time of Lucan's *Pharsalia* and to the several eras of Roman civil war, giving the reader a first introduction to one of his epic's major arguments, that it was in the very act of fighting Hannibal that Rome set itself on a course toward civil war.

b. *Punica* 13: Virrius and Taurea

The strongest links made by Silius to the Saguntines' mass suicide occur in later descriptions of Capua, especially in *Punica* 13, where we first see Virrius and several other opponents of Roman power commit suicide before their city falls to Roman troops; shortly thereafter a Capuan named Taurea commits suicide in front of the Roman consul Fulvius.

Silius first makes a connection between Capua and suicide in *Punica* 11, when he narrates Capua's transfer of allegiance from Rome to Carthage. After Rome has vehemently rejected an arrogant Capuan proposal of alliance and the

Capuans have decided to send envoys to Hannibal declaring their support for him, a lone voice of protest is raised by Decius, whom Silius punningly describes as *solum Capuae decus* (11.158). Decius delivers an impassioned speech, laden with Stoic overtones, to his fellow Capuans (11.160-188), in which he reminds them of all the Romans have done for Capua in the past, assures them of the nobility and even divinity of the Romans' minds, and paints an ugly picture of Carthaginian violence and tyranny. Decius' speech has absolutely no effect on his fellow citizens, as Silius notes in a single line (11.189, *haec vana aversas Decius iactavit ad aures*). It does, however, earn him Hannibal's anger, and when Hannibal enters the city he has Decius arrested; Decius has expected this, but he makes a great show of his lack of concern.

All of this is narrated in Livy's history of the war;[32] but Silius makes a crucial change in his version of the incident, for he has Decius close his first speech with a clear suggestion of his own intent to commit suicide in order to evade the Carthaginian tyrant:

> "non ita, non Decio permixtum fasque nefasque,
> haec ut velle queat. nullo nos invida tanto
> armavit Natura bono, quam ianua mortis
> quod patet et vita non aequa exire potestas."
> (*Pun*.11.185-188)

> "I have not confused the lawful and the unspeakable so completely that I could want what you want.

---

[32] Livy, 23.7-10.

However grudging, Nature has armed us with one great weapon: the fact that the doorway to death stands open, and it is possible to depart from an unfair life."

Decius' words thus encourage the reader to anticipate his suicide, and indeed his name itself adds to such an expectation, for the Decii of early Roman history made a name for themselves by devoting their lives on Roman battlefields to save their country.[33] But despite his name and despite his promotion of suicide to his fellow countrymen, Decius never follows through on the course of action that he promotes. Instead, he bides his time until Hannibal arrives, at which point he is arrested and sent overseas. His change of mind is fortunate, for when Hannibal sends him on a ship to Carthage for imprisonment and more leisurely punishment at the end of the war, the ship is driven by storm to Cyrene, and Decius, sent from there to Alexandria, lives the rest of his life in Egypt under the protection of Ptolemy (11.377-384).

Silius makes no comment on Decius' failure to act upon his own endorsement of suicide, but his description of Decius, the sole Roman loyalist at Capua, stands in sharp contrast to several Capuans who, having supported an alliance of Capua with Hannibal, commit suicide when the Romans retake the city in *Punica* 13. To the extent that these Capuans remain true to their decisions they are more praiseworthy than Decius; but in describing their suicides Silius raises again the more

---

[33] For recent discussions of the Decii and *devotio*, see Janssen (1981), and T.J. Cornell (1986).

troublesome effects that suicide engenders, and so the image of suicide that he leaves us with in *Punica* 13 might suggest that Decius' course of action (or non-action) is the wisest.

There are two separate instances of suicide in *Punica* 13, a group suicide led by a Capuan named Vibius Virrius and committed by the most prominent of the Capuans who opposed maintaining Capua's connections with Rome (13.256-298), and the individual suicide of a Capuan named Taurea, committed in front of the Roman commander Fulvius. It is important to recognize the key shift in these scenes' representation of suicide--for it is now happening in response to *Roman* domination. Whatever the merits and demerits of the act of suicide itself, the final instances of suicide in the *Punica* leave us with images of brave defiance to Roman conquest and provide us with a sympathetic view of the victims of Roman imperialism.

In the case of the group suicide of Vibius Virrius and his supporters, Silius initially presents the suicide as the final price they pay for their earlier perfidy. He describes Vibius as the instigator of Capua's treachery (13.261, *ductor perfidiae*), and he later notes Fulvius' lawful execution of those who had acted against Rome. And yet, as the suicide scene progresses, Silius undercuts the negative aspects of the action--the firm resolution of these Capuans and their acceptance of their previous actions' consequences are impressive, and Silius links them in several respects with the proverbially loyal Saguntines of *Punica* 2.

The chief link to the Saguntum episode comes in the presence at Capua of the goddess Fides, who was prominent in a large portion of *Punica* 2 (and conspicuous by her absence at the close of that book). She appears in *Punica* 13 watching over the Capuans while a disembodied voice reminds them of her powers, and it is this voice that finally drives the conspirators to suicide.[34] Her presence has a vengeful aspect about it--the voice's words suggest that Fides wants to make sure that the Capuans get their due punishment for breaking faith with Rome. But in fact the Capuans are preserving their loyalty to their more recent alliance by their suicide, and so, in a sense, they respect the voice's warnings about keeping their faith.

Silius has also included here a definite echo of the suicide of Aeson and Alcimede in *Argonautica* 1 in his description of the cup of poison tendered by the Fury: *Punica* 13.294-5, *ipsa etiam Stygio spumantia pocula tabo porrigit* clearly recalls *Argonautica* 1.816-817, *adstitit et nigro fumantia*

---

[34] See *Pun.*13.281-291:
  despectat ab alto
sacra Fides agitatque virum fallacia corda.
vox occulta subit, passim diffusa per auras:
"foedera, mortales, ne saevo rumpite ferro,
sed castam servate fidem. fulgentibus ostro
haec potior regnis. dubio qui frangere rerum
gaudebit pacta ac tenuis spes linquet amici,
non illi domus aut coniunx aut vita manebit
umquam expers luctus lacrimaeque. aget aequore semper
ac tellure premens, aget aegrum nocte dieque
despecta ac violata Fides."

pocula tabo contigit. Like the suicide of Aeson and Alcimede too, this one has a particularly Imperial cast to it. Several of the details point to the more notorious suicides of the Claudian and Neronian eras (preserved in the post-Flavian accounts of Tacitus)--the funeral pyre standing ready,[35] the convivial setting,[36] and the use of poison.[37]

From Decius' glory to Virrius' punishment, the specter of suicide remains linked to Capua throughout. Nor are we yet finished with Capua and suicide. After the Romans capture the city, the consul Fulvius gathers together for execution the rest of the nobles who had sided with Hannibal. At this point a Capuan names Taurea boldly confronts Fulvius (having earlier backed down from a duel with a Roman named Claudius Asellus--see 13.142ff) and defiantly commits suicide:[38]

> hic atrox virtus--nec enim occuluisse probarim
> spectatum vel in hoste decus--clamore feroci
> Taurea "tune," inquit, "ferro spoliabis inultus
> te maiorem anima? et iusso lictore recisa
> ignavos cadet ante pedes fortissima cervix?
> haud umquam hoc vobis dederit deus." inde, minaci
> obtutu torvum contra et furiale renidens,
> bellatorem alacer per pectora transigit ensem.
> *(Pun.*13.369-376)

---

[35] Cf. Tacitus, *Ann.*11.3.2, where Asiaticus dines and examines his pyre before opening his veins.

[36] Compare the cheerful recitations, conversations, and dinner that attend Petronius' death at *Ann.*16.19.2-4.

[37] See *Ann.*15.64.3 for Seneca's attempt to die by poison.

[38] The parallel passages in Livy are 23.46-47 for the duel and 26.16 for his suicide.

> At this point an instance of ferocious courage took place, one that I could not possibly allow to be hidden, even if it does credit to the enemy. Taurea bursts into a fierce tirade, "Do you think that you can deprive your superior of his life without paying for it? Do you really think that a brave man's head can be cut off and laid at the feet of cowards, just by issuing an order to the lictor? May no god ever grant this to you all." And then with a threatening glare and a savage and ferocious grin of opposition he quickly drives his warrior sword into his breast.

We have seen much, if not all, of this before. The suicide follows the pattern of Maeon's suicide in *Thebaid* 3, coming in a heated face-to-face encounter between oppressor and oppressed. Taurea's expressions reassert the tendency, present in several of these suicides, for the suicidal figure to adopt expressions more suggestive of tyrannical figures themselves: his fierce gaze (13.374-375, *minaci obtutu*) recalls that of Aeetes in *Argonautica* 5 (5.519, *vultu...minaci*), while his grin (13.375, *torvum contra ac furiale renidens*), mimics Creon's phony smile in *Thebaid* 12 (12.688 *fictum ac triste renidens*). Finally, Silius' approval of the act affirms one final time the bond that the Flavian poets create between their poetry and acts of suicide. He says that he could not approve the passing over of such a deed, even if done by an enemy (13.369-370), and his term of honor for Taurea's action, *decus*, also recalls the honor of Decius' defiance in *Punica* 11.

Conclusions

It is appropriate that Capua provides the setting for the final scenes of suicide in the *Punica*, for Capua, more than anywhere else in the entire epic, mirrors Rome of the first centuries BC and AD:

> nec vitiis deerant vires: non largior ulli
> Ausoniae populo (sic tum Fortuna fovebat)
> aurique argentique modus; madefacta veneno
> Assyrio maribus vestis medioque dierum
> regales epulae atque ortu convivia solis
> deprensa et nulla macula non illita vita.
> tum populo saevi patres, plebesque senatus
> invidia laeta, et collidens dissona corda
> seditio. sed enim interea temeraria pubis
> delicta augebat, pollutior ipsa, senectus.
> nec, quos vile genus despectaque lucis origo
> foedabat, sperare sibi et deposcere habenas.
> quin etiam exhilarare viris convivia caede
> mos olim, et miscere epulis spectacula dira
> certantum ferro, saepe et super ipsa cadentum
> pocula respersis non parco sanguine mensis.
> *(Pun.*11.38-54)

The Capuans did not lack resources to satisfy their pleasures. They were Fortune's favorites: they had more gold and silver than any other Italian race; even the men wore clothes steeped in Syrian dyes; their parties were fit for a king, starting at noon and carrying on to dawn. Their lives were tainted by the stain of every vice. At this time, with the Senate brutalizing the people, and the people reveling in their own hatred of the Senate, civil strife pitted discordant hearts against each other. In the meantime, the city elders, lechers

> themselves, were increasing the number of reckless crimes one usually associates with youth; and there were some in Capua who sought and demanded the reins of government, even though they bore the blemish of worthless blood and unilluminated birth. It was even their long-standing custom to liven up their celebrations with human slaughter and to provide horrifying exhibits of armed combat between courses. Often the tables would be soaked with impressive sprays of blood as bodies toppled amid the drinking cups.

There can be no question that Silius' Rome sits behind much of the description here of Capua (much in the same manner as it sits behind Statius' description of Thebes at *Thebaid* 1.144-170)--in the mentions of wealth and luxury, of senators and plebeians, and of lavish banquets and gladiatorial combats. Indeed, the comparison of Capua in the third century BC to Imperial Rome is one that Seneca also makes in his fifty-first epistle. Silius' location of several suicides (and Decius' near suicide) at Capua thus enhances the Roman atmosphere that he has already created in the city, while turning the act into one of defiance against Roman oppression.

But the suicides at Capua also give final reinforcement to several of the patterns we have found in the suicides of all three epics; and we might briefly review these common points in closing this chapter.

First, at Capua, as in other instances, suicide appears primarily as an act prompted by immediate political realities, and laden with political significance. We do find in the *Punica* occasional glimpses of suicide in less political contexts (most often in battle scenes, where soldiers carried away by their battle-lust set off on suicidal forays into the enemy's ranks), but the chief suicide scenes repeatedly embody one party's refusal to submit to another's authority.

As honorable as such a motive might be, it is at this point that Silius, like Valerius and Statius, might be seen to diverge to the greatest degree from philosophical justifications of suicide. Seneca, for example, in his philosophical discussions of suicide, consistently presents suicide as the rational act of the *sapiens*.[39] The suicides that we find in the Flavian epics, on the other hand, regularly the product of political conflict, are hardly the cool, rational acts of *sapientes*; most of these suicidal figures provides a distorted and grim vision of conviction and madness. Even the most noteworthy exception to this pattern, Menoeceus' altruistic suicide in *Thebaid* 10, only paves the way for Capaneus' demonic assault of Thebes' walls, and for his own father's rapid transformation into a fierce and cruel Theban tyrant.

In the *Punica* too, suicide is tied in subtle ways to speech and silence: Decius promotes suicide in word, but not in deed; Taurea's suicide comes in the midst of his verbal rebuke of Fulvius; and Fulvius treats Taurea's suicide as an argument demanding his own rebuttal, for he answers his dying opponent, reminding him at he could have attempted to die in battle if he truly wanted to die honorably (13.377-380). Silius' voice comes into play in these scenes as well: he expresses his

---

[39] See, e.g., *Ep.*70.4, *Itaque sapiens vivit, quantum debet, non quantum potest.*

inability to leave Taurea's brave action hidden at 13.369-370, and he voices his confidence at *Punica* 2.696 that the Saguntines' achievements, which he has just narrated, will never be equaled.

This connection between poetic voice and suicidal moment helps to differentiate the Flavian writers from their Augustan and Neronian predecessors, but it also takes on an added irony when we reflect on the place these poets occupy in the Latin epic tradition. In order to fully appreciate this issue, we should turn now to a final and brief exploration of their position in the epic tradition--both what the epics themselves say about poetry and what we know of the epic tradition subsequent to the Flavians.

CHAPTER 6: EPIC SILENCE

It might seem curious that a book on Roman epic should propose silence as one of the keynotes for an entire generation of epic composition: after all, epic is by definition an expansive literary genre (one of the Flavians--Silius Italicus--has the distinction of being the author of the longest of all surviving Latin epics), and furthermore, contemporary satirists suggest that Rome was filled with would-be Vergils and Ovids at the end of the first century AD.

Yet the preceding chapters offer a different perspective on the state of epic at the end of the first century, a perspective based on the imagery found in the epic poems themselves, and in concluding this study we might consider the extent to which these poems do grapple with the issues of poetic voice and poetic silence.

The Dead Poets Society

Perhaps the most surprising comment made by any of our authors regarding the status of poetry in the Flavian era comes at the end of *Argonautica* 1, when Valerius describes the descent of Aeson's and Alcimede's shades to the underworld:

>   lucet via late
> igne dei, donec silvas et amoena piorum
> deveniant camposque, ubi sol totumque per annum

> durat aprica dies, thiasique chorique virorum
> carminaque et quorum populis iam nulla cupido.
> (*Arg*.1.843-845)

The path gleams ahead of them with the god's light, until they reach the forests and cheerful haunts of the blessed, and the fields where sunshine and balmy days last throughout the year, and there are dances and choruses of men, and poetry and things for which people no longer have any desire.

As we noted in the previous chapter, the fact that Valerius allows his suicidal characters to enter the realms of Elysium is important in its own right, for in Vergil's earlier representation of Hades suicides were relegated to more marginal districts of the underworld. Aeson and Alcimede arrive at an Elysium familiar to readers of Latin poetry, one that recalls the Elysian Fields of both Tibullus and Vergil, where the shades of right-living people are rewarded with an idyllic life of recreation and song.[1] But in Valerius' picture of Elysium there is a significant shift away from the Vergilian and Tibullan models, for by including the words *et quorum populis iam nulla cupido* he contrasts the activities found in Elysium to those of his own day, suggesting that *carmina* might be classed with

---

[1] *Aen*.6.642-644:
>> pars in gramineis exercent membra palestris,
>> contendunt ludo et fulva luctantur harena;
>> pars pedibus plaudunt choreas et carmina dicunt.
> Cf. also Tibullus 1.3.57-60:
>> sed me, quod facilis tenero sum semper Amori,
>>> ipsa Venus campos ducet in Elysios.
>> hic choreae cantusque vigent, passimque vagantes
>>> dulce sonant tenui gutture carmen aves...

other things for which there is no longer an interest in his own time. Like the suicides themselves, poetry increasingly belongs to the realms of the dead.

We might infer a similar point in Silius' *Punica*, for he too reserves one of his few comments about poets and epic poetry for his description of the underworld in *Punica* 13. His first reference to poetry occurs at the beginning of the Sibyl's description of the layout of Hades to Scipio; she says that 10 gates offer access to the world of the dead, each of them restricted to particular classes of people (*Punica* 13.531-561). The exclusive structure of the admissions process raises some questions about various classes who have no gate reserved for them--honest, male, city-dwellers, for example, don't seem to qualify at any gate--but Silius does make room for poets in Hades: the Sibyl says that the fourth gate is reserved for artists and (good) poets:

> exin, qui laetas artes uitaeque colendae
> inuenere uiam nec dedignanda parenti
> carmina fuderunt Phoebo, sua limina seruant.
> (*Pun.*13.537-539)

> Next, those tend their own doorway, who discovered pleasing occupations and a way to enrich life, and who produced songs not unworthy of their ancestor Phoebus.

Later, however, Silius focuses on one poet in particular, when Scipio spots a distinctive figure on the fringes of the Elysian landscape:

Atque hic, Elysio tendentem limite cernens
effigiem iuuenis, caste cui uitta ligabat
purpurea effusos per colla nitentia crines,
"dic," ait, "hic quinam, uirgo? nam luce refulget
praecipua frons sacra uiro, multaeque sequuntur
mirantes animae et laeto clamore frequentant.
qui uultus! quem, si Stygia non esset in umbra,
dixissem facile esse deum." "non falleris;" inquit
docta comes Triuiae "meruit deus esse uideri,
et fuit in tanto non paruum pectore numen.
carmine complexus terram, mare, sidera, manes
et cantu Musas et Phoebum aequauit honore.
atque haec cuncta, prius quam cerneret, ordine terris
prodidit ac uestram tulit usque ad sidera Troiam."
Scipio perlustrans oculis laetantibus umbram
"si nunc fata darent, ut Romula facta per orbem
hic caneret uates, quanto maiora futuros
facta eadem intrarent hoc" inquit "teste nepotes!
felix Aeacide, cui tali contigit ore
gentibus ostendi! creuit tua carmine uirtus."
                              (*Pun*.13.778-797)

And here, seeing the image of a youth making its way
along the Elysian border whose hair was piously bound
by a purple fillet and flowed back along his shining
neck, Scipio said, "Tell me who this one is, Sibyl. For
his sacred brow gleams with a remarkable glow and
many admiring shades follow along and accompany him
with happy cries. What features he has! If he were not
in the shadows of Hades I would readily say that he
was a god." The learned companion of Hecate
answered, "You are not wrong; he deserves to appear
godlike, and no small amount of divinity was in his
heart. He embraced earth, sea, stars, and the shades
with his poetry; he matched the Muses in song and
Apollo in honor. He passed on all these things here in
fixed order to the earth before he even saw them, and he
raised your own Troy up to the stars." Scipio looked at

> the shade with a cheerful gaze and said, "If only fate would allow this prophet to sing of Romulean deeds throughout the world; these same deeds would impress future generations even more with this one as their witness. Achilles, you were fortunate, being revealed to mankind by this singer--your virtue grew with his song."

Silius' description of the shade of Homer, including Scipio's comments about him, reverberates against the backdrop of Rome's literary history in several respects. First, the Sibyl suggests that part of Homer's fame rests on his immortalization of Troy, Rome's ancestral city, but Scipio longs for Homer, or a Homeric voice, to sing of Rome's own achievements and inspire future Romans. The passage seems to be looking ahead to the time when Vergil will create a uniquely Roman epic, and yet--though at other points Silius feels free to nod openly to his Augustan predecessor--Scipio receives no reassurance that a poet of Homer's caliber might be waiting in the wings for Rome. We are left, instead, with a vision of the archetypal epic poet wandering along the edges of Elysium, admired by the crowd of shades that follows him, with no hint that a worthy successor might follow.

The physical description of Homer here is jarring and unexpected, calling immediate attention to the passage: Homer-- usually old and blind--here seems youthful and handsome (*effigiem iuuenis*..."*qui uultus*!..."). But such a description of the poet places him in close conjunction with another handsome youth encountered in the epic Underworld--the young and ill-starred Marcellus of *Aeneid* 6. Marcellus too is characterized as a *iuuenis*,² and attended by a crowd of followers,³ though his face is clouded with gloom while Homer's shines radiantly.

Silius' assimilation of Homer's ghost to Vergil's Marcellus confounds the interrelationship of history, literary tradition, and the contemporary world set forth in Silius' underworld, for it casts Homer, the canonical founder of epic, in the role of Vergil's model for Rome's frustrated and stillborn hopes for its own future, as if Homer himself--or any Roman who might attempt epic on a grand and Homeric scale--would undertake a task ultimately doomed to frustration were he to attempt a more Roman song.

Scipio's remarks about Homer and fortunate Achilles recall a further literary resonance that seems to be operating in Scipio's encounter with the ghosts of Hades, namely the possible connections between the *Punica*'s Scipio and the senior Africanus of Cicero's *De Re Publica*. Cicero's philosophical dialogue closes with a description by the younger Scipio Africanus of a dream in which his grandfather, the senior Africanus, reveals to him the mechanics of the universe in order to give him better perspective on man's fate and on the foolishness of man's vanity. It closes with the clear message that one should not be at all concerned with fame or glory, but

---

² *Aen*.6.861. I recognize the ambiguity of the form *iuuenis* here--it could be a nominative form referring to Scipio; but its position in the hexameter after *effigiem*, and the regularity with which *effigies* entails a descriptive genitive in Latin make the identification of *iuuenis* here with Homer quite plausible.
³ *Aen*.6.865.

should live a life independent of such vain concerns,[4] and the two Africani stand as exemplary Roman statesmen.

The comments of Silius' Scipio regarding Achilles' Homeric reputation stand in ironic contrast to the ultimate lesson imparted to the younger Africanus by the elder in his dream. Silius' Scipio is repeatedly motivated by the prospects of *fama* and *gloria*, as we saw earlier in his encounter with Alexander, and as is clear here in his envious remark about Achilles. Indeed, Scipio's words here recall the remarks of Alexander when he himself visited Troy and reflected on Achilles' good fortune in having a poet like Homer to glorify his deeds;[5] not coincidentally, Scipio has just left Alexander's ghost when he encounters Homer.

To return to Silius himself, however, the appearance of Homer in his underworld, redolent as it is with echoes of Cicero and Vergil (not to mention possible allusions to Ennius and Lucretius[6]), places Silius' own vision of the epic tradition (and his relation to it) in a particular light. The very mention of Homer underscores the fact that epic is for the Romans a secondary and non-native genre adopted from the Greeks, and thus a genre in which all Roman work must, almost by definition, be self-conscious. The alignment of Homer with Vergil's youthful, but doomed, Marcellus and the Sibyl's

---

[4] Cicero, *Rep.*6.19-23.
[5] See Plutarch, *Alexander* 15.7-9.
[6] Lucretius and Ennius too make significant references to the ghost of Homer. See Ennius *Ann.*I.iv; Lucretius *RN* 1.112-126.

failure to mention Vergil himself cast onto Roman epic the shadow of frustrated expectations, consigning the consummate figure of epic poetry to the margins of Elysium and suppressing any promise of Rome's own successor to Homer.

Statius: from ghosts to madness

For Silius and Valerius, then, there are various connections, both implicit and explicit, between epic and the world of the dead; in his *Thebaid* Statius offers a different perspective on epic poetry's place in his world, particularly in the opening and closing lines of the poem.

There is, first of all, the madness that Statius claims is necessary to sing his song, the *Pierius calor* of *Theb.*1.3. Given Statius' topic, the equation between maddened frenzy and poetic voice is grimly appropriate; yet Statius suggests that a similar madness might be required for other epic topics as well, for he would only sing of Domitian's military campaigns if he were made bolder by a Pierian gadfly (1.32-33). Indeed, the latter topic might require an extra degree of madness before it could be undertaken, for Statius would then be competing in his poetic material with Domitian himself, who also wrote of his own Germanic campaigns.

Statius returns to the connections between his epic and madness in *Thebaid* 10, when he narrates the assault of Capaneus on the walls of Thebes:

> hactenus arma, tubae, ferrumque et vulnera: sed nunc
> comminus astrigeros Capaneus tollendus in axis.
> non mihi iam solito vatum de more canendum;
> maior ab Aoniis poscenda amentia lucis:
> mecum omnes audete deae!
>
> (*Theb.*10.827-831)
>
> Weapons, trumpets, the sword and its wounds have brought us this far: but now Capaneus is at hand, to be raised up against the star-bearing axes. I cannot sing of this in the usual manner of inspired poets; a greater madness must be sought from the Aonian groves. All goddesses now be bold together with me!

As the *Thebaid* moves closer to its climax--Capaneus' assault is the final prelude to the fight between the Theban brothers--Statius demands greater madness, *maior amentia*, from the Muses, and this furor imbues the narrative through the following two books: the ghosts of earlier generations of Thebans are let out of Hades to watch the final duel between Eteocles and Polynices (11.420-423), and are pleased that their own crimes are being surpassed; the Furies themselves are reduced to mere spectators when the brothers' rage exceeds their own (11.537-538); and Statius himself, as we have already seen, makes clear his increasing reluctance to tell his story.

The *Thebaid*'s subject matter and Statius' comments regarding the madness required for epic composition call into question any earnest reading of the poet as the Muses' inspired prophet, the *vates*. For Statius' vatic and inspired voice owes much to the increasingly frenetic and parodic representations of divine inspiration that appear in Roman epic of the first century

AD. The progression of the *vates* from inspiration to madness is first suggested in Roman epic in *Aeneid* 6, where the Sibyl's first moments of divine inspiration are marked by a physical torment and wild turmoil.[7] The maddened and parodic aspects of inspiration are pushed to further extremes by Lucan in the scenes of the *Pharsalia* that involve the Delphic priestess and Erictho,[8] and by Valerius Flaccus, who pits the prophetic voices of Mopsus and Idmon against each other in *Argonautica* 1 and thereby raises the question of each prophet's reliability.[9] These figures of prophecy stand behind Statius' characterizations of his own inspiration and mark the extremities to which he is pushed in composing his poem.

We find further comment regarding poetry in the Flavian era in the epigraph with which Statius closes his poem, one in which he specifically invokes the *Aeneid*, claiming that his own poem should follow respectfully in the *Aeneid*'s footsteps:

> durabisne procul dominoque legere superstes,
> o mihi bissenos multum vigilata per annos
> Thebai? iam certe praesens tibi Fama benignum

---

[7] *Aen.*6.45-51 and 77-82.
[8] *Phar.*5.86-193 and 6.604-776.
[9] Mopsus gives a pessimistic prophecy for the voyage at *Arg.*1.207-226 and is followed by Idmon who offers a more reassuring vision of the future at 1.227-239. It is worth noting that, while Mopsus' prophecy is generally accurate, Valerius subsequently includes details in his narrative that do not conform to Mopsus' vision of the same events--Mopsus suggests, for example, that Hylas will disappear when he goes off in search of water (1.218-220); but Hylas is snatched away by nymphs while hunting a stag (3.545-550).

> stravit iter coepitque novam monstrare futuris.
> iam te magnanimus dignatur noscere Caesar,
> Itala iam studio discit memoratque iuventus.
> vive, precor; nec tu divinam Aeneida tempta,
> sed longe sequere et vestigia semper adora.
> mox, tibi si quis adhuc praetendit nubila livor,
> occidet, et meriti post me referentur honores.
> <div align="right">(<i>Theb.</i>12.810-819)</div>

> I have already watched over you for a dozen years, *Thebaid*; will you now survive, and if you outlive your master will you be read? It is clear already that Fame attends you and has set a friendly path for you to follow; though you are just finished she is ready to introduce you to future generations. Already, too, great-souled Caesar deigns to make your acquaintance, and already Italian youth enthusiastically learn and cite you. So live on, I beg you. Don't try to surpass the divine *Aeneid*; follow at a respectable distance and always honor its footsteps. And, even if now some darker feelings do cast shadows over you, soon they will pass, and after I am gone you will gain the honor you deserve.

Statius begins the epigraph with a question addressed to his own poem, a question which alludes in its language to Ovid, as he asks his poem whether or not it will survive its *dominus*, or master. The reference is to Ovid's *Tristia* 1.1, where Ovid, speaking to his poem as it departs for Rome, refers to himself as the book's *dominus*.[10] But by Statius' day, as we've already discussed, the term *dominus* has taken on new meaning; for by the end of the first century *dominus* is a title

---

[10] *Tr.*1.1.1-2:
> Parve--nec invideo--sine me, liber, ibis in urbem.
> ei mihi, quod domino non licet ire tuo!

enjoyed by the *princeps* himself (Suetonius, *Domitian* 13; c.f., perhaps, Martial 10.72). Statius' ambiguous words thus link his poem's survival in a paradoxical way to the figure of Rome's *princeps*, or *dominus*, for on the one hand the *Thebaid* requires an authority figure like the *princeps* in order for its anti-authoritarian message to make sense; on the other hand, its only chance of being read by future audiences depends on its outlasting Domitian, the *princeps* and *dominus*.

Statius' salute to his poem is hardly a ringing, claim of self-assurance and confidence when compared to similar Horatian and Ovidian epigraphs, though the epigraph contains important references, both formal and linguistic to its Augustan predecessors. Statius, for example, states that his poem will receive honor after Statius' own day (12.819, *et meriti post me referentur honores*), a comment which effectively creates a split between the poet's identity and that of his poem. Ovid, on the other hand, claims that so long as his poem is read and he is spoken of, he himself will live; while Horace states that he will not entirely die and a large part of himself will live on, so long as his durable poetry lasts.[11]

---

[11] Horace, *Carm.* 3.30.1-2, 6-7:
> Exegi monumentum aere perennius
> regalique situ pyramidum altius...
> ...non omnis moriar, multaque pars mei
> vitabit Libitinam...

Ovid, *Met.*15.871-872:
> Iamque opus exegi, quod nec Iovis ira nec ignis
> nec poterit ferrum nec edax abolere vetustas...

Moreover, unlike Horace and Ovid who both confidently assert their poems' invincibility, Statius' epigraph begins with a question (12.810, *durabisne...*), one that calls into doubt his poem's chances of survival. True, he follows up his initial questions with some observations of his poem's immediate popularity (he notes that the Italian *iuvenes* already learn its verses, and that Caesar has familiarized himself with it), but when the epigraph closes, his initial questions remain unanswered, and his poem closes on a note of self-reflection and doubt.

The uncertainty and diffidence voiced by this epigraph, and even some of the language itself, will be echoed in the next generation of writers by Tacitus, when he describes the Domitianic era:

> Quid, si per quindecim annos, grande mortalis aevi spatium, multi fortuitis casibus, promptissimus quisque saevitia principis interciderunt, pauci et, ut dixerim, non modo aliorum sed etiam nostri superstites sumus, exemptis e media vita tot annis, quibus iuvenes ad senectutem, senes prope ad ipsos exactae aetatis terminos per silentium venimus?
> (*Ag*.3.2)

> What? For fifteen years--a huge span in a man's lifetime--many have died by accidents of chance; the most active have been victimized by the savagery of the *princeps*; and a few of us, I would say, are survivors not only of all the others, but even of ourselves: with so

---

...ore legar populi, perque omnia saecula fama,
siquid habent veri vatum praesagia, vivam.

> many years removed from the middle of our lives, years in which youths have become old men, and old men reached the very end of their life's passing, do we reach this point in silence?

Tacitus describes Domitian's fifteen year reign as an immense span of mortal time, *grande mortalis aevi spatium*, during which the most active Romans earned their own deaths. Appropriately enough, the 12 year span to which Statius refers might also roughly encompass the years of Domitian's rule, up to the year of the *Thebaid*'s publication: such a suggestion on the part of Statius at his epic's close that his poem is intimately connected with the years of Domitian's reign would provide fitting closure for the parallels he developed at the outset of the poem between his material and Rome's imperial family.

But Tacitus also refers to himself and other Romans who survived Domitian's reign as "survivors of ourselves," *superstites nostri*, as if a part of everyone was silenced by that era. His words evoke the despondent tone of Statius' salute to his poem, and testify to its truth, confirming from a post-Flavian standpoint the doubts that might preoccupy a poet finishing off a poem as overtly politicized as the *Thebaid*.

Silence of the genre

Statius, Silius, and Valerius, then, all remark in one way or another on epic poetry's waning presence in their world: Valerius openly asserts this fact; Silius, who according to Pliny would reverently visit the Vergil's tomb as if it were a temple, when he was in Naples on the poet's birthday, places his most eloquent figures of poetic power and popularity in the Underworld; and Statius not only adopts the voice of a vates driven mad to sing his *Thebaid*, but he also recasts Augustan statements of poetic power in his final epigraph to reflect the greater instability of epic in his own day.

These allusions to epic's status in the Flavian era become more understandable when we consider some facts of literary history first noted in the preface to this study. For Silius, Statius, and Valerius are practitioners of a genre of poetry that is itself growing silent in their own generation: Bardon, in his survey of Latin literature that did not survive, is able to identify only four epic poets contemporary with the three examined in this book;[12] more surprising, during the entire period from Trajan's accession to Commodus' death, a period of almost 100 years, Bardon can name only two epic poets, one of whom, Calpurnius Piso, composed didactic poetry.[13] In the reign of Augustus, on the other hand, he is able to name twenty epic poets, not counting those who wrote didactic

---

[12] Bardon (1956), 229-230. The four are: Domitian; Cordus, mentioned by Juvenal at *Sat*.1.1; Julius Cerealis, mentioned by Martial in 11.51; and Carus, mentioned by Martial at 9.23 and 24.

[13] A Calpurnius Piso, mentioned by Pliny (*Ep*.5.17), wrote a didactic epic on astronomy; a friend of Apuleius, named Clemens, was working on a *Gigantomachy*. A third poet, named Albinus and mentioned by Priscian, might have written during the late Antonine period, but more probably belongs to the Severan era; he wrote a patriotic epic entitled *Res Romanae*. See Bardon (1956), v.2, 230-231.

hexameters.[14] Nor does one find a similar diminution of poetic activity in other genres: satire, epigram, lyric, and tragedy all find their own practitioners through the second century.[15]

Bardon's statistics, imperfect as they might be, create a different picture of the Flavian literary scene from that which one might deduce from the comments of contemporary poets in other genres--if one were to believe Martial or Juvenal, one could assume that Rome was bursting at the seams with epicists, all of them clamoring for the attention of the public and of their fellow poets.[16] But Martial's and Juvenal's comments might better be read as attempts to privilege their own poetic genres and to distinguish their own literary voices from their fellow poets', for Bardon's review of available evidence and much of the material in this study testify to epic's increasingly marginalized position.

---

[14] Bardon (1956), 61-75.
[15] Ibid. 213-229.
[16] Juvenal, 1.1-2:
> Semper ego auditor tantum? numquamne reponam
> vexatus totiens rauci Theseide Cordi?

Martial, 3.38.7-10:
> "Si nihil hinc veniet, pangentur carmina nobis:
>   audieris, dices esse Maronis opus."
> Insanis: omnes gelidis quicumque lacernis
>   sunt ibi, Nasones Vergiliosque vides.

Conclusions

Near the end of *Change and Decline*, his analysis of literature in the first century AD, Gordon Williams presents a summary of several factors that he feels contributed to the lowering of standards of literary quality in the Flavian and Antonine eras: the tension created during the principate between monarchical government and the idea of free speech; a growing Hellenic focus in literary tastes; the preference of style over substance; an increasing fascination with irrationalism and emotionalism; and the resolution of Republican ideals and Imperial power brought about by the Trajanic accord between emperor and Senate.[17]

Williams' analysis would seem to accord to some degree with much of the material encountered in earlier chapters of this study--certainly the emphasis in the Flavian epics on suicidal activity and civil war would fit into his analysis of irrationalism in Imperial literature; and the Flavian depictions of tyranny and autocracy can be seen to reflect the tensions between free speech and authoritarianism.[18] But the preceding chapters make a case for a far different assessment of Flavian poetry from that offered by Williams and endorsed more generally by scholars of Roman literature.

---

[17] G. Williams (1978), 292-297.
[18] See especially chapter 4, titled "Authoritarianism and Irrationality," (1978), 153-192.

Unlike Williams, who, in an attempt to emphasize stylistic and rhetorical characteristics, effectively obscures the question of substance in Imperial Roman poetry, the several chapters of this book argue strongly for recognition of substantial issues raised in these poems. For example, while the emphasis on suicide scenes in these poems might suggest that the poets are preoccupied with irrationalism, our reading of these scenes suggests that, rather than replicating the irrational in their verse, the Flavian poets were offering their own rational analysis of what is seemingly an irrational and paradoxical act of political defiance. Their representations of civil strife and tyranny can also be seen to be grounded in the historical circumstances of Flavian Rome, testifying to the effects of Imperial succession and Imperial strife on the mentality of the public that lived under the Principate.

The material of these epics presented in the preceding chapters, connected as it is to the public and political world of Flavian Rome, suggests that the Flavian writers adopted the epic genre because it offered a means of analyzing and exploring difficult and often dangerous issues of the day (as it did Ennius, Vergil, and Lucan in earlier generations); and yet the Flavian writers of epic seem to sense the fact that epic is becoming a less effective vehicle for analysis or critique. There might be several reasons for the genre's marginalization--the increasing permanence of the Imperial system; the co-optation of literary patronage within this system; and even, perhaps, the predilection of literary-minded emperors like Nero and

Domitian to write epic themselves (Valerius and Statius both might be suggesting in their proems that the *princeps* himself is the sole person entitled to write about his family's deeds).

The hesitancy and reluctance the Flavian poets convey in their remarks about writing epic and their preoccupations with maddened strife, tyranny, suicide, and, finally, silence, suggest that the disappearance of epic in the next generation would have come as no surprise to these writers. And yet, despite their all too reasonable doubts, they were willing to confront the burden of the literary past and the more dangerous burden of contemporary present, in attempting to craft poems appropriate both to their genre and to their generation.

SELECTED BIBLIOGRAPHY

Ahl, F.M. (1976) *Lucan. An Introduction.* Ithaca.
---(1984) "The Art of Safe Criticism in Greece and Rome," *AJPh* 105, 174-208.
---and M. Davis and A. Pomeroy (1986a) "Silius Italicus," *ANRW* II.32.4, 2492-2561.
---(1986b) "Statius' *Thebaid*: A Reconsideration," *ANRW* II.32.5, 2803-2912.
Bardon, H. (1956) *La littérature latine inconnue. Vol.2.* Paris.
Barton, C. (1992) *The Sorrows of the Ancient Romans: The Gladiator and the Monster.* Princeton.
Barnes, W.P. (1981) "The Trojan War in Valerius Flaccus' *Argonautica*," *Hermes* 109, 360-370.
Bartsch, S. (1994) *Actors in the Audience: Theatricality and Doublespeak from Nero to Hadrian.* Cambridge.
Baumann, R.A. (1974) *Impietas in Principem.* Munich.
Bayet, J. (1951) "Le suicide mutuel dans la mentalité des Romains," *L'Année Sociologique*, ser. 3, Paris, 35-89.
Boyle, A.J., ed. (1990) *The Imperial Muse. Ramus Essays on Roman Literature of the Empire. Volume 2.* Bendigo.
---and J.P. Sullivan, eds. (1991) *Roman Writers of the Early Empire.* New York.
---ed. (1993) *Roman Epic.* New York.
Brown, E.J., ed. (1973) *Major Soviet Writers: Essays in Criticism.* London.

---(1982) *Russian Literature since the Revolution.* Cambridge, MA.
Burck, E. ed. (1979) *Das römische Epos.* Darmstadt.
---(1981) *Vom Menschenbild in der römischen Literatur,* v.2. Heidelberg.
---(1984) *Historische und epische Tradition bei Silius Italicus.* Munich.
Capaiuolo, F. (1976) *Itinerario della poesia latina nel primo secolo del impero.* Rome.
Carradice, I. (1983) *Coinage and Finances in the Reign of Domitian: A.D. 81-96* (BAR International Series 178). Oxford.
Coleman, K.M. (1986) "The Emperor Domitian and Literature," *ANRW* II.32.5, 3087-3115.
Colish, M. (1985) *The Stoic Tradition from Antiquity to the Early Middle Ages.* Leiden.
Conquest, R. (1989) *Tyrants and Typewriters: Communiques from the Struggle for Truth.* Lexington.
Cornell, T.J. (1986) "The Annals of Quintus Ennius," *JRS* 1986, 244-250.
Courtney, E. (1970) *C. Valeri Flacci Argonauticon Libri Octo.* Leipzig.
Davis, M. (1990) "*Ratis Audax*: Valerius Flaccus' Bold Ship," in Boyle (1990),46-73.
Delz, J. (1987) *Sili Italici Punica.* Stuttgart.
d'Espèrey, F.S. (1986) "Vespasien, Titus, et la littérature," *ANRW* II.32.5, 3048-3086.

Dewar, M. (1991) *Statius. Thebaid IX.* Oxford.

Dominik, W.J. (1990) "Monarchical Power and Imperial Politics in Statius' Thebaid," in Boyle (1990), 74-97.

--(1994a) *The Mythic Voice of Statius: Power and Politics in the Thebaid.* Leiden.

---(1994b) *Speech and Rhetoric in Statius' Thebaid.* Hildesheim.

Dunham, V.S. (1976) *In Stalin's Time.* Cambridge.

Dunkle, J.R. (1967) "The Greek Tyrant and Roman Political Invective of the Late Republic," *TAPhA* 98, 151-171.

---(1971) "The Rhetorical Tyrant in Roman Historiography: Sallust, Livy, and Tacitus," *CW* 65, 12-20.

Dutoit, E. (1936) "La thème de la force que se détruit elle-même," *REL* 14, 365-373.

Earl, D.C. (1961) *The Political Thought of Sallust.* Amsterdam.

Evans, E.C. (1969) "Physiognomics in the Ancient World," *TAPS* 59.5, 5-101.

Fantham, E. (1996) *Roman Literary Culture. From Cicero to Marcus Aurelius.* Baltimore.

Feeney, D. (1991) *The Gods in Epic.* Oxford.

Griffin, M. (1976) *Seneca: A Philosopher in Politics.* Oxford.

---(1986) "Philosophy, Cato, and Roman Suicide," *G&R* 33, 64-77 and 192-202.

Grimal, P. (1960) "L'elogie de Néron au début de la *Pharsale*: est il ironique?" *REL* 38, 296-305.

Grisé, Y. (1982) *Le suicide dans la Rome antique.* Paris.

Gruen, E. (1984) *The Hellenistic World and the Coming of Rome*. Berkeley.

Hanfmann, G.M.A. (1975) *Roman Art*. New York.

Hardie, A. (1983) *Statius and the Silvae: Poets, Patrons, and Epideixis in the Graeco-Roman World*. Liverpool.

Hardie, P. (1993) *The Epic Successors of Virgil: A Study in the Dynamics of a Tradition*. Cambridge.

Henderson, J. (1993) "Form Remade / Statius' *Thebaid*" in Boyle (1993), 162-191.

Jal, P. (1963) *La guerre civile à Rome*. Paris.

Janssen, L.F. (1981) "Some Unexplored Aspects of *Devotio Deciana*," *Mnem*. 34, 357-381.

Jaworski, A. (1993) *The Power of Silence: Social and Pragmatic Perspectives*. Newbury Park.

Johnson, W.R. (1988) *Momentary Monsters: Lucan and his Heroes*. Ithaca.

Jones, B.W. (1979) *Domitian and the Senatorial Order: A Prosopographical Study of Domitian's Relationship with the Senate, A.D. 81-96*, (Memoirs of the American Philosophical Society, v.132). Philadelphia.

---(1992) *The Emperor Domitian*. New York.

Juhnke, H. (1972) *Homerisches in römischer Epik flavischer Zeit* (Zetemata Monographien, Heft 53). Munich.

Kissell, W. (1979) *Das Geschichtsbild des Silius Italicus*. Frankfurt.

Klotz, A. (1973) *P. Papini Stati Thebais*. Leipzig.

Küppers, J. (1986) *Tantarum Causas Irarum: Untersuchungen zur einleitenden Bücherdyade der Punica des Silius Italicus.* Berlin.

Lefèvre, E. (1971) *Das Prooemium der Argonautica des Valerius Flaccus.* Wiesbaden.

Loseff, L. (1984) *On the Beneficence of Censorship: Aesopian Language in Modern Russian Literature*, (J. Bobko, trans.). Munich.

Malamud, M. and D. McGuire (1993) "Flavian Variant: Myth. Valerius' Argonautica," in Boyle (1993), 192-217.

Mandelstam, N. (1970) *Hope Against Hope: A Memoir*, (M. Hayward, trans.). New York.

Masters, J. (1992) *Poetry and Civil War in Lucan's Bellum Civile*. Cambridge.

Mayakovsky, V. (1975) *The Bedbug and Selected Poetry*, (M. Hayward and G. Reavey trans.; P. Blake, ed.). Bloomington.

McDermott, W and A.E. Orentzel "Silius and Domitian," *AJPh* 98, 24-34.

McGuire, jr., D.T. (1990) "Textual Strategies and Political Suicide in Flavian Epic," in Boyle (1990), 21-45.

--(1995) "History Compressed: The Roman Names of Silius' Cannae Episode," *Latomus* 54, 110-118.

Millar, F. (1977) *The Emperor in the Roman World.* Ithaca.

Milosz, C. (1981) *The Captive Mind*, (J. Zielonko, trans.). New York.

Mozley, J.H. (1928) *Statius*. Cambridge.

Newman, J.K. (1986) *The Classical Epic Tradition*. Madison.

Nicol, J. (1933) *The Historical and Geographical Sources Used by Silius Italicus*. Oxford.

Pomeroy, A. (1990) "Silius Italicus as *doctus poeta*," in Boyle (1990), 119-139.

Powell, A., ed. (1992) *Roman Poetry and Propaganda in the Age of Augustus*. London.

Preiswerk, R (1934) "Zeitgeschichtliches bei Valerius Flaccus," *Philologus* 89, 433-442.

Quint, D. (1992) *Epic and Empire*. Princeton.

Reitz, C. (1982) *Die Nekyia in den Punica des Silius Italicus*. Frankfurt.

Rist, J.M. (1969) *Stoic Philosophy*. Cambridge.

Rogers, R.S. (1960) "A Group of Domitianic Treason Trials," *CP* 55, 15-23.

Rutz, W. (1960) "Amor Mortis bei Lucan," *Hermes* 88, 462-475.

Schetter, W. (1959) "Die Buchzahl der *Argonautica* des Valerius Flaccus," *Phil.* 103, 297-308.

Schubert, W. (1984) *Jupiter in den Epen der Flavierzeit*. Frankfurt.

Sherwin-White, A.N. (1985) *The Letters of Pliny*. Oxford.

Skutsch, O. (1985) *The Annals of Q. Ennius*. Cambridge.

Sullivan, J.P. (1985) *Literature and Politics in the Age of Nero*. Ithaca.

---(1991) *Martial: The Unexpected Classic*. Cambridge.

Syme, R. (1929) "The *Argonautica* of Valerius Flaccus," *CQ* 23, 129-137.

Talbert, R.J.A. (1984) *The Senate in Imperial Rome*. Princeton.

van Hooff, A.J. (1990) *From Autothanasia to Suicide: Self-Killing in Classical Antiquity*. London.

Veeser, H.A., ed. (1989) *The New Historicism*. New York.

Venini, P. (1969) "Silio Italico e il mito tebano," *RIL* 103, 778-783.

---(1978) "La visione dell' Italia nel catalogo di Silio Italico (*Punica* 8.356-616)," *RIL* 36, 123-227.

Vessey, D.W.T.C.. (1970) "Notes on the Hypsipyle Episode in Statius, Thebaid 4-6," *BICS* 17, 44-54.

---(1973) *Statius and the Thebaid*. Cambridge.

---(1974) "Silius Italicus on the Fall of Saguntum," *CP* 69, 28-36.

---(1984) "The Origin of Ti. Catius Asconius Silius Italicus," *CB* 60, 9-10.

---(1985) "Lemnos Revisited. Some Aspects of Valerius Flaccus, *Argonautica* ii," *CJ* 80, 326-339.

---(1986) "*Pierius menti calor incidit*: Statius' Epic Style," *ANRW* II.32.5, 2965-3019.

von Albrecht, M. (1964) *Silius Italicus. Freiheit und Gebundenheit römischer Epik*. Amsterdam.

Williams, G. (1978) *Change and Decline*. Berkeley.

Williams, R.D. (1972) *Thebaidos Liber Decimus*, (*Mnemosyne* suppl. 22). Leiden.

Wilson, M. (1993) "Flavian Variant. History. Silius' *Punica*," in Boyle (1993), 218-236.

Zanker, P. (1988) *The Power of Images in the Age of Augustus*. Ann Arbor.